Stealing a Gift

JOLITA PONS

Stealing a Gift:
Kierkegaard's Pseudonyms and the Bible

FORDHAM UNIVERSITY PRESS
New York ■ 2004

Perspectives in Continental Philosophy Series, No. 39
ISSN 1089-3938

Library of Congress Cataloging-in-Publication Data

Pons, Jolita.
    Stealing a gift: Kierkegaard's pseudonyms and the Bible / Jolita Pons. — 1st ed.
        p. cm. — (Perspectives in Continental philosophy series, ISSN 1089-3938; Bd. 39)
    Includes bibliographical references (p.) and index.
    ISBN 0-8232-2369-8 (hardcover)
    1. Kierkegaard, Søren, 1813-1855. 2. Bible — Use — History — 19th century.
3. Hermeneutics — History — 19th century. I. Title. II. Perspectives in continental
philosophy; Bd. 39.
    B4378.B52P66   2004
    198'.9 — dc22

                                                                              2004019062

Printed in the United States of America
07 06 05 04   5 4 3 2 1
First edition

To Eric, for *Naked Lunch*

Contents

Acknowledgments

I wish to thank John D. Caputo, without whom this book would not have come out. Thanks go to Hugh Pyper and David Ford for their helpful comments and suggestions. I am grateful to Hongs Kierkegaard Library for its hospitality and invaluable resources. Cynthia Lund and Gordon Marino make sure to create ideal research conditions, and I was lucky to benefit from them. Kierkegaard Research Centre in Copenhagen has always welcomed me; conversations with Niels Jorgen Cappelorn and Joakim Garff have stimulated my thought. Trinity College, Cambridge, provided me with a research grant for three years.

My deepest gratitude goes to George, for his unfailing support and generosity, and for being a utopian reader—understanding the author better than she herself.

Introduction

> It is as if an error slipped into an author's writing and the error
> became conscious of itself as an error—perhaps it actually was not a
> mistake but in a much higher sense an essential part of the whole pro-
> duction—and now this error wants to mutiny against the author, out of
> hatred toward him, forbidding him to correct it and in maniacal defi-
> ance saying to him: No, I refuse to be erased, I will stand as a witness
> against you, a witness that you are a second-rate author (SUD 74).

This book is a study of the use of biblical quotations in Søren
Kierkegaard's pseudonymous works, as well as of Kierkegaard's
hermeneutical methods in general, using the biblical quotations as a
point of departure. Quotation is of crucial importance for both
Christianity and modernity, and I suggest that in Kierkegaard's
pseudonymous writings the two meet in a particularly fruitful and
challenging way.

Although Kierkegaard's philosophical vision was one of the chief
inspirations for the "existential hermeneutics" that largely contributed
to the formation of hermeneutics as a discipline in the twentieth century
(Karl Barth, Rudolf Bultmann, and Martin Heidegger, all deeply
influenced by Kierkegaard, inspired the originator of hermeneutics in
its present-day form, Hans-Georg Gadamer), there is no comprehensive study of hermeneutic theory and practice in Kierkegaard's own
writings. My research, approaching Kierkegaard's biblical quotations

not from a theological but rather a hermeneutical point of view, contributes to filling this gap.

Kierkegaard scholarship has suffered from underestimating the role of the Bible in his so-called philosophical or aesthetic writings. It is not uncommon for commentators to approach Kierkegaard from a philosophical point of view without even a rudimentary knowledge of the Bible. This is not a matter of the researcher's personal belief, but rather of her or his knowledge of the text of the Bible as a historical, literary, and ideological resource for Kierkegaard's writing.

The Bible is at least as important a text for Kierkegaard as the works of, for example, Hegel or Kant. It is therefore my intention to show that readings ignoring the role of the Bible in Kierkegaard's pseudonymous works overlook many nuances of meaning that depend on his use of the Bible. Thus they miss an important dimension of the texts.[1] It is even more surprising that despite many theological interpretations of Kierkegaard's work, few theologians have looked at how he actually uses the Bible in his texts. Such an analysis would provide a constructive basis for further discussion, both for theologians and for philosophers.

This book is not about the language of the Bible but about its presence.[2] It is about the presence of the Bible in the modern age, where the relationship with God has to be rediscovered or re-envisaged. Kierkegaard suggests that it is possible to relate to God only through becoming contemporary with God's Word by repeating the Bible and internalizing it in a spiral movement of "deviations."[3] *Imitatio Christi* begins for Kierkegaard with imitation of the Word. It will be my task to give content to such concepts as imitation, contemporaneity, and appropriation in relation to the biblical word.

The tension between reason and revelation or between autonomy and heteronomy, problems bequeathed by the Enlightenment, necessarily affected the way in which Kierkegaard read the Bible. But it does not make much sense to ask whether he read the Bible in a philosophical or in a theological way. There is no such dichotomy in his works. He offers an original perspective, and one that could perhaps serve as a way out of these kinds of conflicts. In keeping with this view, one of the main aims and expectations of this book is to contribute to the demolition of the artificial separation of the religious and the philosophical (aesthetic) in Kierkegaard's authorship.

Despite flexible and expandable definitions such as "Kierkegaard was a religious and philosophical thinker who possessed a touch of a poet,"[4] in their actual analysis and interpretation most researchers have approached Kierkegaard from one of four major perspectives: biographical, philosophical, literary theory/deconstruction, or theological. Having chosen one point of departure, they have usually excluded the other perspectives.[5] The sharpest distinction has been made between Kierkegaard's philosophy and his theology.[6] This distinction is based on the supposedly irreconcilable division in the human self, namely, the division between the passive (faith, grace, passion) and active (reason, will).

In my opinion, Kierkegaard never subscribed to such a dichotomy, putting forward instead a more balanced and more ingenious view of the human self. The tension is mainly due to the fact that Kierkegaard relates most of the important "philosophical" questions and conceptual constructions to the question of faith. Quite often the distinction between Kierkegaard the philosopher and Kierkegaard the theologian begins with the presupposition that the pseudonymous works are philosophical, while the "veronymous" are theological.[7] For example, Steven Emmanuel stresses that his analysis is a philosophical reconstruction of Kierkegaard's views on the nature of Christian revelation.[8] The reason seems to be none other but the fact that the book on which he bases his study is a pseudonymous work (ergo aesthetic, ergo philosophical), and bears the title *Philosophical Fragments*. In this line of interpretation there is a predisposition to reduce all religious and specifically Christian issues to general philosophical questions, and God is soon interpreted as "the highest principle." It is noticeable that as a "real" philosopher, Kierkegaard has been mostly analyzed comparatively (Kierkegaard and Kant, Kierkegaard and Hegel, and so on), and this tendency has contributed to making his writings more univocal than they are. Such attempts have perhaps partly resulted from the need to justify Kierkegaard's place in the history of philosophy and to remove the label of "irrationalist," but they have led to one-sided reading.

On the other hand, once one has decided to treat Kierkegaard as a theologian, everything is subjected to this presupposition. For example, Arnold Come says: "First, it must be noted that when Kierkegaard says he is a poet, he almost always adds, 'and thinker' (Taenker). This term is his equivalent for 'theologian.' Just as he writes 'discourses' and not 'sermons' because he is 'without authority' of ordination, so he uses 'thinker' to indicate that he is 'a theologian but not appointed.' "[9] Moreover, a "theological" reading of Kierkegaard's works often leads to quite extreme descriptions, for example: "It is fundamental to any understanding of his writings and to this analysis, that Kierkegaard was a theologian in the classical, catholic, and orthodox sense."[10] This kind of interpretation has ignored Kierkegaard's dialectics and done incredible damage to his reception; it has rarely done justice to Kierkegaard's rich and varied reading of the Bible.

The present study involves combining the three modes of thinking and writing, corresponding to three prominent aspects of Kierkegaard's works: the aim is to see *how* he writes the religious in the philosophical. It will become clear that Kierkegaard's way of being "religious" is never merely ascetic (i.e., world-denying), and that the relation between the aesthetic and the religious in his writing is not at all a case of either-or. If I succeed in showing the extent to which the Bible is present in the pseudonymous writings and in unveiling something of the many different and subtle ways it is incorporated in them, it will become clear that the meaning of Kierkegaard's "philosophical" or "existential" discourse is developed in a constant dynamic relation to the Bible.

The ongoing dialogue and interaction with the Bible means that a much greater vigilance is required in reading Kierkegaard and reconstructing his views and concepts than is exhibited in much secondary literature. The more original the author, the more thoroughly he or she has absorbed various possibilities in the history of writing—but also the more urgent is the need for readers to recognize these and, as far as possible, integrate these multiple contexts into their reading.

Apart from illuminating the relationship between the philosophical and the religious, the study of Kierkegaard's use of the Bible casts new light on several other important issues, such as authority, appropriation, repetition, contemporaneity, tautology, and negative theology. One of the key terms in my discussion of Kierkegaard's use of the biblical quotations will be his concept of contemporaneity. Appropriation then becomes the means of achieving this. The term "appropriation" has been much abused, but I hope that my concrete discussion will give it a substantial content. I will also explore the ambiguity of appropriation, the inherent tension between justified and illegitimate ways of appropriating a text. A good metaphor for this tension in appropriation can be found in the Bible itself when Isaac blesses Jacob despite the theft of Esau's birthright.[11] The discussion of all these issues will help to situate Kierkegaard's dialectics between authority and uncertainty.

I shall argue that Kierkegaard's use of the Bible is an essential part of his indirect communication. The presence of the Bible in his pseudonymous works could be called a kind of invisible omnipresence. Kierkegaard's aim is not to *im*pose certain truths or beliefs, but to *ex*pose them, and to do so in such a way that it becomes impossible to ignore their presence, even if the reader retains freedom to engage with them or not. Such a mode of indirect communication has implications for Kierkegaard's understanding both of religiousness and of ethical relations.

In the course of writing the book, it became clear that the majority of the important issues in Kierkegaard's pseudonymous writings are either introduced by biblical quotations or are at least set up in relation to the Bible. However, this often involves changes in the meaning or in the biblical text. For example, in *Philosophical Fragments* Climacus quotes the Bible but changes the plural of Luke 13.27 — "But he shall say, I tell you [*Jer*], I know you [*Jer*] not whence ye are" — into singular [*dig*]. As this change is commented upon in the text itself it is, of course, not accidental and is significant in the context of Kierkegaard's emphasis on the individual and his personal relation to God (see the final chapter of this book).

In the *Sickness unto Death*, speaking about the transition from understanding to doing, Kierkegaard reinterprets the Cartesian *cogito* in biblical terms. "And the secret of modern philosophy is essentially the very same, for it is this: *cogito ergo sum* [I think therefore I am], to think is to be (Christianly, however, it reads: according to your faith, be it unto you, or, as you believe, so you are, to believe is to be)" (SUD 93). In this way he uses a biblical reference to introduce one of the most important issues in his authorship, that of modern philosophy vs. Christianity. The reference is to Matthew 8.13: "As thou hast believed, so be it done unto thee," and it also highlights his key idea, namely the idea of being as believing rather than being as thinking (note: not knowing).[12]

Another relevant example can show how even very tiny changes can be meaningful and reveal a larger presupposed context. In *Philosophical Fragments*, Kierkegaard says: "Thus, belief [*Tro*] believes what it does not see, it does not believe that the star exists [*er til*], for that it sees, but it believes that the star has come into existence [*er bleven til*]" (PF 81).[13] This contains an allusion to Hebrews 11.1, "Now faith is the substance of things hoped for, the evidence of things not seen." However, the biblical "hoped for" has been changed to "has become" (*er bleven til*), a change that reflects the way in which the logic of becoming and existence is one of the major issues for Kierkegaard in *Philosophical Fragments*.

The nature of faith itself is affected if one shifts from the purely futuristic mode of hope (which expresses a total uncertainty of the present and means that the whole existence is held together by the trust and hope that things are as they are or as they seem to be and that there is a binding (*telos*) to the past tense of the process of becoming, which emphasizes the creation. The crucial difference between *er til* and *er bleven til* puts faith in between uncertainty and certainty, but the uncertainty of faith (which is unknown to immediate sensations and cognition) turns out to be a certitude that "wriggles itself out of uncertainty."

These are only two of many examples that show the degree to which the meaning of Kierkegaard's texts relies on the biblical references. However, a great sensitivity in discerning these is needed, especially because Kierkegaard often deviates from the original text in creatively reinterpreting it, so that the resulting meaning is not the outcome of a simple transposition but of an interactive process.

As I have mentioned, to my knowledge there is no comprehensive treatment of the actual use of the Bible in Kierkegaard's works. Of course, there have been several isolated attempts that have been valuable.[14] There is, however, only one book that expresses the ambition of giving a general overview of Kierkegaard's use of the Bible: L. Joseph Rosas III, *Scripture in the Thought of Søren Kierkegaard*.[15] Since it is a major study I feel I should justify why I shall not refer to it further in my work.

Although I agree with Rosas's chief claim about the important role of appropriation through inwardness and the creative use of the Bible, I do not think he supports his claim by analysis or arguments. More important, I do not share his guiding principle: "Kierkegaard's biographical crises are the foundations for understanding the function of Scripture in his thought."[16] The first difference in our approaches is one of scope: I concentrate only on the pseudonymous writings (and already find these to be a very broad field), whereas Rosas aims at covering all of Kierkegaard's authorship. His book is arranged work by work, and apart from some very general (and dubious) remarks about a given work's nature and themes, it amounts to enlisting biblical quotations in the cause of Rosas's monological and tendentious argument. He claims that "Kierkegaard worked from and assumed the truth of biblical material."[17]

I hope it will become apparent from my work that his relation is not so straight or clear-cut. Kierkegaard constantly engages in dialogue with the biblical material. In the *Concept of Anxiety*, for example, he says: "I freely admit my inability to connect any definite thought with the serpent. Furthermore, the difficulty with the serpent is something quite different, namely, that of regarding the temptation as coming from without. This is simply contrary to the teaching of the Bible, contrary to the well known passage in James, which says that God tempts no man and is not tempted by anyone, but each person is tempted by himself" (CA 48).[18] My study of various deviations will further confirm the dynamic nature of Kierkegaard's relation to the biblical text.

Second, Rosas treats the biblical quotations as literary devices, whereas I want to show that far from being merely literary elements or ornaments, they play a constructive role in Kierkegaard's thought and writing.[19] Third, Rosas represents just the kind of reification of the abyss between the religious and the aesthetic that I find so unfortunate. Since Rosas sees the pseudonyms as caricatures, he naturally and predictably draws the conclusion that "Kierkegaard, writing as the consummate aesthete, restricted his use of Scripture to an aesthetic appropriation of the Bible."[20] I argue that this is wrong.

Likewise, Rosas finds that a text belonging to the ethical stage "appeals to the Bible as a source for corroboration of universal law" and that "in general, the hermeneutical pattern of each [caricature, i.e. pseudonym] corresponds roughly to the existence sphere it represents."[21] This is too schematic, as is Rosas's final evaluation, a condemnation of the use of the Bible in the pseudonymous works: "In many respects, the various approaches to the Bible exhibited by the various Kierkegaardian pseudonyms are 'ways' of appropriating the Scripture. However, the majority of these are ultimately unsatisfactory."[22]

I would like to present a less biased reading of Kierkegaard. It has never been my intention to judge whether Kierkegaard used the Bible "in the right way," but to see what models of reading the Bible he incorporated in his writing and thus also (indirectly) offered his readers.

I have defined my book as an attempt to show *how* Kierkegaard writes the *religious* in the *philosophical,* thus performing a synthesis of the three modes of Kierkegaard's writing. This is an interdisciplinary project, within which I have allowed myself to read the texts from several perspectives at the same time. This may be perceived as somewhat eclectic and not completely scientific, but I believe it to be both an appropriate and a fruitful way of reading Kierkegaard and, in a very remote sense, to echo Kierkegaard's own copious and multilayered writing. I have called this interdisciplinary approach "hermeneutical" fully conscious of the abuse of the term. This point has been well put by Vattimo in a preface to his *Beyond Interpretation:* "In contemporary philosophy, hermeneutics has begun to acquire an 'eucumenical' form so vague and generic that, in my view, it is losing much of its meaning."[23]

The reasons for which I nevertheless claim that my project is indeed a hermeneutical one include the following: first, the constitutive characteristics of hermeneutics—ontology and *Sprachlichkeit* (linguisticality)—apply well to my project. As a study of biblical quotations, my project completes the notion of hermeneutics as an art of interpretation that has departed from its demythologizing and rationalistic roots and led to the rediscovery of religion.[24] A further link to hermeneutics comes through the responsibility of reading, and particularly the responsibility involved in reading a text that should affect one's life, namely the Bible. Instead of inducing relativism, "recognition of the linguistic-interpretative character of our experience of the world also entails a clear ethical directive."[25] In my view, Kierkegaard is one of the rare authors who not only reflect on ethical issues but also have a genuinely ethical relation to their readers (I will cover more aspects of hermeneutics in Chapter 2).

The present study is a propaedeutic one. It does not so much answer questions as raise them. My work frequently focuses on tiny (insignificant) points or details; it is not about overarching conceptual constructions, but rather about the fine grain of Kierkegaard's writing. In a very explicit way it is not only about *what* he writes, but *how* the "what" is created. By proceeding in this way, I have tried to follow the curved line of Kierkegaard's writing in order to arrive at concepts rather than begin with them. Thereby I hope to show how Kierkegaard's texts call for reading in the strictest and most intimate sense.

It has become necessary, in writing anything about Kierkegaard, to clarify one's position regarding his pseudonyms.[26] I shall often use the name "Kierkegaard" while speaking of his pseudonymous production, without however at any point assuming that his views *either* in the pseudonymous *or* in his signed works are directly his own. Occasionally I may use the name of the respective pseudonym, but I do not attach any special significance to that. I treat both the name Kierkegaard and his pseudonyms symbolically, as when stating that "Plato" says something in *Timaeus* 25e when in fact it is Critias who speaks.

The objection that could be raised to such a position is that by not drawing a strict line between Kierkegaard and his pseudonyms or between different pseudonyms, one runs a risk of constantly finding that "Kierkegaard" contradicts himself. This is a fair objection, but the issue of apparent contradictions (contrasting views taken from different contexts of Kierkegaard's writing) is not a real danger for my study, since I do not argue anywhere that Kierkegaard contradicts himself, but merely that in his multilayered authorship he discloses diverse sides of the same issues, depending on the immediate and particular constellation of the problems discussed in the text. It has not been my aim to compare different pseudonymous works, but merely to make a kind of involute by tracing interrelated features.

It should also be noted that I have used Kierkegaard's journals to elucidate or complement many points. There are, of course, problems of chronology and evolution involved here, and unfortunately I have not been able to do these full justice since that would require an extensive comparative study of the development of Kierkegaard's writing.

What do we understand by a biblical quotation? To address this question adequately would involve the whole issue of quotation in general.[27] For the purposes of introduction, it will suffice to define quotation as an interdiscursive relation between two texts. Quotation is not a static graft but a relation, and as such it has multipolar functions. However, quotation has also formal, fixed characteristics that establish its authenticity and should be respected in transmission. It is important to note that in the context of Kierkegaard's pseudonymous works, quotation is not a direct or reported speech, but on the contrary an indirect element.

A few words need to be said about the formal characteristics of Kierkegaard's biblical quotations. Most of these in his pseudonymous works are not attributed; they are latent or "assumed" references. On the other hand, even those that are given in quotation marks may contain inaccuracies. In fact, it seems that there is no explanation for the presence or absence of quotation marks or accompanying introductory words such as, "as it is said in Scripture," and the like. In any case, there is substantial evidence that these devices are not connected to the level of accuracy. It is, of course, a debatable issue whether they are quotations, allusions, references, paraphrases, or other devices, but it is not fruitful to try to determine that at a general level, and certainly not for the purposes of a hermeneutical analysis of the biblical quotations in Kierkegaard's pseudonymous works. For the sake of convenience, I will use "quotation" as a generic term for all these "foreign elements" in Kierkegaard's texts.

It has not been my ambition to cover all the pseudonymous works equally, and some get more attention than others. This is inevitable when dealing with such a vast field. Having looked up all the quotations in all the pseudonymous works, I selected those that brought the interesting questions into sharpest focus.[28] Unfortunately many fascinating and noteworthy examples had to be left out due to the restrictions of volume. Had it been possible to take them into account, Kierkegaard's use of the Bible would have appeared even richer.

The attention that I paid to each work depended on many factors, such as the density of biblical quotations (which varies from book to book).[29] For example, despite the quite explicitly Christian character of *The Sickness unto Death*, biblical quotations do not abound there. Thus I have not discussed it extensively. However, the title itself is an interesting case, since it is a reversed quotation of John 11.4: "This sickness is not unto death." Likewise the special character of *The Concept of Anxiety*, and the fact that the presence of the Bible is required by the nature of one of its main themes — the dogma of hereditary sin — meant that the nature of quotations is more exegetical and explicit.

It should be remarked that I did not identify the biblical quotations myself. In this I have relied on several combined commentaries and indexes.[30] It is reasonable to suspect that there are still some unidentified references or that some of the identified ones are attributed falsely, but it would hardly affect my work substantially.[31]

I worked in Danish and converted Kierkegaard's quotations into English only at the very end. In the majority of cases I used the Hongs' translation for convenience's sake. Sometimes, however, I found it necessary to modify their translation. In several places, when I thought it particularly important to appreciate the finer points of the original text, I gave quotations both in English and Danish.

The structure of my book is characterized by a movement from the more general to the concrete, and by my attempt to put the general context and the concrete analysis together in a new synthesis in the concluding remarks. This is true of both the overall structure and that of individual chapters.

Chapter 1 deals with the issue of quotation in general. I give a brief historical overview of the main functions of quotation, notably the tension between its functions as "ornament" and as "authority." I cover a wide range of issues, from the framework of mimesis in ancient rhetoric to quotation as "symptom" in modern times. The historical overview remains rather superficial, but, I hope, sufficient to provide a context for my concrete analysis of Kierkegaard's use of biblical quotations. In the second part of this chapter I introduce several important issues related to quotation, such as appropriation, repetition, authenticity, and manipulation, which later resonate in my examination of Kierkegaard's works.

In Chapter 2, I indicate Kierkegaard's contribution to the development of modern hermeneutics and present his relation to the issues of writing and reading and his peculiar understanding of the authority of an author. I discuss his notion of indirect communication and its correlatives, such as teleological suspension of truth, in order to provide a horizon for my claim that the use of the biblical quotations is one of the crucial tools of indirect communication. I address the question of pseudonymity and attempt to clarify some issues related to the supposed antithesis between Kierkegaard's aesthetic and religious works.

Chapter 3 focuses on Kierkegaard's explicit views on the nature of the biblical text and its reading. I begin with a short overview of changes in biblical studies in early nineteenth century Europe, and in Denmark in particular. The discussion of Kierkegaard's views regarding the biblical hermeneutics is set in the framework of the problem of faith and knowledge, subjective and objective appropriation of truth. The important questions to consider are his understanding of literal and nonliteral reading, inspiration, and the transition from reading to action.

In Chapter 4, I focus on the recreation of biblical stories in *Fear and Trembling* and *Stages on Life's Way*. I present a very detailed analysis of the variations of the biblical texts in these works. I then argue that the phenomenon of reinvented biblical stories in the pseudonymous works is related to a subjunctive mode of Kierkegaard's writing, the emphasis on possibility as the only ethically and religiously challenging form of representation, and to a peculiar form of imagination that plays an important role in appropriation and the transition to faith. The question is also linked to the presence of negative theology in Kierkegaard's authorship.

Chapter 5 concentrates on alterations in the biblical quotations in Kierkegaard's pseudonymous works, arguing that these deviations can contribute to the advance of indirect communication. The implications of biblical "misquotations" are discussed from a nonjudgmental point of view: instead of assuming that "misquotations" are a deficiency or fault, they are held to play a hermeneutical role in Kierkegaard's complex relation to the Bible.

In Chapter 6, I draw attention to the fact that Kierkegaard himself was conscious of the problems formulated in my book and was concerned with the legitimation of quoting and the hermeneutical procedures that this involves. The first part of this chapter is based on the hypothetical dialogues between the author and the imaginary interlocutor in *Philosophical Fragments*. In the second part I move from the issues specific to *Philosophical Fragments* to a discussion of tautology, reduplication, and repetition in the pseudonymous works. With the help of these concepts I try to shape the notion of contemporaneity and appropriation.

I hope that the exposition of Kierkegaard's use of biblical quotations will disturb my reader. Kierkegaard is a troubling author, but he does not blur the issues: rather, he stirs them up. As always, he himself says it best (with the help of the Bible): "Only he really has a style who is never finished with something but 'stirs the waters of language' whenever he begins, so that to him the most ordinary expression comes into existence with newborn originality" (CUP 86).

"For an angel went down at a certain season into the pool, and troubled the water: whosoever then first after the troubling of the water stepped in was made whole of whatsoever disease he had" (Jn 5.4).

List of Abbreviations

E/O I	Either/Or I
E/O II	Either/Or II
EPW	Early Polemical Writings
EUD	Eighteen Upbuilding Discourses
CA	The Concept of Anxiety
CI	The Concept of Irony
CUP	Concluding Unscientific Postscript
FSE	For Self-Examination
FT	Fear and Trembling
JP	Journals and Papers
K	Komentarer
P	Prefaces
Pap.	Søren Kierkegaards Papirer
PC	Practice in Christianity
PF	Philosophical Fragments
PV	The Point of View for My Work as an Author
R	Repetition
SLW	Stages on Life's Way
SKS	Søren Kierkegaards Skrifter
SUD	The Sickness unto Death
WA	Without Authority
WL	Works of Love

Stealing a Gift

Quotation Theory

Le texte est un tissu de citations issues des mille foyers de la culture.
— **Roland Barthes,** *Le Bruissement de la langue*

As my book concentrates on the hermeneutical analysis of biblical quotations in Kierkegaard's pseudonymous works, it seems best to begin by a brief discussion of quotation as such. In this chapter I shall, therefore, attempt to provide a context for the concrete analysis of Kierkegaard's biblical quotations by looking more generally at the theory of quotation. Many of the issues touched upon in a rather general manner in this chapter will be further developed later in the book, particularly such topics as the relation to authority, models of appropriation, and repetition.

The question of quotation is central to any discussion of textuality, and in particular of intertextuality. In this context, quotation is often understood rather loosely: it becomes little more than an echo or a trace of previously absorbed layers of culture and education (including nonliterary media, such as music or art). It is, indeed, not easy to give an adequate and satisfactory definition of quotation. This is partly because it is a relatively small element, and partly because, given that quotation can be inexact or modified, we have to determine the minimal requirement of identity for there to be a quotation. This is necessary in order to allow even the slightest allusion to form a link between two texts, but at the same time to exclude artificially imposed links when coincidental details are made the basis for claims regarding a conscious relation between texts. Preliminarily we can define quotation as an interdiscursive relation between two texts.[1] Quotation is not a static graft but a relation, and, as such, it has multipolar functions. However, quotation also has a formal, fixed characteristic that establishes its authenticity and should be respected in transmission.

Function and Historical Perspective

As it is not the aim of this section to give a full account of the complex history of the practice of quoting, I shall give only an overview, emphasizing several characteristic moments in the history of quotation.[2]

What is the function of quotation? Quotations are often used to adorn texts with what has been well put by other authors or to reinforce arguments by invoking the authority of other authors. Thus the two privileged functions are ornament and authority. Of course, one can discern many others, such as amplification or erudition, and while it is true that the art of quotation has been employed in many different ways in any given period, one can observe that during certain periods, some functions of quotations have been preferred to others according to different perceptions of textuality.[3] The most important periods in the history of quotation coincide with the four main distinct periods in the history of textuality: (a) ancient rhetoric; (b) the Patristic commentary and the Middle Ages; (c) early modernity; (d) modernity. Let us go briefly through these main periods in order to appreciate the variety of ways in which a quotation can function.

Ancient Rhetoric: The Framework of Mimesis

Already Plato and Aristotle both employed quotations and reflected on the implications of quoting when they addressed the issue of mimesis. They took different positions with respect to mimesis and quotation. According to Plato direct discourse implied mimesis, while according to Aristotle both direct and indirect discourse were mimetic.[4] Compagnon has noted that whereas Plato mistrusted repetition and direct discourse but was at the same time willing to employ them in his text, Aristotle claimed that all discourse was mimetic but hardly ever used obviously mimetic structures, such as dialogues, in his own writings. The framework of mimesis will remain of an immense importance for quotation and will later turn into the problem as to whether repetition is at all possible (a problem we will take up in Kierkegaardian context in the final chapter).

Another important figure in ancient rhetoric is Quintilian, according to whom quotation calls for a rereading, because it rearranges a text and gives it a *relief*.

We must return to what we have read and reconsider it with care, while, just as we do not swallow our food until we have chewed it and reduced it almost to a state of liquefaction to assist the process of digestion, so what we read must not be committed to memory for subsequent imitation while it is still in a crude state, but must be softened and, if I may use the phrase, reduced to a pulp by frequent re-perusal.[5]

Quotation thus reflects the author's reading and his work of appropriation; it explicitly combines reading and writing in a single act.[6] Quintilian disagreed with Aristotle about the notion of the *gnome*, which he translated as *sentential*. In Aristotle's *Rhetoric*, *gnome* is presented as close to a proverb or a maxim (*gnome* becomes the medieval *maxima sententia*) and is said to be employed to prove something.[7] Quintilian points to the practice of Cicero, where quotation is sometimes employed as an ornament. Thus the two main functions of quotation, authority and ornament, were described as early as this stage.

Furthermore, from Quintilian's discussion of *figurae verborum* and *figurae sententiarum* it seems that in ancient rhetoric, one made a distinction between the quotation of thought and that of words: *repetitio sententiarum* and *repetitio verborum*.[8] However, from Cicero onward, rhetoric was more concerned with *verba* than with *res*. On the other hand, quotation in the ancient times signified not only an explicit quotation or reference to the author but also a free paraphrase that captured as it were only the overall meaning or spirit of the original saying.

Medieval Theology

Quotations occupy a special place in a discourse concerned with Christian theological matters, because all Christian theological discourse is constructed around biblical quotations. As Compagnon remarks about the origins of theological discourse, "All medieval writing takes place but in repetition of the Scripture."[9] The Bible is both the archetype (content) and prototype (form) of all theological discourse. Theological discourse—as a kind of metalanguage for the Bible—is an extreme case of the relation between one text and the other, and in some sense it is a systematization of the act of quoting.

At the core of both all biblical exegesis and the use of biblical quotations is II Corinthians 3.6, "The letter kills but the spirit gives life," because this distinction between letter and spirit introduces the possibility of polysemy in the whole of Scripture.

Quotation was, of course, also affected by the four principles of interpretation: literal/historical, tropological/moral, allegorical/mystical, anagogical/eschatological. These opened the way for a variety of readings of the Bible even when they remained rooted in the framework of authority.

Through its exegetical endeavours, medieval theology is the only historical attempt to make quotation central in the theory of text. The Middle Ages produced doctrines relating to the employment of profane quotations in the Old Testament, quotations from the Old Testament in the New Testament,[10] biblical quotations in the works of Church fathers, patristic quotations in theology, and so on. The attention paid to quotation is not so remarkable, given the focal place that quotation necessarily occupies in the biblical commentaries. The biblical quotations in the writings of medieval theologians act for the whole of the Bible, according to the principle of a synecdoche: *pars pro toto*.[11]

A quotation did not need to be justified, but simply introduced — as in the case of "as it is said in the Scripture" — and its power was limitless to the degree to which it bore the Logos in itself. In a sense, the biblical quotation can be read as an abridgement of the Word. Indeed, we will come back to this in relation to tautology in Kierkegaard's writings, in Chapter 6.

There are two other important aspects of quoting within the theological domain. The first is the issue of implicit quotations in the Bible and their subsequent requoting. The second is the interaction between theological texts, where authors not only quote each other but also requote biblical passages quoted in the works of others. Implicit quotations are various textual units that witness the appropriation of earlier cultural heritage, as well as those quotations from the Old Testament within the New Testament that do not form part of typological interpretations. These quotations in the Bible have always been problematic, as it has often been unclear whether they too (or whether all of them) were inspired.

This remained undecided until French theologian Father Prat founded a general theory of quotation, and the Biblical Commission of the Vatican reacted to the problem of implicit quotation by passing a decree to restrain reference to implicit quotation — which, as Compagnon says, was a way of denying it.[12] When patristic authors start quoting each other, quotation acquires a serial character. The quoted authors are called *auctoritas*, whose writings can be interpreted but not contested. Compagnon seems to think that the function of *auctoritas* is proper only to a quotation that refers to an author, to a particular utterance, and to a name of the author, and thus stands in opposition to *exemplum*, which is a more general kind of quotation.

However, it cannot be said that only explicitly referenced quotations invoke authority. In the patristic discourse, it was not important to refer to an author by name (although it is true that in a certain sense this was implied due to common knowledge of the texts referred to). Furthermore, because of the *pars pro toto* each phrase stood for the whole *corpus*. The same is true of the Bible itself, because of the schooling in the biblical language that all authors of the period absorbed. The Venerable Bede, who put the initials of the father he quoted in the margin, was an exception, and it was Thomas Aquinas who started making precise references in *Catena aurea*.

The net woven by quotation in the Middle Ages is even more complex if we bear in mind the multiple layers of receptions contained within the texts themselves: first with respect to the biblical text itself, and then in the sense of the universalization of the quotation source, since when one author cited another he was in fact invoking the entire tradition of reception.[13]

Early Modernity

The major event that affected literacy in the sixteenth century was, of course, the invention of print in Europe.[14] Print mobilized textuality and dissolved differences between the original copy and subsequent copies, and thus arose new principles of regulating discourse. The invention of print affected biblical quotations in particular. Previously copyists often quoted biblical citations found in the writings of patristic authors by heart, or according to the version they had learned, or from the Vulgata, and thus quotations often differed every time a text was recopied.

This was a period of the early modern breakthrough, when it was no longer sufficient simply to repeat. Instead, the same material had to be reworked. A quotation was no longer a guarantee of truth. Instead of expressing the integrity of writing as something different but still belonging essentially to the same corpus, it began to point to another as radically different and alien. The combination of utterances, the context and the interplay of texts became crucial in determining the value and meaning of separate segments and of the whole. The medieval *auctoritas* of quotation became dissolved. At the same time the active, constructive role of quotation in the creation of texts was acknowledged. Compagnon observes that quotation in this period did not so much point outside the text as it called or invited other texts to the "host" text and incorporated them.[15]

One of the best representatives of this epoch is Montaigne. In his works Montaigne quotes extensively, sometimes giving the name of the author or the work he is quoting, but most of the time leaving his quotation unattributed. Montaigne never uses the term "citation"; instead he calls it "allegation" or "borrowing." His relation to tradition is ambiguous. On the one hand, his writings presuppose some knowledge of certain literary and philosophical tradition and refer to them frequently; on the other hand, he is clearly antiauthoritarian. Montaigne claims that just because somebody else said something before him, it does not mean that this same thought cannot be conceived anew by him or another author; that is, according to Montaigne, we should think of texts not in terms of appropriation but in terms of cocreation.

This takes us to another important step in the history of quotation as well as in the history of writing more generally: the introduction of the difference between property and appropriation (Seneca had already made the distinction, but it had to be rediscovered).[16] The notion of the author's copyright, or "intellectual property," developed in the seventeenth century.[17] One can assume that Kant's discussion in *Metaphysics of Morals* of the confusion between the right to a thing (inasmuch as a text or a book is a thing to be reproduced) and the right against a person has generated a broader discussion of these issues.[18] The rise of a consciousness with regard to protection of one's intellectual property and the need to regulate its use subsequently led to laws about literary properties.[19] This, of course, has immense consequences for quoting, since quotation is the place where the property of one author meets that of another.

Modern Quoting

Contrary to the view of ancient rhetoric that public discourse was public property, literary property is now considered as private property from the ethical and legal point of view. One of the early influential works related to this change was Hegel's *Principles of the Philosophy of Right* (1821). In the section on property in *Abstract Right*,

Hegel says: "Intellectual [*geistige*] accomplishments, sciences, arts, even religious observances (such as sermons, masses, prayers, and blessings at consecrations), inventions, and the like, become objects [*Gegenstände*] of contract; in the way in which they are bought and sold, etc., they are treated as equivalent to acknowledged *things*."[20] It is precisely in their capacity as things (*Sachen*) that they are considered as legal possession, and since Hegel claims that human beings have the absolute right of appropriation over all things, once you place your will in any thing and then take possession of it, it becomes yours (§44, §51). In Hegel's view, apart from the purely negative protection of such property against theft, there is little one can do in the way of regulating the use of others' intellectual property. According to him, the endless multiplicity of alterations give the property of another person the superficial imprint of being one's own, so that it becomes very difficult to establish clear property boundaries. He says:

> As for the extent to which the existing store of knowledge, and in particular the thoughts of other people who retain external ownership of their intellectual products, become by virtue of the new *form* which they acquire through repeated expression, a special intellectual property of the individual who reproduces them and thereby give him (or fail to give him) the right to make them his external property in turn—the extent to which this is so cannot be precisely determined, nor therefore defined in terms of right and law. . . . Plagiarism ought therefore to be a matter of *honour*, and honour should deter people from committing it. Thus the laws against *breach of copyright* do attain their end of protecting the property rights of authors and publishers to the (albeit very limited) extent specified.[21]

Although Hegel's account is twofold, the reception of his thought has mainly focused on his conception of an intellectual property as a *thing*. From this point on, in the majority of contexts (excluding perhaps the domain of *belles-lettres*) it is required not only to acknowledge a quotation, but also to remain faithful to the original text. This means first of all to be faithful to the letter in order to maintain the authenticity of the quotation, but also to assume ethical and legal responsibility and to avoid manipulation.[22]

Relation to quotation changes also in another sense, insofar as the quoted author is more acutely conceived as someone different and distinct from the quoter—in other words, as the other. Thus it would seem that until the end of the nineteenth century, or at least until Flaubert—who appears as a transitional figure—writers could borrow freely from the tradition, add to an already existing canon, or struggle with that same tradition to inscribe their names within its boundaries. In contrast, for modernist and postmodernist writers, quotation serves to mark a break with the tradition and to question the nature of the literary text as such.[23]

Contrary to many scholars, such as Bloom, Said, or Compagnon, Jacqueline T. Miller argues that the tension usually attributed to the nineteenth century as a breakthrough to modernity had existed long before its advent: "The tension between the desire for creative autonomy and the pressure of inherited or conventionally accepted authoritative systems is a central artistic concern whose roots extend further back than is customarily acknowledged."[24] A prominent example is, of course, *Don Quixote*, particularly its prologue. Meyer describes it thus:

> A friend instructs him how to insert, on occasions both appropriate and inappropriate, the well-known *loci communes* from the literature of classical antiquity and the Bible. Moreover, tradition requires that he should append an alphabetical index of quoted authors, and he should feel free to appropriate this index from any book he chooses. After all, not a soul will check up on him and notice the deception. It is clear that the device of pedantic quoting, which in countless works of Renaissance and Baroque poetry belongs to the reverently venerated set of decorative literary forms, has become meaningless for the author of Don Quixote. It has been debased to the function of a piece in a puzzle of literary fictions.[25]

In modern times, quotation has become intrinsic to language and writing. From the nineteenth century onward, there has emerged a complex relation to quotation. It is very clearly perceived as a foreign element belonging to the "other." Thus quotation entails some sense of discontinuity with the established tradition, it marks a certain individualism and pragmatism; but at the same time it embodies respect for the other's individual creativity and the right to protect it.

Since quotations create a net of literacy and information, the seeming restriction on them (acknowledging them as somebody else's property) not only does not minimize their use but, on the contrary, encourages an abundance of quotations and gives rise to serial quotation.[26] Compagnon claims that a serial quotation is not a literary reference, nor even a graft or encrustation; it does not send us to the other, to a particular text or author—it is more like a stain, which is on the page even before we start writing.[27]

Surgical and Economical Modes

Two types of metaphors are most frequently employed when quotation is being discussed: surgical and economical.

Surgical metaphors see quotation as something cut off and transplanted into a "host" text, and thus in this sense it is a graft. "A chosen fragment converts itself into a text, not any more a piece of text, a member of the phrase or the discourse, but a chosen piece, an amputated member."[28] Quotations are like foreign bodies, which do not properly belong to us but are "invited" and appropriated and thus enter into the texture of our writings. Sometimes they indicate a distance and do not blend with the host text, but sometimes they, as it were, disappear in our text, either because they do not acquire full significance or because they become assimilated to such a degree that they lose their discrete boundaries and become one with our text. The ensuing merging can be the result of a natural coincidence of style and mode of thinking, or it can be brought about by the author's conscious efforts, usually inflicting some changes on the quotation. Other similar metaphors employed to describe the process of quoting are paternity, filiation, insemination, and castration. All these metaphors enter into the surgical mode of description, as they deal with violence and transplantation.

The other obvious and predominant mode of speaking about quotations is economical. Quotation introduces an object into circulation. This object might acquire a new value from that which it originally had. Because quotation detaches fragments of text from their respective contexts and attaches them to other contexts, there arises a tension between their independent value and the sense that the quotation might have had in its original context. Quotation has a power independent of this sense, because it creates a semantic potential. In the sense produced by the quotation, it is not only the sense of the quotation that acts and reacts but also the quotation itself, the phenomenon. Because of its double value (one taken from the original source and one created in relation to its new context), quoting is an economic operation, subject to the rule of exchange. (I shall later question whether there may be an exception to that, whether biblical quotation is also subject to a rule of exchange, and where, with respect to it, one can speak about violence. See Chapter 6.)

Recent Approaches to Quotation

In recent times the question of quotations has been approached from different perspectives: linguistics,[29] philosophy of language, and literary studies.[30] What is lacking is a more holistic perspective that would first describe the performance of quotation in the immediate experience of reading or writing (in the first instance phenomenologically as the process and not the product), but would then focus on the creation of sense and the interaction of the contexts. The latter should again be viewed from several perspectives: it should not only determine the precise sense acquired as a result of the interplay of the two relative contexts, but also examine how quotation "disturbs" the normal flow of language and relate quoting to such issues as authority and appropriation.

Little or no attempt has been made to examine the hermeneutical function of quotation in a philosophical context. In spite of considerable attention paid to influences in philosophy, there has not been much thought about influence in terms of quotation, and no one has described how the process and phenomenon of quoting affects patterns of thinking and writing, as well as the reader's reception of a multilayered philosophical text. The study of Kierkegaard's use of quotations demonstrates that quotations do play a distinct role in the construction of a philosophical text.

The only area in philosophy where quotation has been discussed extensively is logic, as part of the philosophy of language. "In quotation not only does language turn on itself, but it does so word by word and expression by expression, and this reflexive twist is inseparable from the convenience and universal applicability of the device. Here we already have enough to draw the interest of the philosopher of language."[31] Indeed, the whole discussion of quotation in logic is centered on the conflict between mention and use.[32] This major issue in the philosophy of language does not significantly affect the quotations discussed in the present work, because the majority of the biblical quotations in Kierkegaard's pseudonymous works are "incorporated quotations," and, as Clark and Gerrig have put it, "Incorporated quotations depict, but what they depict is simultaneously appropriated for use in the containing utterance."[33]

Tensions in Quotation

Let us briefly review several interrelated problem fields, all of which are central to any process of writing and in which key issues are brought to light by the question of quotation. In assigning a central role to quotation in the phenomenon of textuality, we should ask whether, apart from the fact that they essentially belong (do they?) to another, quotations function differently from other segments of text.

First, of course, there is the problem of uncertain boundaries and affinities between the concepts of quotation and allusion, and between other parts of speech such as paraphrase or reference. The question whether allusion or quotation should be considered the more encompassing category has been answered both ways. Some have advised making a sharp distinction between categories such as the use of: independent literal quotation, modified quotation, clear or obvious allusion, characteristic word combinations, turns of phrase, or other language, forms, and variations. However, it seems that no one has yet found a stable or valid definition of quotation that would enable us infallibly to draw the line between quotation and allusion and other related forms. I thought it best, therefore, to consider them under a generic term of "quotation," assuming that all these textual variations share fundamentally the same function. The question of whether quotation plays an essentially different role from that of other elements that make up a text undermines the classical model, which draws a sharp distinction between a source text and quotation in terms of "host" and "guest element."

It has been suggested that it is not clear whether the status of the tension between juxtaposition and combination in a quoted text is different from that in "homogeneous" writing, since the whole practice of writing always includes quotation, so that no definition of quotation is possible.[34] Although I agree that no strict demarcation between a quotation and the rest of the text is possible, I think we should also beware of falling into the relativism of "everything is a quotation."

Quotation is a unique segment of text, insofar as it establishes a more or less visible and traceable "public" link between texts. It can, therefore, be rightly treated as a central feature of intertextuality. Also, it is precisely through the tension between assimilation and dissimilation that a quotation participates in the appropriation. This dialectic (which can be also expressed through the paradigm active-passive) is inherent to quotation, and in this way sets it apart from other textual elements. By defining quotation as "a repeated utterance [*énoncé*] and a repeating uttering,"[35] Compagnon points toward this important feature of quotation, namely, the collision between active and passive, distance and proximity. This involves the dynamic tension between distancing and approaching in quotation.

Quotation can mark the distance and shake off responsibility, or it can associate and appropriate. Most often both moments are present. The dialectic between the active and the passive mode is present in the quotation insofar as quotation has an independent meaning, but in the interaction with the host text acquires a new meaning itself and affects the meaning of the host text. We will see how interestingly Kierkegaard reworks this dynamic between active and passive when biblical quotations become an essential tool of indirect communication.

Yet another side of this tension is veiling-revealing. Quotation multiplies the sense, but it can also obscure it either by imposing an "unknown" or indecipherable meaning, or by deferring it. Through the function of authority, quotation is a guarantee of truth (this means that there is at least a trace of *auctoritas* in almost all quotations). As Compagnon puts it, "Quotation masks the question of the truth of utterance under the question of the authenticity of uttering, so that the utterance itself is held to be true."[36]

Quotation seemingly guarantees both the truth of the content and the fact that somebody really said or wrote it. Thus quotation creates a link of confidence between a reader and a writer: even if the reader mistrusts the author's arguments, he is likely to believe that there is some truth, namely, at least the fact that a third party has thought this or that about this matter. Because of this confidence, manipulation is possible on two levels: by inflicting changes on the text of the quotation or by cutting it in a certain way and placing it in its new context so as to give it a different and possibly even an opposite sense.[37] Such manipulation is not necessarily malign. It may involve a deliberate distortion, but it may also be due to an ingenious or insensitive use. It seems that there are no reliable formal criteria to distinguish between these two types of manipulation. An extreme case revealing possibilities of manipulation is parody:

> The charm of parody, one might say in general, is based on sharpened contrast between the original sense of quotation and the meaning newly attributed to it by the act of quoting. If we cling to this as a guiding point of view, then the contrast can be shaded in a series of gradations, according to its constitutive elements. The gentlest form of contrast is found in the tension which results when the quoted words as such are used in the original sense, but, through their *context,* collide with meanings of an opposite sort and are themselves dragged over into a contrary sense. This collision can be primarily in form or in meaning.[38]

The third specific feature of quotation is that it relates reading to writing in a very explicit way. It has been said that "Quotation attempts to reproduce the passion of reading in writing."[39] This, as earlier noted, is particularly relevant for Kierkegaard, who preferred to refer to himself as the reader of his own texts.[40]

Repetition in Appropriation

What, then, are the important issues relating to quotations that affect the present study? First of all, quotation is directly connected to the issues of appropriation and authority, to the dynamics of activity and passivity in reading and writing, and also to the relation to tradition, originality, and authenticity. As Meyer says: "Whether he is oriented toward tradition or against tradition, the writer is concerned with the management of a cultural inheritance that he himself absorbs, preserves, and passes along."[41] Nowhere is the interplay of spontaneity and tradition more obvious than in the intersection between the originality of the author on the one hand and the reception of tradition on the other—that is to say, in the quotation.

The complex relation between an author and the tradition is reflected by the choice of quotations, if it is at all a matter of choice and not a mere submission to cultural conventions. Through the selection of points of reference, an author reveals his attitude toward tradition: he either dreams of a polyvalent, elusive and profuse structure where one can choose selectively, or he accepts a more or less established preselected configuration. "The art of heir is to maintain the greatest possible tension between fidelity and infidelity."[42] In many cases it is likely to be the combination of respect for the tradition and also a wish to overturn it, or to bring to light the forgotten and hidden treasures of the tradition (instead of bowing to immortal authors to resurrect the dead ones). But even in a closed structure of tradition, there is a certain liberty of individual choice, so that the question is why a certain author picks up certain texts from the vast history of literacy and chooses to relate to them in an explicit way.

Related to this is the question as to how a quotation becomes a quotation, that is to say, what in the primary text enables it to take itself off, to penetrate other texts and thus to "prolong" its existence. Even if the relation to tradition is a negative one, the power of tradition is acknowledged by allowing it to continue participating in the history of thought and writing through quotation. Entering into a dialogue with other texts, a given text often takes as a point of departure (and this is part of the natural consequences of education) an idea expressed elsewhere, either for confrontation and innovation or for confirmation, by appealing, implicitly or explicitly, to the authority of the source. The process of quoting can be rightly called dissemination.

Thus one of the functions of quoting is to ensure continuity, by keeping the past alive and renewed in contemporary writings. It is a way of preservation, however, not a static reproduction, but often a creative reinvention. The way quotation relates to the authority of tradition involves the process of legitimation. Perhaps the most effective form of quotation is a familiar quotation, which appeals to our memory. It works as a shortcut to the meaning—instead of spelling it out, it gives us a kind of password, a summary, and then our memory has to clarify the picture, add the missing context. A familiar quotation basically provides another dimension, so that it is possible to read the present text and yet *at the same time* have another text "in mind." As such it is the opposite of a footnote, or perhaps just a successful footnote, since it refers to the outside of the text but itself stays within it.

As we have clarified, quotation was already placed in the framework of repetition and memory in ancient rhetoric.[43] Through memory and imitation, quotations help to weave the net of literacy. We remember that the "text" originally comes from the verb meaning "to weave." It is in this way that the text was imagined: as a fabric (textile) woven from many different threads. One of the aspects of it has to do namely with the reproduction of reading in writing, with repetition in appropriation. When we say that quotation is a repetition, this is to be understood in connection with the inevitable tension between the identical and the similar in repetition. The complex problem of the possibility of repetition arises because: "Identical elements repeat only on condition that there is an independence of 'cases' or a discontinuity of 'times' such that one appears only when the other has disappeared: within representation, repetition is indeed forced to undo itself even as it occurs."[44]

Even a verbally exact quotation that would seem to be a perfect repetition is ambiguous, because it is not clear whether it can keep its integrity in the new context. For what matters is not only *what* a quotation is, but also *how* it is. Roughly, there are three levels of reduplication in the repetition involved in quotation: (1) the original content A in the original form A; (2) the content A in content B (new context); (3) the content A of the form A now in the form B.

The ambiguity of quotation as repetition is intrinsic, because appropriation is the only mode of transmitting tradition, although inasmuch as tradition goes forward it must reinvent itself, and thus it acquires a more or less different form. The tension inherent in the "repetition" of quotation is best illustrated in Borges's story *Pierre Menard, Author of Don Quixote*. Borges describes the ambition of Pierre Menard to produce pages that would coincide—word for word and line for line—with those of Miguel de Cervantes.[45] Borges takes two verbally identical quotations and argues that not only is the meaning different (this could be explained as due to a new context), but also, "equally vivid is the contrast in styles."[46] This statement amplifies the problem of there being not merely similar but identical elements in repetition.

Does quotation aim at repetition but only achieve imitation? It might be said that quotation is a symbol of the problem of repetition, as we encounter it in Kierkegaard's works, where "repetition" is a key existential and religious concept. Quotation is a symbol of the problem, whether it is possible for a repetition to take place and, if yes, on what conditions. We will come back to quotation as repetition in Kierkegaardian context in Chapter 6. It is also interesting to note that in Kierkegaard's use of biblical quotations, the modern use of quotation meets that of an early theological discourse that was a systematic act of quoting.

Quotation is not a marginal feature, and in many modern texts it is far from being merely an ornament. Indeed it is true not only of modern times, since "Similarly metafiction, the way in which one story draws upon another, is not the product of modern critical theory, but is a constant and inescapable presence in the written word, constituting at once a revision of the past and a legitimation of the present."[47] But now, when there is no more such distinction as the main text and inserted fragment, it occupies an even more central place in the intertextuality. I have tried to draw attention to the vast semantic field that is affected or articulated by the presence of quotation, most notably to the issues of authority and legitimation, the dialectic of distance and proximity in the process of appropriation, and the possibility of treating quotation as a symbol of the problem of repetition.

Kierkegaard's Hermeneutics: Hidden Communication

> Indeed, give [somebody] a creative talent like that, and then such
> frail health, and he surely will learn to pray. (PV 74)

In order to appreciate the hermeneutical functioning of biblical quotations in Kierkegaard's pseudonymous works, it is necessary to consider
the question of hermeneutics as such in Kierkegaard's authorship.
Quotation plays a special role in hermeneutics since, as we have seen,
it is a segment of text that manifests the author's interaction with the
tradition and the history of writing *par excellence*. Biblical quotation is a
hermeneutical subject not only because it provides such a uniquely
explicit relation to tradition, but also because it incorporates two
impulses from which hermeneutics has developed as an art of understanding and interpreting, namely, the theological and the philological
impulses.

It incorporates the theological impulse insofar as it invokes and at
the same time incarnates the Bible; the philological impulse insofar as
it transmits one text to the other, and because it often touches upon
the issue of translation. But before assessing its relation to other
texts, it is important to have a notion of the premise on which the writing under consideration is constructed, and to discover the overall
internal structure and the circumstances of the authorship.

In this chapter, I shall first show how various features of modern
hermeneutics are anticipated in Kierkegaard's works. I will then

concentrate on the problem of Kierkegaard's pseudonyms, his understanding of writing and reading, the authority of author and the engagement required from the reader, as well as the theory and practice of indirect communication. It may seem that these questions are not the subject of hermeneutics, which deals with understanding rather than creating. However—even though the link between rhetoric and hermeneutics has often been overlooked—one can argue that such questions do pertain to the domain of hermeneutics.

Indeed, hermeneutics was an integral part of ancient rhetoric. Both Schleiermacher and Gadamer have drawn our attention to the close relation between rhetoric and hermeneutics, but the relation has not been properly explored and has—until recently—remained marginal. Schleiermacher, for example, observed: "The belonging together of hermeneutics and rhetoric consists in the fact that every act of understanding is the inversion of a speech-act [*Akt des Redens*] during which the thought which was the basis of the speech must become conscious."[1] With respect to Kierkegaard's texts, the link between rhetoric and hermeneutics is particularly interesting, since the reflexivity of his writing always betrays a concern with reading. That is to say, in his intra-active hermeneutics there is a certain reflexive twist that bases writing on the anticipation of reading, so that the author's concern is how to write in order to be read in a particular way—this means that it becomes a hermeneutical problem.

The Origins of Modern Hermeneutics: From Text to Being

Before moving on to specifically Kierkegaardian issues, let us briefly consider the origins of modern hermeneutics. I will begin by introducing the chief features of Schleiermacher's and Dilthey's hermeneutics. I will then outline the main hermeneutical questions posed from Heidegger onward. This short outline is not meant to exhaust the complex issues of hermeneutics, but merely to provide a context and indicate Kierkegaard's role and influence in the modern hermeneutical setting. I will focus only on the figures that shaped the development of hermeneutics in general, such as Heidegger, Gadamer, and Ricoeur, and point out several instances where Kierkegaard anticipated their key notions and distinctions. This means, of course, that I will have to leave out many other thinkers, such as Nietzsche and Foucault, whose multiple contributions to hermeneutics, to our understanding of the interpretative context of modern thought, are beyond any doubt; or Bultmann, who freed theological hermeneutics from a view that one needs to attribute a special discursive structure to God's Word and in a rather Kierkegaardian spirit claimed that the text can be heard only by those who are already concerned about their existence.[2] I will, however, deal briefly with the literary hermeneutics because it represents the fusion of literary and philosophical questions, which is one of the prominent features of Kierkegaard's own hermeneutics and has a direct bearing on the question of quotation.

In the nineteenth century, hermeneutics ceased to be exclusively a tool of theology and philology and was made central to all human sciences. As Gadamer observes, it owed its centrality to the rise of historical consciousness.[3] One of the main questions of hermeneutics was to define its task in relation to historical mediation. The two thinkers who are most likely to have influenced Kierkegaard on this subject, Schleiermacher and Hegel, suggest two very different ways of historical mediation; "They may be described as *reconstruction* and *integration*."[4] What rouses both of them to hermeneutical reflection is the consciousness of loss and estrangement in relation to tradition.

Schleiermacher believes that it is possible to replace the loss by various means of historical reconstruction—by reestablishing the "world" to which it belongs, reenacting the intention of the creative artist and his state of mind, and so on. In short, this hermeneutical method aims at a recreation of the creative act and at understanding a writer better than he understood himself. Schleiermacher suggests a fundamental shift insofar as, according to him, the task of hermeneutics is to understand not only the text and its meaning, but also the individuality of author, as well as to identify with the original reader.

In thinking along these lines, however, Schleiermacher overlooks the objection that "Reconstructing the original circumstances, like all restoration, is a futile undertaking in view of the historicity of our being. What is reconstructed, a life brought back from the lost past, is not the original."[5] The past that is "recreated" nevertheless remains estranged from us.

Hegel describes a Schleiermacherian reconstruction with a negative emphasis. For Hegel, our relation to history should be a thoughtful mediation with contemporary life. What we need, he says, is an "*interiorizing recollection* [*Er-innerung*] of the still *externalized* spirit" manifested in the fruits of history/nature.[6] For Hegel, this self-conscious spirit is expressed above all in philosophy.

Another major figure at the origins of hermeneutics was Dilthey, who inserted hermeneutics into the context of his own life philosophy (*Lebensphilosophie*). For Dilthey, hermeneutics involved the right construing of "expressions of lived experience fixed in writing [*schriftlich fixierte Erlebnisausserungen*]."[7] His interpretation was mainly psychological, but one has to bear in mind that he regarded life as accessible only through manifestations, traces, and expressions. He hoped that methods arising from a foundational hermeneutics would be as objectively "valid" as determinations in the natural sciences. Dilthey attempted a critique of historical reason to complement the critique of pure reason and to find the conditions of historical knowledge, or knowledge of history. It was also Dilthey who introduced the couple explain/understand (*erklaren/verstehen*), which made hermeneutics a part of epistemology and played an important role in its evolution.

As Gadamer remarks, the science of hermeneutics as developed by Schleiermacher differs from the techniques of classical philology and the theological hermeneutics of the Church fathers, or of Reformation theologians, because understanding as such becomes a problem for the first time.[8] With Schleiermacher (or rather after him), the task of hermeneutics changes and becomes more universal, because alienation is now seen as inextricably tied together with the individuality of the other.[9]

Gadamer has pointed out that "The art of understanding came under fundamental theoretical examination and universal cultivation because neither scripturally nor rationally founded agreement could any longer constitute the dogmatic guideline of textual understanding."[10] Consequently it became necessary to redefine the relation to tradition. Kierkegaard offered an original model for reappraising this relation, specifically with regard to the Christian heritage, and his emphasis on contemporaneity in spirit (as opposed to contemporaneity due to immediate historical participation) was an alternative to the models of appropriation suggested by Schleiermacher and Hegel.

In the twentieth century, a decisive shift took place from the transcendental tradition to an ontological one, from ideas about knowledge and the interior life of those whose situations and cultural frameworks differ radically from those shaping the inquirer's prejudices, or "cultural grammars," to a problematic of being. This second approach "does not stop with the determination of meanings but is an ongoing critical reflection in which we see ourselves and what matters to us in the light of the text, even as we see the text in the light of ourselves and of our interests."[11]

Indeed the task for Heidegger and Gadamer was to free hermeneutics from the methodological mission of providing correct interpretations of texts and to place the "event" of understanding in its full intentional, existential, phenomenological, historical, ontological, and linguistic context. Instead of being "framed," interpretation was now conceived as "open": it aimed not at an object but at a "fusion of horizons" (*Horizontverschmelzung*).

A hermeneutical operation does not perform an exhaustive comprehension of a certain object, but a "syntony" between the interpreter and the "call" that he has to be able to receive and listen to.[12] There is no longer in the act of interpretation an epistemological dichotomy between the subject as knowing and the object as known. It can be said that this dissolution was begun by Kierkegaard when he introduced and emphasized the role of the "how" in the process of both the communication and the "reception" of communication, and set up the distinction between subjective and objective truth rather than between objective subject and subjective object.

After this "turn" in the modern history of hermeneutics, one often speaks about two directions: a mere interpretation of texts and a new, broader sense of hermeneutics of existence. While it is true that there is now an ontological turn in hermeneutics, the two directions need not be mutually exclusive. It seems that to a certain degree the two directions, or rather levels, have always coexisted, even in pre-Heideggerian hermeneutics. Kierkegaard is an excellent example of hermeneutics where reading a text (the Bible) and interpreting it is directly and deeply concerned with the question of being, inasmuch as reading is about imitation and learning to be in becoming. Vattimo rightly observes that "In its constitutive and universal dimension, hermeneutics first of all concerns the conditions that make communication possible."[13] Kierkegaard was always interested in both the conditions of communication (from the author's as well as the reader's point of view) and its implications for individual existence.

We now move to the main features of the post-Schleiermacherian hermeneutical tradition, in order to indicate Kierkegaard's contribution to its development. I will not attempt to prove Kierkegaard's influence on Heidegger, Gadamer, or Ricoeur; such a task would require a careful and thorough comparative study. I will simply call attention to several decisive concepts and distinctions that Kierkegaard introduced and also to the fact that some of the appropriations of his hermeneutical notions were misguided.

Heidegger: The Hermeneutical Situation of *Dasein*

The new turn of hermeneutics is to be traced back to Heidegger's project of a hermeneutics of facticity. Heidegger breaks with the limitations of discussion about method and takes the hermeneutical problem to the level of the ontology of a finite being, where "to understand" is no longer simply a way of knowing or perceiving, but a way of being. The question about conditions for understanding a text is replaced by another question about the very nature of a being whose being consists of understanding.[14] Heidegger challenges the idea of metaphysical presence and discusses the hermeneutical problem in terms of temporality and movement. "In *Being and Time,* the hermeneutics of facticity assumed the dimensions of a deconstruction of the metaphysics of presence and of a new raising of the question of Being; it had come to mean restoring the original difficulty in Being."[15]

For Heidegger understanding is an event, and to understand means to project a certain horizontal framework within which the being is to be understood. Thus the hermeneutical question becomes part of the larger question of the existential constitution of *Da* and is treated in the framework of three main existential aspects: situation, understanding, and interpretation.[16] In his *Radical Hermeneutics,* Caputo notes that "In *Being and Time* the projective structure of the understanding (the Husserlian principle) derives from the Being of Dasein as repetition (the Kierkegaardian principle), from the forward momentum of 'existing' Dasein."[17] He thus identifies two major influences on Heidegger's hermeneutics of facticity. He suggests that Husserl's "anticipatory" theory of constitution is an essential ingredient in Heidegger's "hermeneutic."[18] In Husserl's phenomenology, the intentional object is always something interpreted. Husserl "takes consciousness to be a composite of focal and marginal components and the work of phenomenology to be an 'unfolding' or 'ex-plicating' of this marginal life, which is what he meant by *Auslegung.* This is the same word, of course, which is used by Heidegger in *Being and Time* and is rendered in the English translation as 'interpretation.' *Aus-legen* means to lay out, or make explicit, the tacit structures of intentional life."[19] Husserl raised the question of the constitution of meaning and objectivity that Heidegger developed further and enriched by "repetition." We will come back to his debt to Kierkegaard a bit later.

The projective structure of understanding is the horizon within which things are set free to be the things that they are. This understanding then has to become more determinate, and that is the role of interpretation. For Heidegger, "interpretation" (*Auslegung*) is the working out (*Ausarbeitung*) of understanding.[20] This working out of understanding into fully developed interpretation consists of accumulating the hermeneutic "fore-structures." The main fore-structures of *Vorverständnis*, the fore-understanding, are *Vorhabe*, fore-having; *Vorsicht*, fore-sight; and *Vorgriff*, fore-grasping. Together these fore-structures make up what Heidegger calls the "hermeneutic situation" (*Being and Time*, 275). This means that "to know the 'meaning' of something is to know that in terms of which it is to be projected, the horizon in terms of which it should be cast, the sphere to which it belongs."[21] Therefore the network of hermeneutic fore-structure is the very condition under which understanding is possible; it is not an obstacle to objective understanding. Rather, it reflects the inherently hermeneutical structure of our consciousness.

In this sense, "Hermeneutics in *Being and Time* invokes a strategy of recovery, of *re-cognitio, Wieder-erkennung*, of knowing again, bringing back on a cognitive level something which is already obscurely understood."[22] Before understanding can be fully articulated, the Platonic "recollection" has to go through the multiple fore-structures. Heidegger asks a radical question about the meaning of meaning: "We do not 'know' (*wissen*) what Dasein and *a fortiori* Being itself mean; we lack a conceptual fix (*begrifflich Fixieren*) on them. But we always and already move about within an 'understanding' of them" (*Being and Time*, 25). "What does 'meaning' signify? . . . meaning is that wherein the understandability [*Verstehbarkeit*] of something maintains itself—even that of something which does not come into view explicitly and thematically" (*Being and Time*, 370–371).

The question about the meaning of meaning and the starting point of interpretation takes us back to the notorious problem of the hermeneutical circle. "The circle can also be put in terms of part-whole relations: we are trying to establish a reading of the whole text, and for this we appeal to readings of its partial expressions, and yet because we are dealing with meaning, with making sense, where expressions only make sense or not in relation to others, the readings of partial expressions depend on those of others, and ultimately of the whole."[23] Heidegger gives the "hermeneutic circle"—which previously bore only an epistemological or methodological sense—an ontological weight and says that "What is decisive is not to get out of the circle but to come into it in the right way" (*Being and Time*, 195).

Heidegger thus makes a double shift in perspective: first he moves from the epistemological framework to the ontological; the understanding is no longer a mere knowledge but also a way of being. The *Dasein* is the privileged object of ontological reflection because it itself manifests a certain interpretation of the meaning of being. Second, he finishes the process of "depsychologization" of the hermeneutical problem, which moves from knowledge and understanding of the other to the problem of understanding one's self, history, world, and understanding itself.

Kierkegaard and Heidegger: Concealed Repetition

Let us now address the question of Heidegger's unacknowledged debt to Kierkegaard. Kierkegaard's biggest contribution to *Being and Time*, and to hermeneutics in general, is no doubt the concept of repetition and the constitution of the self in the flux of temporality.

Greisch observes that far from ending with paragraph 34 of *Being and Time*, as it is sometimes assumed, the theme of hermeneutics only begins there. In order to understand what Heidegger means by hermeneutics, we therefore have to show that understanding, situation, and discourse are the specific modes of temporalization. For example, discourse has to be understood as the articulation of temporality in order to find the possibility of expressing time through "tenses" in language.[24]

Indeed Heidegger's understanding of hermeneutics closely depends on his understanding of the structure of temporality of the human self. Caputo observes that "In Heidegger, the projective character of the understanding is itself rooted in the more profound ontological makeup of Dasein. The structure of the understanding reflects the Being of Dasein as care, existence, and temporality. It is precisely at this point that the ontology of Kierkegaard intervenes in *Being and Time*, and in a particularly decisive manner."[25] In more than one way, it is true that "Kierkegaard set in motion the 'destruction of the history of ontology' and hence anticipated the central ontological argument of *Being and Time* and the whole gesture of 'overcoming of metaphysics' in the later Heidegger. By opposing existential repetition to Platonic recollection and Hegelian mediation, the beginning and end of metaphysics, he mounted a sweeping attack upon the whole history of metaphysics."[26]

Kierkegaard rethought the Platonic recollection, and instead of the backward movement he chose repetition as a forward movement that characterizes the constitution of the human self.[27] In his view, the self produces or creates itself by choosing one's self in repetition. The self is not a static presence, but a possibility in becoming. Obviously such a conception of a human self is accompanied by a redefinition of understanding of temporality and the meeting point of temporality and eternity, thus terms such as "moment," "becoming," "movement," "decision," "paradox," and "possibility" become of crucial importance. This break with the Platonic tradition of recollection is full of ontological consequences, and it is rather strange that Heidegger asserts that Kierkegaard did not make the necessary break with the metaphysical tradition. Heidegger underestimates Kierkegaard's radical understanding of temporality. This is most obvious in his famous footnote in *Being and Time:*

> S. Kierkegaard is probably the one who has seen the *existentiell* phenomenon of the moment of vision with the most penetration; but this does not signify that he has been correspondingly successful in interpreting it existentially. He clings to the ordinary conception of time, and defines the "moment of vision" with the help of "now" and "eternity." When Kierkegaard speaks of "temporality," what he has in mind is man's "Being-in-time" [*In-der-Zeit-sein*]. Time as within-time-ness knows only the "now"; it never knows a moment of vision.

It is true that Kierkegaard rarely treats "time" as a separate issue, and his discussion of time is often implicit and fragmented (except perhaps for the third chapter in *The Concept of Anxiety* and "The Interlude" in *The Philosophical Fragments*) and has to be traced through his treatment of concepts such as eternity, the instant (or moment), the fullness of time, or memory and recollection.[28] However, time necessarily plays an important role in such key concepts as "becoming." The concern with the temporal (and *via negationis*—the eternal) is often a question of actuality and possibility.

In fact, it would not be too much to say that for Kierkegaard, time is constitutive of selfhood in the most eminent sense.[29] This failure to fully appreciate the novelty of Kierkegaard's concepts of "moment" and "repetition" may be due to the fact that Heidegger tried to overcome the metaphysical tradition by incorporating recollection in the moment of repetition, thus making a forward movement at some point coincide with a backward one. "So when Dasein comes *toward* itself in its authentic potentiality for Being it comes *back* to itself and *retrieves* that which it has been all along" (*Being and Time*, 373). This movement, of course, creates a circle. "In Heidegger the movement is more properly *circular*, inasmuch as the movement forward is at the same time a movement back to one's inherited possibilities. Kierkegaard remains within the *linear* model but reverses its direction."[30]

But it seems not entirely correct to say that Kierkegaard has a linear conception of self. His image is, rather, that of a chain of loops, whereby, in a constant movement of repetition, a self is becoming what it is but in such a way that there is a moment, an infinitely fine point, when a self is self-reflecting. In relation to Heidegger, the question remains how decision, or a "moment," is possible in a circle. The same problem is encountered in the question of whether Heidegger ever provided an answer to how to enter the hermeneutical circle "in the right way."

Even though Kierkegaard's repetition is at the very heart of the hermeneutical problem in *Being and Time*, Kierkegaardian "repetition" (*Gjentagelse*) becomes "retrieval" (*Wiederholung*), a forward retrieval that recovers something that was *Dasein's in potential*.[31] The difference in the mode and vector of movement in Heidegger and Kierkegaard may be also due to the fact that Heidegger concentrated much more on the historicity of *Dasein* and on historicity as an essential element of authenticity than did Kierkegaard. While Kierkegaard was conscious of the historical situatedness of existential resolve, he was more interested in the concept of contemporaneity than in that of inheritance.

It has been suggested that one of the things that separates Heidegger's approach to the question of repetition from Kierkegaard's is the way each author incorporates it in his text. "Here we see a certain convergence of the matter (*Sache*) which *Being and Time* addresses and the method which the treatise employs. In Kierkegaard, the matter was existential repetition, but the method was oblique indirection in complex aesthetic thrusting and parrying."[32] I hope that in the course of this book it will become apparent that repetition is also very much a methodical element in Kierkegaard's writings and lies at the very core of his indirect communication. Indeed what is said of *Being and Time*, "Thus the very method of the book, the progress of the treatise, follows the downward-spiralling path of repetition,"[33] is very true of Kierkegaard's pseudonymous works, regardless of whether or not Heidegger himself was influenced by Kierkegaard's way of inscribing repetition in his works.

Equally, when Gerald Bruns claims that Heidegger shifted "the question of understanding from the theoretical plane of seeing from a perspective to the practical plane of involvement and participation in ongoing action,"[34] we note that well before Heidegger, Kierkegaard did just this through his indirect communication, the analysis of "interest" and "passion," the emphasis on transition from reading to acting, existential engagement, and so on.

We thus see that through his concept of repetition and his notion of the temporal constitution of selfhood, Kierkegaard is present at the heart of the ontological turn of hermeneutics.

Gadamer's Truth Beyond Method

Gadamer shaped the methodological horizon of hermeneutics inasmuch as he posed the unity of understanding, interpretation, and application in all hermeneutical approach, no matter what its object and field may have been. Although he continued to develop the notion of understanding as an *event* and tried to emancipate hermeneutics from the limitations of the various techniques of interpretation in order to move toward the philosophy and ontology, Gadamer concentrated mainly on the importance that Heidegger gave to the ontological weight of language, and not so much on another key thought in Heidegger—meditation of metaphysics as the history and fate of a being.

In order for a hermeneutical problem to emerge, "a situation must exist where something remote has to be brought nearer, a strangeness overcome, a bridge built between 'once' and 'now.' "[35] According to Gadamer, "The task of hermeneutics is to clarify this miracle of understanding, which is not a mysterious communion of souls, but sharing in a common meaning."[36] This understanding takes place in the framework of fore-meanings as analyzed by Heidegger. For Gadamer, the text can present itself in all its otherness and thus assert its own truth only when we are thoroughly aware of our own fore-meanings and "prejudices" in the technical sense. "Openness always includes our situating the other meaning in relation to the whole of our meanings or ourselves in relation to it."[37]

Gadamer insisted on the historical dimension of understanding. In all understanding, whether we are expressly aware of it or not, the efficacy of history is at work, and the failure to recognize that can lead to an actual deformation of knowledge: "Consciousness of being affected by history (*wirkungsgeschichtliches Bewußtsein*) is primarily consciousness of the hermeneutical *situation*."[38] Accordingly, the task of philosophical hermeneutics is to retrace the path of Hegel's phenomenology of mind until we discover in all that is subjective the substantiality that determines it, that both prescribes and limits every possibility for understanding any tradition whatsoever in its historical alterity.

There are several aspects where Kierkegaard and Gadamer raise similar hermeneutical issues. One can ask whether the hermeneutical problem of application explicitly articulated by Gadamer does not at least partially coincide with the problem of appropriation in Kierkegaard's works. The questions of contemporaneity,[39] and expressing the limit as found in Kierkegaard's works, find their echo in Gadamer's analysis of the essentially linguistic character of all human experience:

> Hermeneutic work is based on a polarity of familiarity and strangeness; but his polarity is not to be regarded psychologically, with Schleiermacher, as the range that covers the mystery of individuality, but truly hermeneutically—i.e., in regard to what has been said: the language in which text addresses us, the story that it tells us. Here too there is a tension. It is in the play between the traditional text's strangeness and familiarity to us, between being a historically intended, distanciated object and belonging to a tradition. *The true locus of hermeneutics is this in-between.*[40]

However, Gadamer does not take Kierkegaard's notion of appropriation sufficiently radically, and thus remains in the hermeneutical circle: "The movement of understanding is constantly from the whole to the part and back to the whole. Our task is to expand the unity of the understood meaning centrifugally. The harmony of all the details with the whole is the criterion of correct understanding."[41] On the other hand, Gadamer develops Kierkegaard's notion of the blurred line between the creativity of author and that of the reader: "Not just occasionally but always, the meaning of a text goes beyond its author. That is why understanding is not merely a reproductive but always a productive activity as well."[42] As we will see later in this chapter, Kierkegaard's idea of the productive or creative understanding/reading is one of the features that made his writing anticipatingly modern.

The issue of understanding as a productive rather than a passive activity has had a considerable influence in hermeneutics and literary theory, and has contributed to redefining textuality in general. It is also important to note that Gadamer continues and thematizes Kierkegaard's distinction between objective and subjective truth and his notion that meaning cannot be separated from the subjectivity of the interpreter. "Our line of thought prevents us from dividing the hermeneutic problem in terms of the subjectivity of the interpreter and the objectivity of the meaning to be understood. This would be starting from a false antithesis that cannot be resolved even by recognising the dialectic of subjective and objective. To distinguish between a normative function and a cognitive one is to separate what clearly belong together."[43] As observed earlier, the dissolution of the epistemological dichotomy between the subject as knowing and object as known played a major role in the hermeneutical turn.

Ricoeur and Narrative Time

Ricoeur's hermeneutics can be situated between those of Betti and Gadamer. He rejects all forms of psychological interpretation, he does not subscribe to the theory of the transfer of intentionality, but he is concerned with method rather than with ontologizing the problem of hermeneutics.[44] Ricoeur's hermeneutics tries to maintain a dialectical balance between "explain" and "understand," while it seems that Gadamer has resolutely crossed the line without ever looking back.[45]

Although still largely concerned with method, Ricoeur agrees that the question of truth is no longer one of method but rather one relating to the manifestation of being, for a being whose existence consists in understanding being.[46] Ricoeur criticizes Heidegger because the latter's view of hermeneutics does not provide any answer to such questions as how to constitute the historical sciences in distinction from the natural sciences, or how to solve the question of rival interpretations.[47] The difficulty of transition from understanding as a mode of knowledge to understanding as a mode of being is that analysis of *Dasein* is itself influenced by understanding as knowledge, which suggests that it is in language itself that we should look for indications that understanding is a mode of being.

All understanding, ontic or ontological, always takes place in language. Ricoeur sticks to the notion of "text" but enlarges the domain of text. For example, he speaks about meaningful action (such as gesture) as a text, or, in the Freudian context, about dream as "story." Because Ricoeur enlarges the domain of "text" and believes that the same principles of understanding and interpretation apply to many nonlinguistic texts, it is important for him to stay in close contact with the disciplines that exercise interpretation methodically. Ricoeur claims that one should look for what could be called a *hermeneutical knot,* a common element in the architecture of meaning, double sense or multiple sense, the role of which is to show by concealing.[48] Thus Ricoeur situates the hermeneutical problem in the framework of concealing-and-disclosing, disclosing by concealing. This is, of course, particularly relevant for Kierkegaard's indirect communication, which is based on this principle of showing (or rather allowing to see) through deviations, distortions, and concealment. Kierkegaard's indirect communication lies at the very core of Ricoeur's hermeneutics.

Because interpretation is deciphering the secret meaning in the apparent meaning, symbol and interpretation are correlated concepts for Ricoeur. However, he agrees that the semantics of the expression of multiple meanings is not enough for hermeneutics to be philosophical. The logic of double sense is more than a mere formal logic; it is a transcendental logic that establishes itself on the level of the conditions of possibility, the conditions of appropriation of our desire to be.[49] We can fully understand the hermeneutical problem only if we can grasp the double dependence on the self, dependence of the unconscious and on the sacred, because this double dependence is manifest only as a symbol.[50]

Ricoeur raised the question of how it is possible for reflection to take a starting point in the symbolic structure of language without falling into allegorizing or dogmatic mythology. In his view, relating the symbolical language to understanding of one's self is one of the key things in hermeneutics. Reflection has to become interpretation because we can grasp the act of existing only in the scattered signs of the world.[51] Therefore he proposes exploring another way, that of a creative interpretation that is inspired by the original mystery of symbols but that also forms and creates sense by itself, assuming full responsibility for this autonomous thought.

The question is how a thought can be at the same time related and free.[52] This is very much a Kierkegaardian problematic, and we will come back to it later in this chapter in the section on "Reading and Writing," as well as in Chapter 4 in the section on creative and productive imagination.

Ricoeur makes the distinction between "hermeneutics of the sacred," which takes the text as an access to a higher truth, and a "hermeneutics of suspicion," which goes behind the text to the interests guiding its formation. According to him, the major conflict of interpretations is conflict between two opposed hermeneutics: Hegelian phenomenology of religion, with its teleological approach and, derivatively, Heidegger's ontological hermeneutics and psychoanalysis, with their archaeological approach (see Freud). The conflict takes place between phenomenological theory of "truth" and psychoanalytical theory of "illusion." The opposition is between the unconscious and the spirit and two different movements of interpretation: the analytical and regressive toward the unconscious, and the synthetic and progressive toward spirit.[53]

Following Gadamer, Ricoeur thinks that all interpretation purports to overcome a distance between the culture period of the text and that of the interpreter. In overcoming this distance, in becoming contemporary to the text, the exegete can appropriate the sense. He wants to make proper what was foreign, that is to say, to make it his own. "All hermeneutics is thus, explicitly or implicitly, understanding of one's self through the deviation of understanding another."[54] I will try to describe Kierkegaard's model of contemporaneity with one text—the Bible. We will see that it is not so much a matter of overcoming a historical or cultural distance, but of overcoming oneself. This is one of the points where Kierkegaard was more radical than either Gadamer or Ricoeur, because for him the problem of understanding was far from being exhausted by the difficulties of historical mediation.

It is interesting to note that Ricoeur attempts to find a way out of the hermeneutical circle through the concept of second immediacy: "The second immediacy which we are looking for, the second naiveté which we are waiting for, are accessible to us only in hermeneutics; we can believe only in interpreting."[55] It is difficult to imagine that Ricoeur is not influenced by Kierkegaard's thought on double reflection and second immediacy. Kierkegaard's influence is also obvious in Ricoeur's concern with the problem of transition from text to action (only that, as mentioned, a meaningful action for Ricoeur is also a text that needs to be interpreted), most explicitly dealt with in the collection of his hermeneutical essays *Du texte à l'action*.

However, Ricoeur misses Kierkegaard's notion that it is not only meaning that leads to an action; action also defines meaning (for discussion on this, see the last section of Chapter 3). And Ricoeur overlooks Kierkegaard's emphasis on "moment" and "decision" that allow him to refuse entering the hermeneutical circle. In general, it could be said that all the three major hermeneutical thinkers, Heidegger, Gadamer, and Ricoeur, remain within the hermeneutical circle (although they try to redefine problems posed by it), while through his biblical hermeneutics, Kierkegaard offers a way to break the circle.

Many commentators have drawn attention to Ricoeur's guiding idea in *Time and Narrative* that there are kinds of truth that cannot be reduced to a principle, axiom, or thesis; rather, they can be conveyed only by means of a story, a narrative. The "narrativity" of knowledge has indeed had an enormous impact on the discussion of the nature of communication as such, and on the interaction of cognitive and narrative aspects. The present study shows Kierkegaard's use of stories woven into the most complex of theological and philosophical discussions, and demonstrates that these narrative deviations are incorporated in Kierkegaard's indirect communication.

Pragmatism and Literary Theory

A further strand in recent hermeneutics that should be mentioned is that of pragmatism. Richard E. Palmer remarks that both pragmatism and hermeneutics "build their reflection on an empirical reference back to concrete experience and doing. Both recognize that meaning resides in the situation and in the goals of persons in a situation, not outside and beyond them in a metaphysical realm. Both appeal to the Aristotelian practical philosophy as a forerunner of their thought. Both see communicative experience in terms of a language game."[56]

However, there are some major differences. In his *Philosophy and the Mirror of Nature*, Richard Rorty devotes chapters 7 and 8, "From Epistemology to Hermeneutics" and "Philosophy without Mirrors," to the discussion of hermeneutics. Rorty distinguishes two basic styles of philosophy, the foundationalist and the nonfoundationalist, or hermeneutical. He defines hermeneutics as "not a discipline, nor a method of achieving the sort of results epistemology failed to achieve, nor a program of research," but rather a "style of thought,"[57] although he admits that there is a clear and essential link between German hermeneutical thinking and American pragmatism. Very interestingly, the first section of "Philosophy without Mirrors" is entitled "Hermeneutics and Edification." Here Rorty says, "From the educational, as opposed to the epistemological or the technological, point of view, the way things are said is more important than the possession of truths."[58] Of course, for Rorty a hermeneutical activity is edifying without being constructive. What is interesting to us is that without referring to Kierkegaard and speaking mainly about the hermeneutics of Heidegger and Gadamer, Rorty puts the importance of "how" rather than "what" at the very heart of hermeneutics.

On the other hand, American pragmatism and its tendency to reduce philosophy to logic and epistemology has meant that another discipline, literary criticism, has had to assimilate many problems traditionally discussed by continental philosophy. Therefore one could say that in North America, hermeneutics has mainly developed as literary hermeneutics (for example, the Yale school of Bloom, Hartman, and Paul de Man). Literary theory in general was receptive to the Gadamerian hermeneutics, and critics such as Jauss, Iser, Barthes, and Riffaterre integrated hermeneutical and broader ontological issues into their literary theory. The challenge given to the Schleiermacherian tradition by Wimsatt and Beardsley in their "Intentional Fallacy" has had an impact on understanding any kind of text, be it literary, philosophical or theological.

However, it needs to be mentioned that literary theory has for a long time been a victim of historicism and immanent interpretation. It was the advance of the theory of "aesthetics of reception" that enabled literary theory to articulate the moments of understanding and application,[59] and thus to constitute the hermeneutical unity of understanding, interpretation, and application. The assimilation of hermeneutical questions allowed the dialogical dimension of literary texts to become clear: "Hermeneutics is not a hermetic science, but a precious instrument in the praxis of life, in the sense that, through the dialogical understanding in the experience of a text, it enables at the same time to experience another."[60] We note that the hermeneutical turn in literary theory took place when scholars started asking questions about the reader's reception and, in parallel, about writing as reading.

Thus Milton's *Paradise Lost* is given as an example of "productive" literary hermeneutics. The text deals with what happened before events about which we know from another text, events collectively called "the fall." Understanding and interpretation fuse into reinterpretation as creation, "filling in" the original text. Although the practice as such is not new, the theory—to a certain degree—is. The reversibility of the roles of author and reader, the dialogical dimension of reading, writing as reading or rewriting has been masterfully exposed by Kierkegaard, both in what he says about these matters in *The Point of View for my Work as an Author* (now an acknowledged reference work in the field of literary hermeneutics) and in the way his writings are constructed.

Back to Hermeneutics and Rhetoric

Let us now come back to the question of the relation between rhetoric and hermeneutics, which has recently become a major topic in hermeneutics. Although, as mentioned earlier, Schleiermacher drew attention to the vital links between the two and Gadamer claimed that "the rhetorical and the hermeneutical aspects of human linguisticality interpenetrate each other at every point,"[61] the role of rhetoric remained underestimated. It is worth recalling that in the period from ancient times to the Renaissance, rhetoric included the art of expression and thinking (dialectic) and how to read texts (now specialized to hermeneutics). In classical rhetoric, the doctrine of *imitatio* provided the most obvious intersection between the reading of texts and the production of persuasive arguments, not a mechanical reproduction but a complex relation. It was only under pressure of the Reformation that hermeneutics separated from rhetoric and took on a separate life of its own. Today the boundaries blur again, because modern rhetoric deals with preconditions of speaking and hermeneutics with preconditions of understanding. Phenomenology and the ontology of speaking, as well as epistemology, are of interest both for rhetoric and hermeneutics.

Gadamer observed, "The rhetorical competence that informs a text leads hermeneutics in the direction it must go to reach out and engage others."[62] Kierkegaard was much more radical, by claiming that he was his own reader (see the section "Reading and Writing" in this chapter). In my opinion, Kierkegaard is the first to bring rhetoric and hermeneutics together again after their separation. The consciousness of understanding and writing as essentially active and dialogical is, thus, one of the biggest contributions Kierkegaard made to hermeneutics. His concept of repetition also lies at the very intersection of hermeneutics and rhetoric.

Another interesting but underdeveloped link is the relation between rhetoric, hermeneutics, and ethics (I will argue that Kierkegaard has united these three aspects in his own writing). Heidegger says that Aristotle's *Rhetoric* comprised "the first systematic hermeneutics of the everydayness of Being with one another."[63] Indeed the interpretation and preparation of a text, of the other in the text and outside the text, involves an ethical relation. In Aristotle's *Rhetoric,* the ethical is one of the three sources of proof (along with the rational and the emotional); all persuasion that falls within the art of rhetoric is ethical. Altieri remarks that

ontological hermeneutics, both mundane and sublime, are most striking in the ethical possibilities they afford for the modes of agency they describe. Minimally, they avoid every form of subjectivism—whether the subjectivism be attributed to the inferiority of the author or to the demands of the interpreter. One might even say that the author and interpreter become effective collaborators in addressing a problem or situation, since all the emphasis is on who one becomes when exposed to the activity that the text can perform in one's world. Consequently, one is constantly aware of the various contingencies at play in the interaction.[64]

Responsibility becomes inseparable from acknowledging the singularity and, hence, the freedom of the other, first of all, the reader. Through his indirect communication, Kierkegaard attempts to create a truly ethical relation with his reader, and once again is a pioneer. In emphasizing reading of the Bible as an action, he also raises awareness of the ethical dimension of hermeneutics.

Pseudonyms: Kierkegaard Is neither Climacus nor Agnes

I will now address the problem of pseudonymity in order to clarify the tension between aesthetic and religious in Kierkegaard's writings, and in order to justify my treatment of the pseudonyms, which inevitably affects the argument of my book.

The fact that Kierkegaard wrote both works under various pseudonyms and works signed with his proper name has resulted in an ongoing discussion about the importance of the pseudonyms. This discussion has been thoroughly misleading from its very beginnings, because it has been largely motivated by a persistent desire to identify the author with a particular biographical person, and this regardless of whether one would like to separate Kierkegaard from his pseudonyms.

Kierkegaard scholars have been preoccupied with questions ranging from his motives for choosing a particular pseudonym for a particular work to the meaning of the supposedly distinct position of each individual pseudonym. Needless to say, researchers have also sought to interpret the fact that there is more than one pseudonym. Indeed, the plurality of pseudonyms has led Mackey, for example, to say that "Søren Kierkegaard was one of his own pseudonyms. Or perhaps all of them are God's pseudonyms."[65] The question of Kierkegaard's pseudonymity has been discussed as if there had never been a precedent for authorial dissimulation. Rarely taken into account are observations such as Gerard Genette's that "The multiple pseudonym is to some small degree, as the case of Stendhal plainly shows, the true nature of the single pseudonym and the state it naturally inclines towards."[66] Mainly due to scholars' failure to contextualize the problem of Kierkegaard's pseudonyms in both historical and theoretical perspective, the rather vague discussion of pseudonyms and their role in Kierkegaard's authorship has led to many approximations and misunderstandings, such as, for example, the introduction of the term "genuine pseudonym."[67]

If anything, the resulting confusion might be a sign that we ought to readdress the issue of pseudonyms in a radical way. That is, first of all, as Kierkegaard would say, begin with the beginning. We should ask ourselves "what an author is" and then "what a pseudonym is" from the point of view of history (particularly Kierkegaard's literary context—German literature, which was marked by the play of irony and distance from Schlegel to Hoffman) and of literary theory, for only then can one approach this question in Kierkegaard. I do not, of course, exclude the possibility that Kierkegaard understood and employed pseudonyms in an idiosyncratic way, but in order to appreciate that we must know the context. Hitherto the discussion of Kierkegaard's pseudonyms has not properly considered the conceptual nature and function of "pseudonym." However, this is not an easy task, and in the end perhaps there is no distinct concept of the pseudonym at all, since pseudonyms themselves are as elusive as mottos or prefaces. They involve the superfluous, the *esprit* of writing.

The first striking feature of the discussion of the "pseudonym problem" in secondary literature on Kierkegaard is the distinction commonly made between the religious and the aesthetic in Kierkegaard's authorship: the pseudonymous works are supposed to be aesthetic and not reflect Kierkegaard's own thoughts, whereas the signed works are considered to be religious, and to convey reliably (or at least more reliably) Kierkegaard's own views.[68] This is a far-reaching presupposition that has greatly influenced the reading of Kierkegaard in that it has supported a binary scheme of oppositions: pseudonymous/aesthetic/indirect *versus* veronymous/religious/direct.[69] This binary scheme has also affected the role one assigns to the Bible in Kierkegaard's works. It should be noted that this distinction was to some degree suggested by Kierkegaard himself in *The Point of View*, but I hope that in the course of this book it will become clear that his suggestion has been misunderstood.

The second problematic feature related to the pseudonyms is the view held by many scholars that pseudonyms represent different worldviews. Mark C. Taylor best expresses this position: "Each pseudonym represents a particular shape of consciousness, form of life, or type of selfhood."[70] However, this position is hardly ever based on any concrete analysis of texts, and the only argument advanced in favor of such a thesis is that the authors are pseudonyms. But it does not follow that pseudonyms *represent* different perspectives.

Roger Poole is one of the few researchers who have tried to support the theory of different types of selfhood by telling us how pseudonyms differ one from another. He has attempted to show the differences between pseudonyms by tracing different meanings of the concept "ethical" in *Fear and Trembling* and in *Either/Or*, then "sin" in *The Concept of Anxiety*, *The Sickness unto Death*, and *Philosophical Fragments*, as well as "despair" in *Either/Or* and *The Sickness unto Death*. In his endeavour Poole is guided by the following principle: "The pseudonymous authors inhabit thought-worlds which are radically different, and thus concepts in the pseudonyms ought to be distinguished from each other, even when they are verbally identical."[71]

However, one notices that the difference of terms is derived from the unargued presupposition that the "thought-worlds" of pseudonyms are radically different. Moreover, the fact that concepts might differ from book to book does not prove that the pseudonyms reflect distinctively different worldviews. The meaning of terms and concepts is often context-dependent in such a way that "sin" can have very different connotations in *The Concept of Anxiety* and *The Sickness unto Death*, simply because the subject of these two books is different. In his famous "A First and Last Explanation" at the end of *Concluding Unscientific Postscript*, Kierkegaard says: "I am just as far from being Johannes de silentio in *Fear and Trembling* as I am from being the knight of faith he depicts" (CUP 626). This could, of course, be interpreted as supporting the view that one should draw a sharp distinction between Kierkegaard's views and those held by Johannes de silentio, but I think it is important to pay attention to the symmetry "as far . . . as." This alone should be sufficient evidence to discourage one from assuming independent worldviews for pseudonyms; they are authors first, and the usual problems of authors are not solved simply by saying that the author's name is a pseudonym. Johannes de silentio has no more a distinct worldview than does the *havmand* (Merman).[72]

The third highly complex issue posed by the use of pseudonyms is the question of fiction and biography. One of the most interesting confusions that has arisen from reading "A First and Last Explanation" has to do with the role of Kierkegaard's life in his authorship. This confusion has enabled the same researcher to emphasize Kierkegaard's words "in the pseudonymous books there is not a single word by me" (CUP 626), and yet to ignore what he wrote just a few lines later: "What and how I am is absolutely irrelevant to this production" (626). For example, M. Holmes Hartshorne quotes "in the pseudonymous books there is not a single word by me" in the first page of his book,[73] but later pursues a biographical line of interpretation; and thus, after having just quoted from the first of the diapsalmata of the pseudonymous *Either/Or,* he writes, "That Kierkegaard was speaking of his own life is obvious."[74] This selective reading of "A First and Last Explanation" has led to a centaur-like view that in the pseudonymous works there is not a single word by Kierkegaard, but that nevertheless his life itself is to be found in them.[75]

The short but complex text "A First and Last Explanation" has been often simplified, misunderstood, and abused.[76] It has usually been taken to mean that Kierkegaard hereforth renounced his pseudonymous authorship, whereas in fact he had explicitly acknowledged it. Apart from the opening sentence, "For the sake of form and order, I hereby acknowledge," one finds, for example, the interesting sentence toward the end: "Insofar as the pseudonymous authors in any way whatever might have disturbed or made ambiguous any actual good in the established order—then there is no one more willing to make *an apology than I,* who bear the responsibility for the use of the guided pen" (CUP 629, my emphasis).

What could be a better expression of an intimate relationship than making an apology on behalf of someone? In his explanation, Kierkegaard insists only that one should not confuse Kierkegaard the author with Kierkegaard the person.[77] For example, talking about the fact that in both a legal and literary sense the responsibility for authorship is his, Kierkegaard nevertheless writes: "Legal and literary, because all poetic creation would *eo ipso* be made impossible or meaningless and intolerable if the lines were supposed to be the producer's own words (literally understood)" (CUP 627). Although it is hardly ever quoted, this statement gives us a clear idea of how subtle, complex, and modern Kierkegaard's understanding of an author is.[78]

Thus, in order to appreciate the role of pseudonyms in his work one should first of all examine Kierkegaard's notion of an author. Apart from reading "A First and Last Declaration" and *The Point of View,* one can get a better insight into the problem of pseudonyms by *reading* Kierkegaard's prefaces to his works and in general by paying attention to tiny segments of text, such as the comment on the title page of the veronymous *From the Papers of One Still Living:* "published, against his will, by S. Kjerkegaard."[79] In reading Kierkegaard's prefaces, one sees clearly that pseudonyms are not at all the only way of distancing the author from the text in Kierkegaard's authorship. Rather, they enter into a chain of self-distancing techniques. If we take *Lectori Benevolo!* (which serves as a preface) in *Stages on Life's Way,* we are told that the book was left for binding, that its writer, Mr. Literatus, died (the death of an author!), that some time later a small package of handwritten papers was found and the publisher took responsibility to publish it.[80]

As if that were not complicated enough, there is a separate preface to *Guilty?/Not Guilty?* which is called "Notice: Owner Sought" (a title that asks the question about authorship in no uncertain terms). Frater Taciturnus here tells that he found the manuscript of *Guilty?/Not Guilty?* in Søborg lake in "a box of palisander wood." Thus it is clear that the pseudonyms themselves also insist on their detachment and disinterestedness (for example, see Johannes Climacus in *Concluding Unscientific Postscript*) and draw different perspectives within themselves. In fact, pseudonyms make a special effort to tell us that they are not the authors.[81]

Conversely, we might look at the textual plays in Kierkegaard's veronymous works. We soon discover that many of the features said to be specific to pseudonyms are actually common to most of Kierkegaard's works. For example, in the preface to *From the Papers of One Still Living* Kierkegaard tries to describe his interesting relation to the "real author" of the treatise, a complicated relationship in which both parties rarely agree with one another and are engaged in a constant fight, yet are "united by the deepest, most sacred, indissoluble ties" (EPW 55). He further tells us that it is "as if two souls resided in one body"; much the same could be said with regard to Kierkegaard's relation to his pseudonyms and to the relation between the different pseudonyms. At the very end of the preface to *From the Papers of One Still Living,* after the fight with the "other" author, Kierkegaard gives perhaps the best answer to the pseudonym problem with the biblical words: "What I have written I have written."[82]

Reading and Writing

Kierkegaard was the sort of author who takes a very conscious interest not only in what it is to be an author, but also in what it means to be a reader. Indeed he was inclined to consider himself primarily a reader: "I regard myself rather as a *reader* of the books, not as the *author*" (PV 12). And yet the role he assigns to the reader is such an active one that the reader tends to become an author and participate actively in the creation of the work. The boundaries between reader and author, thus, often become blurred in Kierkegaard's writings.[83] Two main hermeneutical features are especially relevant here: first, the author's self-effacement in indirect communication; second, the notion of an author without authority. These issues are important to the present work, in the sense that it is through quotation (in this case biblical quotation) that the reader meets the author in the most tangible way, and that the reader could be said to become the author of the very text he reads. It is when we stumble upon a quotation that the active role of the reader as simultaneously re-creator of the original context and creator of a new interactive meaning is most visible. The reader is the re-creator in both a positive and negative way: in a positive way insofar as he is capable of remembering the semantic value of the original context and applying it to the present text; in a negative way insofar as quotation detaches itself from its original context and perhaps its own meaning. Then the reader's creation is to integrate the difference in the present text.[84]

Kierkegaard's understanding of the reader shows to what degree his writing (which is itself, as we will see, largely a reading of the Bible) is orientated toward reading. His reader is the individual, "the reader whom I with pleasure and gratitude call *my* reader," a formula that is repeated in the prefaces to upbuilding discourses. This has to do not only with the overall emphasis on the individual in his authorship, but also with the requirement of "existential" reading. The repeatedly stipulated requirements are to read aloud, to read slowly, and to read alone (Pap. VII 1 B 148). In cases of "successful" writing, in Kierkegaard's opinion, the reader helps the author in the process of self-effacement. If Kierkegaard focuses mainly on the problem of the author in the prefaces to his pseudonymous writings, in the veronymous works he concentrates on the reader. The reader is seen as somebody who accomplishes the work begun by the author, and this includes not only the creation of the text, but also the work of author's self-effacement.

In a preface to "Four Upbuilding Discourses 1844," the meeting between author and reader is described in the following manner: "The joy of him who sends it, who continually comes to his reader only to bid him farewell, and now bids him farewell for the last time"

(EUD 296). Such is the wish and ambition of the author, but it is the reader who "transforms the discourse into a conversation, the honest confidentiality of which is not disturbed by any recollection of the one who continually desires only to be forgotten" (EUD 232), and thus helps the author to be forgotten. Kierkegaard's view on the overlapping roles of author and reader is best expressed in one of his journal entries:

> The main thing is the interiority with which one reads . . . Even if all the people would read hastily through the book, I would still be misunderstood. On the other hand, if only one read the book that he would appropriate it in his essential interiority, so that in the end it is accidental that it is me who has written it because the reader himself produces it—then I am understood and I am glad (Pap. VII 1 B 86, 281; my translation).[85]

As I have observed, Kierkegaard's understanding of the problem of reading points back to the problem of writing, turning the latter into a hermeneutical issue. Speaking about Kierkegaard's hermeneutics and his particular conception of author, we should always bear in mind the question whether it is possible, as Kierkegaard would seem to have suggested in *The Point of View*, for an author to read himself in the capacity of a third person and not *qua* author, and thus to give an unbiased interpretation of his own work. This in its turn points back to the question about the status of *The Point of View*, namely, whether or not it can be regarded as some sort of metatext that overwrites the others.[86]

Is there a valid foundation for considering *The Point of View* to be a privileged text, transcending all the doubt and obscurity intrinsic to any writing, and for taking it to be a text that stands out from the totality of the authorship, and thus is somehow "beyond" authorship (speaking as if from some kind of eschatological perspective)?[87] Can this text be said to have ceased being part of a larger body of authorship? That is, can it be said to be a text to which one cannot apply what is said (in the text itself) about other texts? And yet it is in *The Point of View* that we find the most instructive descriptions of *how* Kierkegaard writes. For example, he states: "My behavior least of all resembles that of a genius."[88] This points to the tension, in the process of writing, between immediacy and reflection (a theme that is important to Kierkegaard on many levels). Kierkegaard tells us that he uses reflection not because he lacks immediacy (inspiration), but by conscious choice, thereby hoping to transport all qualities of his writing onto a higher level. Reflection is present not only in the contents of writing, but in his very relation to writing. Indeed, this mirror effect of a correspondence between form and content is a recurring feature of Kierkegaard's writing.

We should also register quite a radical break with the romantic model of writing. For Kierkegaard, there is time to write every letter slowly and carefully (PV 73). The question of the voice and the role of Providence in writing leads us to one of the most important features of Kierkegaard's understanding of himself as an author: being outside authority. This essential feature of his writing has crucial implications for his employment of biblical quotations, since the latter directly involves the relation of the author to the authority of the Bible.[89]

Author Outside Authority

Although the concepts of "author" and "authority" have become significantly detached from one another and alienated in contemporary usage, they are fundamentally linked. The Latin word *auctoritas* is derived from *auctor*. According to the *Oxford Latin Dictionary*,[90] the first meaning of the word (the "principal in sale") has nothing to do with our topic,[91] but the next three meanings describe an *auctor* through "authority": "a person with a title to take action or to make a decision; one who attests or vouches for the truth, a guarantor; one who sanctions or authorises the actions of another, etc." As the arrangement of the dictionary entries testifies, "author," in the present sense of the word, derives from the legal sense of *auctor qua* "authority" (cf. 9: "A writer who is regarded as a master of his subject or as providing reliable evidence, an authority"). In medieval usage, the meanings of *auctor* as "performer, maker, creator" and "author" in the present sense merge in the conception of God as the Author of the Universe (which is often visualized as the Book of Nature). God's "authorship" is echoed by his "authority" expressed in the Holy Scripture. In the notion of *auctoritas Sanctae Scripturae*, "authorship" and "authority" are inextricably interwoven.

While it is obvious that an author creates authority, the opposite also seems to hold true.[92] This is because authority enables the author to be an author in a public sense and makes his discourse valid and paradigmatic, as distinguished from a mere (private) speaker's discourse. Thus it is only natural that every author has some kind of authority or pretends to have it.

Yet we find Kierkegaard refusing any authority. He keeps on claiming, "All is done without authority" (PV 78), or "I am like a spy in a higher service, the service of the idea. I have nothing new to proclaim; I am without authority, being myself hidden in a deception" (PV 87), or "'Without authority' to *make aware* of the religious, the essentially Christian, is the category for my whole work as an author regarded as a totality" (PV 12). In *The Point of View* Kierkegaard does not discuss the nature of the concept "authority," but repeatedly declines having authority. This is a rather strange thing to do in a book that claims to be a "report to history" and "to explain once for all, as directly and openly and specifically as possible, what is what" (PV 23) — that is to say, in a book that aims to tell the truth, and thus to define it authoritatively. Paradoxically Kierkegaard declines authority in a book that is authoritative in its internal structure.

From the very beginning of his reflections on this concept, Kierkegaard treats the term "authority" in a demanding and peculiar way. And although he does not attempt to demarcate and to set apart distinct usages of the word, the crucial point is that by "authority," Kierkegaard means something very different from what it now ordinarily means.[93] He reserves this word for one restricted and homogeneous meaning — to designate the divine Authority, the authority of the one who gives the very condition for understanding truth. In his *Journals,* Kierkegaard calls authority "perhaps the most important ethical-religious concept" (JP 6447). Kierkegaard abides by the theological, "sacred" origin of the later-secularized concept of authority, and thus invariably perceives authority as either divine or apostolic. In all the other cases (for instance, in a professor's authority), when the authority does not come from God we deal, as it were, with what is really only a parody or misuse of authority. According to Kierkegaard, the category of authority is beyond any reflection or aesthetics; in fact, there is a mutual exclusivity: "The apostolic quality is authority — not brilliance" (JP 635). Kierkegaard's strict treatment of the term renders it impossible for him to say that he has any authority without declaring himself an apostle first.[94]

Understandably he is keen to ensure that no such mistake is made: "Am I perhaps the 'Apostle'? Abominable! I have never given an occasion for such an idea" (PV 78). According to him, one who has received a command to proclaim Christian truth has a certain degree of authority. A command to proclaim is not in itself sufficient, however; it is only a potentiality that must be helped into becoming a reality and a power by supporting it with one's own life. The requirement of consistency between proclamation and existence is of crucial importance here: it means that only the person whose life conforms to what he proclaims has a genuine authority to validate his proclamation: "Where my own personal life expresses what I speak about, there I use and should use *some kind* of authority. But if what I describe is higher than my life, then for the sake of truth I must admit that I am only a poet" (JP 6503, my emphasis). We see that Kierkegaard is here in the collision between *some kind* of authority and *the* authority.[95]

Kierkegaard finds himself caught in a paradox: being an author, he must inevitably present the claim for authority—yet he cannot and does not do this. What results is a reinscription of his abdication of authority into his text, by means of dialectical method or indirect communication and specific self-representation of the author. Kierkegaard's aim is double: to present truth without being present as authority, or in fact even as an author. Apart from being a means of escaping an author's authority, Kierkegaard's pseudonymity also often simulates authority (cf. the assumption of the names of spiritual—real or imagined-masters, e.g. "Johannes Climacus" and "Victor Eremita"). One way in which he does this is to transfer authority to the reader: in *The Point of View* and in many prefaces to Kierkegaard's works, the author is said to be without authority, but at the same time he is an authoritative reader. Quite often one can observe a double movement in the preface: it performs a *captatio benevolentiae* as regards the book, but simultaneously carries out an act of straightforward self-authorization as regards the preface. That is, the author claims not to have authority but yet be an authoritative reader.

In this book, I try to examine among other things the status of the authority of the Bible in the authorship of one who either declines being an author or presents himself as being an author without authority.

Indirect Communication: Dialogue and Deception

A short discussion of indirect communication will provide a perspective for considering biblical quotations in the pseudonymous writings as an important element of indirect communication. Without making direct appeal to the authority of the Bible, Kierkegaard's biblical quotations create an invisible but omnipresent web, since most of the important issues discussed in the pseudonymous works interact with the Bible. In this way, the Bible's presence is woven into the text but not imposed on it.

In order to appreciate the mechanism of indirect communication, we should first ask whether it is really confined to the pseudonymous writings. Is it not, rather, true that the whole authorship involves indirect communication,[96] and that if one is to speak about the differences between pseudonymous and veronymous works in this respect, one should think in terms of the difference between a method and a mode?[97] To say that the ultimate reason for the necessity of indirect communication is the impossibility of otherwise communicating the Absolute Paradox, and at the same time that this need is embodied in the so-called aesthetic writings but not in the Christian ones (because they have, as it were, a more direct approach to the Absolute Paradox) seems contradictory, or at least confused. It is even stranger in the light of Kierkegaard's saying "Only the God-man is in every respect indirect communication from first to last" (Pap. X 3 A 413), which clearly gives indirect communication as an example of ideal communication, not as something to be abandoned at the first opportunity.

Indirect communication is needed not only in Kierkegaard's "present age" or ours, and not only in the pseudonymous works, and not only in respect to the Absolute Paradox. George Pattison observes, "Kierkegaard's indirect approach was not simply a tactical ploy, determined by the cultural situation of the modern world or by his own combination of lay status and literary ability—it was rather an instantiation of an essential element in *all* Christian communication."[98] I would like to extend this thesis to all *essential* communication, and not limit it to the Absolute Paradox, even though this is undoubtedly the crux of Kierkegaard's problem. What Kierkegaard would call essential communication is communication of *Kunnen* (or, in the case of ethical and religious, *Skullen-Kunnen*). Essential communication is not necessarily Christologically determined.[99]

In his journals Kierkegaard says, "All communication of *Kunnen* is indirect communication" (Pap. VIII 2 B 83). Indirect communication can deal with the aesthetic, the ethical, and the religious. What unites all of them is that they have no object and are rooted in the subject's relation (to the matter at issue); what separates them is the degree to which one can properly say that they belong to indirect communication. The aesthetic does not belong to indirect communication unconditionally, whereas the ethical does; the religious does not belong to it unconditionally, insofar it contains the communication of

Viden. What makes the religious (Christian) indirect communication conditional and complicated (one could even say communication in the second degree) is that in it there is a *Viden* that is incorporated in a *Kunnen,* and this *Viden* is of the eternal God incarnated in time.

Having said that, we can define indirect communication (as a method) as a series of specific communication techniques (dialogue, Socratic midwifery, double reflection, teleological deception, and — as I will argue — the peculiar use of biblical quotations), the (secret) aim of which is to communicate that which is not communicable directly: the essential truth. The task is to convey the truth respecting the integrity and freedom of an individual, thereby enabling him to have a personal relation to truth. The essential truth mostly concerns religious truth, but we might also include the ethical and other determinations of the spiritual development of an individual.

Kierkegaard's indirect communication is not, therefore, a simple lack of directness in the sense of its being a cryptic or incoherent collection of hints (which would constitute indirect discourse, in a sense), but a certain "reversed" language that aims at overcoming the impossibility of directness. Indirect communication, according to Mark C. Taylor, is a way of communicating the lack of language: "Kierkegaard explores the possibility that the unthinkable can be *written.* To write the Other of thought, it is necessary to devise alternative strategies of writing. Having recognized the impossibility of writing *about* the impossibility of thought, Kierkegaard develops a style of indirect communication, which has as its aim the communication of the incommunicable. In the strange folds of Kierkegaard's pseudonymous texts, discourse 'communicates' the lack of language."[100]

Indirect communication is, among other things, an attempt to bring the abstract language of thought closer to concrete reality — which is not the same as reconstructing that same concrete reality. Kierkegaard was worried about the abstractedness of language and the existential consequences of this (cf., for example, Pap. X 2 A 235; Pap. XI 2 A 106). Besides, as Bigelow has remarked, Kierkegaard employs indirect communication to try to describe phenomena, the nature of which is to resist the description of the specificity of their nature, so that even indirect communication is bound to be inadequate.[101] Nevertheless, indirect communication is the only way to approach or articulate these phenomena. Such phenomena are: silence, boredom, oblivion/forgetfulness, time, difference (which, according to Hegel, entails a contradiction in itself). Bataille calls them *les mots glissants.*

This inadequacy is far from being a banal linguistic confusion. It reflects a quite legitimate dissatisfaction with possibilities of expression, which is caused by an essential incapacity of language to embrace "becoming." Particularly painful is the way in which this affects the phenomena in which "becoming" is not only a development in time, but something that is directly implied in the definition of essence of that thing. Thus in the *Concluding Unscientific Postscript*, Kierkegaard writes: "Precisely because he himself is constantly in the process of becoming, that is, in the inwardness, he can never communicate directly, because the movement is precisely the opposite one. Direct communication requires certainty, but for the one who is becoming certainty is impossible and is precisely the deception" (CUP 61). Likewise Kierkegaard attempts to rediscover God's Word, the language of the Bible that corresponds to the uncertainty of faith.

According to Kierkegaard, there are two different subject matters that require two different forms of communication. The different subject matters are due to two different conceptions of truth, as either objective or subjective. When it is a matter of subjective truth, only indirect communication is possible, because only indirect communication respects the individual sufficiently to let him reach the truth himself. With respect to subjective truth, the only way of comprehension is the way of appropriation. Appropriation means to make truth your own (proper to you), to internalize it, to convert it into a reality within yourself.[102]

It is important to pay attention to the term "reality" in this context, as it has two meanings. On the one hand, reality is the reflection of truth in life: "'Reality' is an existential reduplication of that which is said. In reality/really to learn that truth is mocked and etc., is to teach it when you yourself are being mocked and laughed at" (Pap. VIII 2 B 85, 17). The movement is double: the appropriation of truth — the deepest possible internalization — is at the same time a practical "realization," which transports internal appropriation to the level of action.[103]

Thus the direct communication of essential truth is not possible because of the nature of the content to be communicated. Direct, objective communication cannot pay attention to a certain negativity of existence, to the fact that existence is a process of "becoming" and that it is volatile. Direct communication would not only intrude on the freedom of the individual, it would also distort the content of truth, because it could not convey all those aspects of truth and the play of contradictions through which the truth actually emerges. Thus direct communication would only damage and betray the truth.

Another feature of indirect communication is the justification of the suspension of truth and deception employed as method. Speaking about the teleological suspension of truth in *Concluding Unscientific Postscript*, Kierkegaard gives an analogy of a person with a mouth so full of food that he cannot swallow any of it, and thus is facing death from starvation—a perfectly paradoxical situation. The analogy introduces the need for a certain purification and for a necessary negativity in the process of communication. The indirect communication of truth does not take place in a blank space of ignorance, but, on the contrary, in a space crowded and burdened with much superficial, unessential knowledge.

Therefore for truth to be appropriated, one needs first to discard the misconceptions of truth. This is the justification of deception, since it indirectly (namely negatively) allows us to replace these misconceptions with truth. Of course, the very mention of deception as a method arouses opposition, because it is perceived as a moral fault. Anticipating this criticism, Kierkegaard replies: "But a deception that is indeed something ugly. To that I would answer: Do not be deceived by the word *deception*. One can deceive a person out of what is true, and—to recall old Socrates—one can deceive a person into what is true. Yes, in only this way can a deluded person actually be brought into what is true—by deceiving him" (PV 53). The invisible or seemingly inconsequential use of the biblical quotations, which is, as will be argued, very important for the construction of Kierkegaard's argument and direction of his thought, could be an instance of such a deception.

The necessity of indirect communication (and deception) begins with the very surface, with the level of expression in language, because there is confusion and deception: a name is given to something that it is not, a thing does not correspond to the name, but only pretends to be; there is a gap between "to appear" and "to be."[104] Kierkegaard is acutely aware first of the monstrous discrepancy between Christianity and Christendom, between a Christian as a conscious individual believer and a Christian in the sense that everybody is held to be a Christian, because of historical and cultural determinations. According to Kierkegaard, in the situation of Christendom, to communicate directly would be a triple deception: of God, of the individual himself, and of the other (CUP 63).

Indirect communication needs to deceive or is itself a necessary deception. It is a deception not in the sense of an illusion, but a deception on the part of the author that should become truth in the hands of the reader, a kind of relative deception that aims not at success (in a straightforward sense), but rather at its own downfall.

The use of indirect communication gives Kierkegaard's authorship a dialectical character (which is also prominent in his use of biblical quotations). In this context, we should approach the term "dialectical" in connection with its origin as a philosophical term, that is, when we read it as a derivation from a dramatic dialogue.[105] Dialectic is a kind of dialogue, and, as is the case with Kierkegaard, a kind of dialogue that is suggestive and provocative rather than imposing any definite point of view. This kind of dialogue could hardly take place if one side had authority and exercised it (this is particularly relevant for the biblical quotations, since they seem to suggest an inherent authority; the task then is to suspend the authority). For, although having an authority would not exclude the dialectical, it would dissolve the dialogical. Taylor points out that Kierkegaard's authorship is dialogical in two senses: first, it contains the dialogue within itself, the dialogue that is enacted between the individual writings; second, it is a dialogue between the whole *oeuvre* and the reader.[106]

Consequently the adoption of an authoritative stance would undermine the very aim Kierkegaard strives to achieve, by employing the method of indirect communication. Instead of giving the form of direct dialogue as Plato did (even though again, in Plato there is a dialogue not only between Socrates and, say, Alcibiades, but also between Socrates [and Plato] and the reader), Kierkegaard composes his authorship in such a way that the dialogues are between author and reader and also between different dialogues, as well as between Kierkegaard and the Bible.[107] Kierkegaard's recurrent wish "to draw attention" is another example of the dialogue technique. Socratic midwifery, which is an essentially dialogical mode of appropriation, is the other side of it. To be the midwife of the other person's "subjectivity" is, according to Kierkegaard, the highest relation between two human beings.

The maieutic method is, however, problematic because Kierkegaard tries to reconcile two different conceptions of truth and the individual's relations to truth: the Greek and Christian. From the Christian point of view, fundamentally significant truth is only the truth of subjectivity, but subjectivity in itself is not the truth. The focus on subjectivity does not guarantee the attainment of truth (for the Greeks truth is in ourselves, it is just a matter of discovering it), since the sinful individual has turned from the truth and by himself has no condition to find it in himself.[108] In *Philosophical Fragments,* Kierkegaard seems to suggest that there is, however, an analogy between these two conceptions of truth, in the sense that through a maieutic method the Greeks discover the truth in themselves, while the Christians discover the untruth—sin—in themselves.

I have tried to cover some of the main hermeneutical issues in Kierkegaard's authorship in order to provide a context for my concrete discussion of the biblical quotations. These issues will resonate throughout the book. My discussion of the biblical quotations will take place in the framework of indirect communication, and I will try to show that Kierkegaard's peculiar use of the biblical quotations is an essential element of his indirect communication.

Explicit Views: Kierkegaard on the Use and Reading of the Bible

> The little bit I have wanted to do is easily stated: I have wanted to
> make people a little aware and to make the admission that I find the
> New Testament very easy to understand, but so far I have found
> tremendously great difficulties in my own self when it comes to acting
> literally according to what is not difficult to understand. (JP 2872)

In discussing Kierkegaard's use of the Bible, it is important to bear in
mind the radical changes in biblical studies in Europe in the later
eighteenth century and throughout the first half of the nineteenth.[1]
The most important event was the rise and dominance of the historical critical method. New literary, philological, and historical tools
were applied to the study of the Bible, and naturally this affected the
understanding of the biblical text, as well as the way it was to be
quoted. These changes preoccupied Kierkegaard and served as an
impulse for one of the important themes in his authorship, namely,
the relation between faith and knowledge.

In this chapter I will address the question of faith and knowledge,
and some related issues such as the relationship between the literal
and the nonliteral reading of the Bible, Kierkegaard's emphasis on
scandal and "hard sayings" (for example, hatred), his definition of
action and the transition from reading to action. An introductory
exposition of these issues helps to situate Kierkegaard's biblical quotations in the context of subjective appropriation. Kierkegaard's

explicit views about the nature of religious truth and the individual's relation to it shape the mode of employment of biblical quotations in his pseudonymous works.

The Danish Context and Strauss

The first half of the nineteenth century in Denmark was, of course, affected by developments in European biblical studies, particularly in Germany. At the same time Denmark saw several popular religious movements, which also affected theological discussion. Schematically speaking, theology in Denmark in the first half of the nineteenth inherited from the eighteenth a combination of supranaturalism, neology, Enlightenment theology, and rationalism.[2] In Kierkegaard's immediate theological context in Denmark, the most important figures were J. P. Mynster, H. C. Martensen, N. F. S. Gruntvig, and H. N. Clausen.[3] To take a closer look at these influences in that order:

1. Bishop J. P. Mynster (1775–1854) was conservative in his theological, political, and Church-political views. His theology has been described as "a stoical enlightenment deism in orthodox Christian dress";[4] however, it may have been not so much deism as romanticism. He pursued an aggressive state-church policy, the best example of which is the way he dealt with the Baptists. "The most notorious instance of Mynster's proclivity to use legal force and official state sanctions against the efforts of the lower classes to lead an independent religious life was his compaign against Baptists forcibly seized and baptized against their parents will."[5] As regards the presence of the Bible in his writings, not every sermon is based on a specific biblical text, even though such was the general requirement. "Quite a number of Mynster's sermons seem to come no further than the general message of Providence, duty, and conscience."[6] Niels Thulstrup observes that his late sermons were more marked by the presence of the Bible.[7] But it is certainly very far from what we shall see as Kierkegaard's organic use of the Bible.[8]

2. H. C. Martensen (1808–1884), professor of theology and later bishop, was an influential figure in Kierkegaard's time. Thulstrup claims that if one were to choose one book that best expresses the general tendencies in early- to mid-nineteenth-century Danish theology, it would be Martensen's *Christian Dogmatics*. Despite being labeled as a Hegelian, in this book Martensen claims that Christianity is a religious relationship with God that can be defined

as an existential relationship (*sic!*) expressed in the conscience. As Bruce Kirmmse puts it: "For Martensen dogmatics is not only a science about faith, but is a knowledge in faith and from faith."[9]

In his dogmatic system Martensen, however, makes place for fantasy, and claims that one gains knowledge of religion not only through reason but also through the help of fantasy. "Martensen did not deny (any more than idealism did) Christianity's positive, historical character, but he confronted Christianity as the object of faith with the specific epistemological problem of the relation between the objective and the subjective, and he poses the issue phenomenologically, that is, as seen in the light of self-consciousness as the final goal, and within which Christianity too, is to be found."[10] In *The Christian Dogmatics* (1849), Martensen considers Scripture as the formal principle to be inseparable from the material or subjective principle of spirit. Kierkegaard criticizes Martensen by saying that his dogmatics is populistic, and that there is not much in the way of concepts (Pap. X, 1 A 553).

Martensen was influenced by the late romantic, idealistic movement. This is reflected in his choice of words. Words like "talent," "hero," "enthusiasm," "admiration," "genius" are frequent. The presence of this romantic vocabulary is perhaps the most prominent feature of his use of the Bible. The biblical quotations usually are given with an exact reference;[11] they do not truly participate in the discourse, but stand out as objects or illustrations.

3. N. F. S. Gruntvig (1783–1872), minister, social reformer, and educator, started with Romantic pantheism and later moved to "biblical Christianity," where the biblical message was not obscured by exegetes. For Gruntvig, biblical Christianity was also mixed with the ancient Norse pagan religion. In *Philosophical Fragments*, Johannes Climacus mocks Gruntvig's translation of the Bible precisely because of this heavy presence of Old Norse motives in his translation: "But is a jubilant, triumphant generation such as this, which, as you say, goes through life singing and ringing—which reminds me, if I remember correctly, of a jaunty, ale-Norse [*olnordiske*] translation of a Bible verse by a popular genius—is a generation such as this actually supposed to be a believing generation?"[12] (PF 107).

However, in one formal respect Gruntvig's use of the Bible is closest to Kierkegaard's—they both integrate the Bible in their manner of writing; for both of them it is not only a subject of discussion, but also the structuring power behind their discourse. Despite his own "biblical Christianity," Gruntvig claims that what is fundamental in the Christian faith is not the Bible, but the sacraments. "This is Gruntvig's 'matchless discovery': that an oral tradition, carried in the congregation, precedes and validates Scripture instead of being validated by it; that this oral tradition is particularly to be found in the Lord's Prayer, the words of institution of baptism and Holy Communion, and in the Apostles' Creed, all of which are direct sayings 'from the mouth of the Lord.'"[13]

Thus God's word is to be found not in the written, but in the oral form. Thulstrup observes that this understanding of the sacraments corresponds to a performative action; as they are pronounced, they create their subject by asserting it.[14] Moreover, Gruntvig maintains that they have reached us unchanged and unchangeable, whereas the Bible has always been subjected to various exegetical interpretations, and thus its content is not stable or reliable. On the other hand, one also finds in Gruntvig's writings an invitation to read the Bible with the simple faith of a child, and to avoid the doubt that Christ's words may not be his words after all. It is the precondition of the consolation to be found in the Holy Scripture that one firmly believes that God's word has reached us unchanged. Supporting his statement that God's words are given in transparent form as the shining truth and should be understood in all their simplicity and directness, Gruntvig says that otherwise, simple people would not have an access to them. They would be forced either to believe lies or to believe in the words of other men as if they were God's.[15] He observes that the supposed need of learnedness and special skills of exegesis would go strictly against what Jesus says in Mt 11:25: "I thank thee, O Father, Lord of heaven and earth, because thou hast hid these things from the wise and prudent, and has revealed them unto babes."

4. H. N. Clausen (1793–1877) was a prominent academic theologian. He claimed that a special hermeneutical method should be applied to the biblical hermeneutics, and within that a further special method for the New Testament.[16] Clausen describes the relation of hermeneutics to exegesis as an immediate relationship (as theory to praxis), and its relation to dogmatics as a mediated one. In his book *The Hermeneutics of the New Testament*, Clausen gives a detailed study of the meaning of selected separate words in the New Testament and also discusses the principles of philological analysis. According to Clausen, the specificity of New Testament language is due to Christian ideas that served as the formative principle of the language of the apostles. One can partly understand its meaning from the etymology

and from its employment in classical works and the Old Testament, but there remains something that can be understood only in the light of New Testament language itself.[17]

Clausen also gives a list of the words that appear sometimes in the literal, sometimes in the metaphorical meaning.[18] However, he does not give any rules as to how to determine whether the meaning is literal or metaphorical. Pedersen says that "As a representative of the rationalist tradition, yet renewed within the sphere of romanticism and through his contact with Schleiermacher, H. N. Clausen wanted to cling to and advance Protestant spiritualism (with a corresponding doctrinal form free of strict orthodoxy and Church authority), by way of balanced philological, historical, and theological interpretation."[19] According to Clausen, the Bible as Holy Scripture gives to subjective interpretation its objective character as a spiritual possession.

Danish theological context followed closely the new trends coming from Germany. A landmark in the new biblical debate was Strauss's *Leben Jesu*. We should briefly introduce this book, since it did much to define the kind of positions Kierkegaard was most concerned to contest.

D. F. Strauss's *Leben Jesu* (1835) was an epoch-breaking book. The difference between Strauss and the naturalist or rationalist interpreters of the Bible is that Strauss did not want to explain the historical, but to reject it altogether. "The novelty of Strauss's approach to the Gospels is that he cuts the Gordian knot which had baffled both rationalism and orthodoxy. So long as both sides assumed that biblical narratives must be accepted as factual records, there could be no hope of agreement, or of an end to constant battles."[20] Strauss argued that the historical facts behind the most important religious claims turned out to be myths. "Strauss had demonstrated that historical exegesis of the gospels does not justify basing the dogma of divine-human reconciliation on the historical factuality of Jesus' story. He effectively subverted what was agreed by all shades of theological opinion to be an indispensable tenet of conservative and mediating theology."[21] By his detailed analysis of each Gospel incident and by demonstrating the contradictions between the four Gospels, Strauss opened the floodgate for modern historical criticism.

Having discussed in his introduction various earlier modes of interpretation, Strauss concludes that all the previous efforts were deficient—"It was impossible to rest satisfied with modes of proceeding so unhistorical on the one hand, and so unphilosophical on the other"[22] — but concedes that they prepared the way for the mythological interpretation.[23] Early representatives of this school defined myth as the representation of an event or an idea in a form that is historical, but at the same time characterized by the rich pictorial and imaginative mode of thought and expression of the primitive ages. The influence of this tradition on the narratives was emphasized, and several kinds of myth were distinguished: historical, philosophical, and poetical. Representatives of the mythical school made complicated distinctions between, for example, historical myth and mythical history.

But Strauss complains that there is only one essential difference between an ancient allegorical mode and the new mythical one as adopted by theologians: in the allegorical mode the higher intelligence, which influences the historian to make use of a historical semblance merely as a shell of an idea, is the immediate divine agency; whereas for mythical theologians that divine agency is the spirit of a people or a community.[24] Strauss sets out to radicalize the mythical interpretation.

In his view one can recognize the mythical in individual cases of narrative in two ways, negatively and positively. Negatively, there are two main laws. The first occurs "when the narration is irreconcilable with the known and universal laws which govern the course of events. Now according to these laws, agreeing with all just philosophical conceptions and all credible experience, the absolute cause never disturbs the chain of secondary causes by single arbitrary acts of interposition, but rather manifests itself in the production of the aggregate of finite casualties, and of their reciprocal action."[25] The second law is the law of succession: "An account which shall be regarded as historically valid, must neither be inconsistent with itself, nor in contradiction with other accounts."[26]

On the positive side the mythical, according to Strauss, is sometimes recognizable in the form, sometimes in the substance of a narrative. "If the contents of a narrative strikingly accord with certain ideas existing and prevailing within the circle from which the narrative proceeded, which ideas themselves seem to be the product of preconceived opinions rather than of practical experience, it is more or less probable, according to circumstances, that such a narrative is of mythical origin."[27]

However, Strauss did not limit himself to a critical historical destruction of the biblical narrative; he also had a positive interpretation of the religious mythical language of the Bible. It is in the unhistorical material of Gospels that he found religious significance.[28] His novel theological proposal was to translate the mythical material into the Hegelian philosophical scheme. Influenced by Shelling's thought that the idea of God embraces all reality, he transferred the mythical apprehension of God to the human race as a whole. Inspired by Hegel's idea of God as the universal process of Spirit through history as a whole, Strauss suggested that rather than being expressed in the particularity of one historical individual, the union of the human and the divine applied to the human race and not just Jesus.

Strauss's theological proposal has not left a very deep impact, but his critical historical reasoning has led to many reconstructions of Christian belief and anticipated important trends in the twentieth century, in particular the history of tradition research, eschatology, and the history of Gospel tradition.

Faith and Knowledge

Although Kierkegaard does not engage directly with Strauss's *Leben Jesu*, he is contesting Strauss in two ways, theoretically and practically.[29] Theoretically he emphasizes the uniqueness of the Christian story of incarnation and says that it cannot be a human invention, a myth, and therefore there can be no analogies to it in the strict sense. He contests Strauss practically in the very manner of reinscribing the Bible in his writings and in stressing the existential dimension of reading. Questions brought into focus by Strauss are constantly present in Kierkegaard's philosophical debate with Hegel and in his discussion of the relation between faith and knowledge.

Kierkegaard was notoriously very critical of the temptation to confuse knowledge and faith. According to him, the attempt to approach the Bible through knowledge can never lead to "anything more than approximation, and there is an essential misrelation between that and a personal, infinite interestedness in one's own eternal happiness. Nothing pertaining to faith results from critical theological scholarship" (CUP 25). One can infer that Kierkegaard himself attempts to find a mode of approaching the biblical text that would not lead to such an approximation, but would enable an appropriation; one of the ways to achieve this is his peculiar treatment of biblical quotations.

Kierkegaard seems to agree with Luther's distinction that in relation to the Bible one is allowed to argue, but not in relation to the

Holy Scripture. He observes that what is true for philosophy does not hold true for theology, and even though the Bible and the Holy Scripture are the same book, the way in which it is considered makes a difference (Pap. X 1 A 361). In the same entry Kierkegaard says that there is no immediate transition from, say, reading and studying the Bible as an ordinary human book to presuming that it is God's Word, Holy Scripture.[30] There is a leap, which defines the qualitatively new, even though this remains *allo genos*.

The issue is the difference between "what" (related to the historical) and "how" (the subjective perspective, faith), as well as the incommensurability between a historical truth and an eternal decision (knowledge and faith). The latter is discussed in detail in *Philosophical Fragments* and *Concluding Unscientific Postscript*. The main problem is that an event in time, the Incarnation, precisely *qua* historical is professed as having a decisive significance for a person's eternal happiness. Analogously, two distinct ways of approaching the truth of Christianity present themselves: the objective and the subjective. The objective way corresponds to the historical approach. In historical inquiry, the text of the Bible is a crucial document. But, as Kierkegaard says, the most consummate fulfillment of scholarship and the greatest certainty with regard to the historical is only an approximation (CUP 23), because everything that is historical is contingent.[31]

The historical inquiry into the historical aspect of Christianity provides no link to the eternal. Kierkegaard's main objection to scholarly research, however, is not so much that it is only an approximation, but that it keeps an individual from taking the decision now: "The subject's personal, infinite, impassioned interestedness (which is the possibility of faith and then faith, the form of eternal happiness and then eternal happiness) fades away more and more because the decision is postponed, and is postponed as a direct result of the results of the learned research scholar" (CUP 27). The historical avoids the "now," "this" moment, *the* moment of decision, which is the link to the eternal through the present.[32] The subjective approach to the Bible is the way of existential engagement with infinite passion.[33] As regards the secondary level, the communication of the possibility of such a relation, it can be achieved only by means of indirect communication, which in the case of biblical quotations is instantiated by the unauthorative and discreet, yet decisive use of the Bible.

In the *Postscript*, Kierkegaard says that demonstration does not prove anything with regard to the Bible. Even if one assumes that an exhaustive knowledge is possible, if the enemies of Christianity succeed in proving anything they want with regard to the Scriptures (for example, that certain books are not authentic), the person who does not believe will not be a single step closer to faith. On the other hand, "The believer is still equally free to accept it, equally free, please note, because if he accepted it by virtue of a demonstration, he would be on the verge of abandoning the faith" (CUP 30).

For the believer, proof does not mean anything, because faith and demonstration are mutually exclusive.[34] Indeed, the goal of any scholarship—certainty—would be the end of faith, since dizziness and uncertainty are fundamental properties of the latter. "Whereas up to now faith has had a beneficial taskmaster in uncertainty, it would have its worst enemy in this certainty" (CUP 29).[35] Uncertainty as the nature of faith is determined by the ontological constitution of the world, by the very fact of it being imperfect. In eternity, uncertainty but also faith is abolished. It is essential for Kierkegaard's understanding of faith that infinite reflection is every-where accompanied by the dialectical. "Even the most certain of all, a revelation, *eo ipso* [precisely thereby] becomes dialectical when I am to appropriate it" (CUP 35).

Even the Bible, then, does not offer Kierkegaard certainty of an objective kind and could not, therefore, be the source of certainty for faith, but chiefly an occasion for creating a transparent relation to God through the individual himself.[36] There are two reasons for this limitation on the biblical authority. The first is the language as such, which serves as a prism for the correspondence between truth and reality, and imposes the fractured image of truth. The second reason that even the Bible cannot be a source of certainty is the peculiar way in which God speaks (and reflectively: the way we can hear or understand his Word). Take the following passage:

> But *if it were* so that God had once and for all spoken, *for example*, in Scripture, then, far from being the most powerful, God would be in the tightest squeeze, for a person can easily argue with something like this if he is allowed to use himself against it. But such an assumption is an airy notion without any basis, for *this is not the way God speaks*. He speaks to each individuality, and the instant he speaks to him, he uses the individual himself in order to say through him what he wants to say to him. *Therefore in Job it is a weakness in the plot* that God appears in the clouds and also speaks like the most skilful of dialecticians (SLW 316; Jb 38.1–2, my emphasis).[37]

One significant element in the conflict in this passage is the aspect of time and continuity. It seems important for Quidam (the character who is writing these words in his diary) to emphasize that God is not a God of the past who has once spoken and is silent now, but a God of the present, engaged in a present relationship with an individual. There are therefore two sources of uncertainty pointed out in this passage: continuity, which leads to uncertainty because of its openness, and subjectivity and reflectivity, which are a constant source of uncertainty inasmuch as God "uses the individual himself in order to say through him what he wants to say to him."

Yet another aspect of uncertainty is the "veiled" language of the Bible. Speaking about the many cases of inconsistency and (seeming) contradiction in the Bible, Kierkegaard justifies them as a challenge to and a test of faith. In fact, it is not so much a test as the possibility, the "condition" of faith, since otherwise faith would be identical with knowledge. "A Holy Scripture requires 'faith' and for that very reason there must be discrepancies so that the choice and that the possibility of offense gives tension to faith" (Pap. X 3 A 702, 451).[38]

Literal vs. Nonliteral

At the core of the discussion arising from the historical critical method was the question of the choice between the literal and the nonliteral reading of the Bible. A brief overview of this question contributes to understanding Kierkegaard's employment of the biblical quotations in his pseudonymous works, because it is closely related to his definition of action and the transition from reading to action. The issue of figurative or literal language and interpretative fidelity becomes crucially relevant, for example, for Abraham's story in *Fear and Trembling*. Kierkegaard's use of the biblical quotations takes into account multiple levels of the biblical text and various aspects of its reading, in order to create the best possible conditions for the reader's existential reception of the biblical text. Given Kierkegaard's repeated invitation to read "literally" in the framework of his indirect communication, it is necessary to clarify his position.

Kierkegaard is opposed to excessively figurative reading because such a reading loses the element of the imperative, just as he is against too scholarly an approach in which the element of interestedness fades away more and more because scholarship leads to the postponement of the decision (CUP 27). On the other hand, he notes that slavish literalness can also result in evasion: "Now when you read, 'But by chance a *priest* came down the road, and when he saw him he passed by,' then you shall say to yourself, 'It is *I*' . . . You are not to say, 'It is not I; after all, it was a priest, and I am not a priest'" (FSE 40, my emphasis). In the course of this section, I will try to cast some light on what Kierkegaard means by "literal." It appears that while stressing the need of careful, literal reading Kierkegaard is not speaking about a kind of realism/literalism, but about the spiritual sense of "literal" when the meaning of the Bible becomes concrete for an individual reader.

In its basic form, the tension between literal and nonliteral reading revolves around the following: if one accepts the human origins of biblical writings, then it follows that they may be factually unreliable; therefore the religious claims expressed in the Bible are not absolute, but relative. On the other hand, if one holds the view that the biblical writings are inspired, then it follows that they are not only true, but also factually reliable, which in turn confirms that the claims are absolute. Two fundamental options present themselves: literal or nonliteral reading. Nonliteral reading, then, can take many different forms, from classical allegorical to sheer metaphorism of fiction (for example, from a nonbeliever's point of view). "Literal sense" can also have at least two meanings: a philological and lexical meaning, or a directly descriptive sense.[39] But even the literal meaning is not "given"; rather, it needs to be interpreted: "the literal meaning is itself a text to be understood, a letter to be interpreted."[40]

The literal reading had a great tradition in the Lutheran religion and the verbal literalism of Pietists. Frei observes:

> Concerning the hermeneutical issue, as it arose especially in German biblical scholarship, mainly under the pressure of the question of the positivity of revelation, the basic problem was simply this: Was the sense of the writings ostensive? If not, just what was their meaning? The basic issue in hermeneutics appeared to be that of covering the gap between statements that appeared sufficiently history-like to warrant their being considered historical, and their "real" meaning if they were not.[41]

The need to solve this problem also partly explains the popularity of the mythical school that attempted to bridge the gap between words and meaning, claiming that they were neither ostensive nor allegorical. In his "Kierkegaard's View of Scripture," Pedersen argues that the Lutheran tradition also largely affected Kierkegaard's views on this subject.

The specific background of SK's understanding of the Bible is to be found in the Reformation's scriptural principle and its history. . . . The Lutheran view of Scripture . . . is based on the doctrine of Christ himself as the Word of God revealed in time and present with the spirit in the proclamation. The Word is the true means of grace and communicates the Spirit, but it is embodied in Scripture and speaks primarily through the biblical testimony, yet without being identical with it.[42]

The latter necessarily leads to a conflict between personal interpretation on the one hand and "clarity" of the Bible on the other.

An interesting aspect of this problem is the relation between the two Testaments. This relation is a hermeneutical one, because the New Testament is to a large degree a rereading of the ancient Scripture. In a sense, the movement from history and letter to spiritual meaning is inscribed in the very relation between the two Testaments. The same tension is also reflected in Kierkegaard's comments on the difference between Old and New Testaments with respect to the issue of literal vs. nonliteral reading. Kierkegaard says that Christianity is more rigorous than Judaism:

[Christianity] is literally in earnest about letting go, giving up, and losing what is earthly, constantly suffering and dying to the world. In another sense, Christianity is infinitely milder, because it is the manifestation of the eternity. But to be transformed into being consoled solely by the eternal is to have become spirit, but of all sufferings the suffering of becoming spirit is the most agonising, even more so than the "test" of the Old Testament (Pap. X 4 A 572).

This entry clearly suggests that Kierkegaard's understanding of "literal" is unconventional and complex. It is, after all, Abraham who draws the knife, that is, literally obeys and performs a tangible action; whereas, for example, when the obedience of the Virgin Mary is tested in the Annunciation, there seems to be no action, just anxiety and the victory of faith. Hers is an inward test. Yet in this entry Kierkegaard argues that in the Old Testament it is not the action, but the test that is *Alvor* (seriousness), whereas in the New Testament it is the action itself.

In the same entry we find two terms that can help to define action for Kierkegaard: suffering and continuity. The spiritual inward test is an action because it involves the task of becoming Spirit, which in its turn causes most suffering: "to become Spirit is the most painful of sufferings, more dreadful than 'tests' in the Old Testament" (Pap. X 4 A 572). The other feature that makes an inward action *Alvor* is that it is stretched out in time; it is a process and not an event. In the Old Testament God tests "occasionally"; in the New Testament, the action and the proof of faith required is a continuous, never-ending process (we have seen that this aspect of temporality is also related to the essential uncertainty of faith).[43] This qualification of "action" as suffering (passion) and continuity can perhaps cast light on quite a few cases where Kierkegaard invites us to read literally and to act literally upon the message of New Testament (which mainly consists of parables, and parables *per se* are not to be taken literally). Accompanied by the notion that God speaks through and with the individual himself, the literal meaning perhaps often connotes a concrete meaning for the individual, a literal sense that is spiritual but embodied.

Kierkegaard's focus on language, from etymological subtlety and philological nuances to the precision of the semantic field, adds another dimension to the issue of literal vs. nonliteral reading. Kierkegaard derives his hermeneutics from a very close reading. For example, in the *Postscript* he writes, "When Scripture says that God dwells in a broken and a contrite heart, this is not an expression for an accidental, transitory, momentary condition (*in that case the word 'dwells' would be very unsuitable*) but rather for the essential meaning of suffering for the relationship with God" (CUP 445, my emphasis). We can see from such comments that Kierkegaard is quite clearly concerned with the philological side of theology.[44]

There are many more cases where he bases his reading of a certain passage on the most literal meaning. However, it is clear that he is not literally advocating a literal reading.[45] He says, for example: "Obtuse pastors do indeed appeal very literally to a Bible verse literally understood—that no one enters the kingdom of God if he does not enter it as a little child" (CUP 292; Mt 18.3).

At this point we should recall that in Kierkegaard's view, spiritual communication depends on the metaphorical structure of language.[46] In the *Works of Love* he says, "All human speech, even the divine speech of Holy Scripture, about the spiritual is essentially metaphorical speech" (WL 209). He then proceeds by first determining the most literal meaning of "build up." Thus the literal in spiritual communication is literal only within the metaphorical structure; the important thing is not to get lost in the word but to let the Word build up. Kierkegaard says about a person who distorts the meaning and resists the love message of the Bible: "then he immersed himself [*fordybede sig*] in the words; he refused to allow the words [*Ordet*, Word] to draw him up to themselves, to forget the metaphorical for the actual, but the words of comfort and the words of power became for him the seed of doubt" (EUD 130).

Hard Sayings

Before moving to a closer examination of the transition from reading to action, let us briefly concentrate on several quotations. These exemplify Kierkegaard's reading of the Bible and present the question of literal vs. nonliteral in a particularly incisive way, because they deal with "strong expressions" such as hatred. Kierkegaard was quite preoccupied with the "harshness" of the New Testament, partly in an attempt to explain it (turning categories upside down, as when a seemingly negative action becomes an expression of love in the transformation of faith) and partly in order to accentuate the need for the possibility of offense.

For example, in *The Sickness unto Death* we read: "Christ went around in the form of a lowly servant, poor, despised, mocked, and, as Scripture tells us, spat upon" (SUD 91; Mt 27.67, Lk 18.32), and "a life that is too spiritless to be called sin and is worthy only, as Scripture says, of being 'spewed out'" (SUD 101; Rev. 3.16). What is interesting here is not so much the quotations in themselves, but the insertions "as Scripture tells us/says." In both cases the Scripture is invoked as if to justify these strong expressions. The violence of biblical images is readily admitted and perhaps even stressed.[47]

These quotations acquire their full meaning when we bear in mind Kierkegaard's emphasis on offense, on the scandal of incarnation. For Kierkegaard, the "sign of contradiction" of the Incarnation is not a formal contradiction: "A sign of contradiction . . . is a sign that contains a contradiction in its composition. To justify the name of 'sign,' there must be something by which it draws attention to itself or to the contradiction. But the contradictory parts must not annul each other in such a way that the sign comes to mean nothing or in such a way that it becomes the opposite of a sign, an unconditional concealment" (PC 125).

Gouwens has suggested that the contradiction is passional: "The sign signifies rather than cancelling itself, and yet the situation the sign creates is a contradiction not between the elements of the portrayal (God and human), but between the reader of the gospel and the figure presented."[48] In the "Acoustical Illusion" in *Philosophical Fragments*, Kierkegaard relates paradox to offense, which "does not understand itself but is understood by the paradox. Thus although the offense, however it expresses itself sounds from somewhere else — indeed, from the opposite corner — nevertheless it is the paradox that resounds it, and this indeed is an acoustical illusion" (PF 51).[49] He also says that offense is fundamentally a suffering and always an act, not an event (50). We notice that the problematic of offense brings us back to the question of action. Taking offense thus could be said to be an action issuing from a literal reading of the Bible that has not been transformed or clarified [forklaret] by the spiritual dimension of the literal. The spiritual literalness is the incarnation of Word in our lives; only in this way does Incarnation cease to be scandalous.

An obvious target for concern is the offensive Luke 14.26: "If any man come to me, and hate not his father, and mother, and wife, and children, and brethren, and sisters, yea, and his own life also, he cannot be my disciple." Indeed we find Kierkegaard addressing it several times (most crucially in *Fear and Trembling*; see Chapter 4), and also in a somewhat ambiguous way.[50] In a journal entry called "Love-Cruelty" (related to Mt 8.22) Kierkegaard says:

> Is it not cruel to say to a person who only begs to be able first to bury his father — let the dead bury their dead — and it is love that says it. But it is obvious that for us, Christianity has become something very different than it used to be, since now precisely this love, which lovingly buries the dead and remembers him, would be considered as Christianity. Now, in Christendom, Christianity does not make any division, no, no it copulates. (Pap. X 4 A 642; JP 2439).

Love and hatred curiously become central to the issue of literal vs. nonliteral, because there is a seeming contradiction in the Bible. The task is to not understate this collision, but yet to explain it in some way, which would be subdued to love. Kierkegaard returns to these particularly "difficult" texts in the Bible because they are very explicitly concerned with action, given that the principle action in the New Testament is love, the "work of love."

It is instructive, in relation to the issue of literal vs. nonliteral, to have a look at one passage in the *Postscript* where Kierkegaard criticizes the sentimental view of the child's innocence and analyzes Matthew 19.13–15: "Leave the small children alone and do not forbid them to come to me, for to such belongs the kingdom of heaven." Kierkegaard says, "The whole chapter speaks of the difficulty of entering the kingdom of heaven, and the expressions are as strong as possible" (CUP 592), and then he adds that the meaning in Matthew is not difficult. Christ says the words to the disciples who rebuke the children: his primary concern is not with the children, but he uses the children against the disciples (CUP 593) — "he turns to the small children, but he is speaking to the apostle" (CUP 594). For an adult to become a child is the most powerful expression of difficulty. But perhaps the most interesting thing about Kierkegaard's exegesis is his sophisticated footnote:

> *Toioutoi;* precisely this word adequately shows that Christ is not speaking about children or literally to children, but that he is speaking to the disciples. Literally understood, a child is not *toioutos; toioutos* implies a comparison, which presupposes a difference. Therefore, this does not say anything about children literally, does not say that a child (literally understood) has free admission, but it says that only a person who is like a child can enter into the kingdom of heaven. But just as for the adult it is of all things most impossible to become a child (literally understood), so for a child it is of all things most impossible to be *like* a child, simply because it is a child.

It is clear that Kierkegaard bases his nonliteral interpretation on *word,* on its true, literal meaning. This is one reason that it may see as if Kierkegaard often contradicts himself. In fact, he often wants to do several things on different levels at the same time: (1) not re literally; (2) read literally in the sense of an immediate acting on what we understand the text to mean; (3) read literally in the sense of paying scrupulous attention to grammatical, stylistic, etymological details.

Perhaps in some sense one could say that Kierkegaard's position with respect to literal vs. nonliteral is what Strauss says about Origen: "For when he says, in illustration of the above-mentioned passage, that among other things, it is not to be understood literally that Satan showed to Jesus all the kingdoms of the earth from a mountain, because this is impossible to bodily eye; he here gives not a strictly allegorical interpretation, but merely a different turn to the literal sense, which, according to him, relates not to an external fact, but the internal fact of a vision."[51]

Can One Act without a Meaning?

When Kierkegaard speaks about literal meaning, this can be redescribed as ethical-literal because the literal is valued insofar as it leads to action.[52] Understanding is mediated and at the same time embodied by action. This is put very well in *For Self-Examination:* "God's Word is given in order that you should act according to it, not that you shall practice interpreting obscure texts. If you do not read God's Word in such a way that the least fragment you do understand instantly binds you to act according to it, you are not reading God's Word" (FSE 29). Reading and action (in the form of imitation) are thus essentially interrelated.

We have already attempted to define "action" through suffering and continuity. An important aspect of the definition of action can be found in the *Postscript.* "The actuality is not the external action but an interiority in which the individual annuls possibility and identifies himself with what is thought in order to exist. This is an action" (CUP 339). Accordingly one can say that in relation to reading, action is the transition from the possibility presented by the text to the actuality, by making it concrete (identifying with it). But "Between the thought-action and the actual action, between possibility and actuality, there perhaps is no difference at all in content; the difference in form is always essential. Actuality is interestedness by existing in it" (CUP 340).

Action becomes "real" when it takes the form of personal existential interestedness. Kierkegaard speaks about responsibility for the meaning, about assuming the meaning (see Abraham, who acted upon that little that he understood): "Submission to authority of the adviser becomes a cunning way to derive advantage from the authority. But is that consulting? Is this submitting to what is called the divine authority of the Bible? It is, after all, a cowardly attempt to push away all responsibility by never acting on one's own—just as one has no responsibility for the manner in which one finds a Bible passage on one's side" (CUP 603). This passage brings forth two issues: first, it shows that Kierkegaard was very aware of the possibilities of manipulation of biblical quotations; second, it suggests that in order to prevent such manipulation, the hermeneutical responsibility should be at the same time an existential engagement. However, whether we speak about a literal or a nonliteral meaning, about imposed or assumed meaning, there remains the basic problem of determining the content of this meaning. How does the meaning of the New Testament convey itself to us? Does it ensure that we get the "right" meaning, and, if so, in what way? Or can we act without making sure that we have understood the text rightly? And how does all this relate to the uncertainty of faith?

There are at least two things to consider here. First, how does an individual come to discover the meaning? In quite a few entries in his journals, Kierkegaard declares that it is very easy to understand the Bible if one is ready to understand it literally, which means to act according to what it says. Understanding the Bible is thereby reduced to the will to understand ("but it is tough for flesh and blood to will to understand it," FSE 35), and it seems that there is no hermeneutical issue.

> A Christian Perception. It is a very simple matter. Pick up the New Testament, read it. Can you deny, do you dare deny, that what you read about forsaking everything, about giving up the world, being mocked and spit upon as your Lord and master was — Can you deny, do you dare deny, that this is very easy to understand, indescribably easy, that you do not need a dictionary or commentary or a single other person in order to understand it? (Pap. IX 1 A 221; JP 2865).

That is: If we want to understand, if we do not make obstacles and evasions ourselves, we can easily understand. It is, in other words, as if it were a matter of willing. We should be careful, however, not to confuse the "will" meant here with a "volition"; it is a will qualified by imagination that in its turn plays an important role in transition to faith.[53]

Apart from this will, another condition for understanding seems to be an immediate confrontation with the Word of God, a certain nakedness, a state in which one is stripped of all external help and considerations. This need for personal transparency and confidence in order to establish a transparent relation to God is beautifully expressed in the journal entry where Kierkegaard compares reading the New Testament to a letter from a beloved: "The Principal Rule. Above all, read the NT without a commentary. Would it ever occur to a lover to read a letter from his beloved with a commentary! . . . With the help of God, I understand it all right. Every commentary detracts" (Pap. X 2 A 555; JP 210).[54]

Secondly, what shall we do about the uncertainty of faith and the possibility that we do not understand "rightly" despite our goodwill? There is an entry devoted to the question of whether one can act without having understood the meaning. In his journals, Kierkegaard says that the fundamental confusion is that Christianity has been made into a doctrine (Pap. X3 A 169). In relation to a doctrine, it is true that one first of all needs to put oneself in relation to the "whole" and seek the perspective of totality, but the opposite is true with regard to the New Testament. It stands in relation only to the ethical, and therefore only requires that the reader begin by taking a single thing (*et Enkelt*) and doing it.

> However, one cannot act according to something, which one has not understood. Of course not, that is why God has always arranged it so, that that according to which one has to act, is so easy to understand, that even the most stupid person can understand it immediately. What is easier to understand, then: Give your fortune to the poor — but here there are other difficulties. What is easier to understand than all the demands about self-denial and renunciation? . . "But is it not absolutely important first of all to understand?" No, ethically the important thing is that you do that which is so infinitely easy to understand that you understand it immediately, but your flesh and blood wants to prevent you from doing it (Pap. X 3 A 169).

We see that it is not only meaning that leads to an action, but also action defines meaning; the "meaning" can be divided. One need not aim to exhaust the totality of meaning, but should act upon the little that one can understand. It is in action that the meaning fully reveals itself (perhaps sometimes remaining mysterious for the actor himself). In other words, Kierkegaard refuses to enter into the hermeneutical circle: "To understand a text, it is necessary to believe in what the text announces to me; but what the text announces to me is given nowhere but in the text."[55]

It is important to bear in mind the issues discussed in this chapter in order fully to appreciate the use of the biblical quotations in Kierkegaard's pseudonymous works. Kierkegaard's sensitivity to the text, his sophisticated and complex view of the "literal," shows that his use of the Bible presents the reader with the requirement to reduplicate its meaning and content, while at the same time emphasizing the element of freedom in faith. Kierkegaard's understanding of literal and nonliteral meaning, his definition of action and relation between reading and acting, enables him to make the Bible more translucent to his reader. By lucidity we do not mean absolute clarity, but rather the creation of a prism, of a possibility for the reader to see himself, to see through it without going further than it.

Fictitious Stories

It is supposed to be difficult to understand Hegel, but to understand Abraham is a small matter (FT 32).

In this chapter I should like to discuss what I shall call a hypothetical
or subjunctive use of biblical quotation. This is only one of many different ways Kierkegaard uses the Bible in his pseudonymous works,
but it is particularly interesting because it nicely illustrates his understanding of subjectivity (in the sense of becoming a subject, becoming
a self) and of the individual's relation to truth. By "subjunctive" I
mean not a grammatical mood (although that is also often used), but
a subjunctive existential mode, which means that the representation
of reality takes the form of possibility.

Kierkegaard's texts contain not a description of reality nor a pre-
scription, but a possibility of reality, which can be turned into actuality
only by the individual reader himself. The possibility, in its turn, is
not presented as a defined idea but as a dialectical horizon, which
keeps different moments of reality in tension. The realization of
possibility demands not a random surrender to it, but a conscious
exercise of freedom.

The subjunctive is, for example, expressed in the reinvention of
biblical stories and particularly in the "diffusion" of the same story in
several variations. The presence of variations links the subjunctive
mode to repetition, since repetition discloses the essence by exhibiting

possibilities.[1] As we will see later, repetition plays an important role in appropriation and ensures its elasticity and reflexivity.

The most prominent example of such a reinvention of the biblical story is to be found in the four variations of Abraham's story in *Fear and Trembling*. Much has been said about Abraham, his silence, the sacrifice, the teleological suspension of the ethical, and so on, but little attention has been paid to what Abraham's story in *Fear and Trembling* exactly is.[2] Other relevant examples of rewriting the biblical material can be found in *Stages on Life's Way*, including stories concerning Solomon, Simon the Leper, and Nebuchadnezzar. The aim of this chapter is to draw attention to the presence of recreated biblical stories in Kierkegaard's pseudonymous works, and to point out some of the implications of this phenomenon.

The rewriting may strike us as very modern (and to some extent it is), but there is, of course, a precedent in the Bible itself. Stanley observes:

> Within the Jewish sphere, moreover, a long standing tradition allowed for repeated reinterpretation and even rewriting of certain parts of the biblical record so as to draw out its significance for a later time. Already within the canonical text, the book of Deuteronomy covers much the same ground as the books of Exodus, Numbers, and Leviticus, while the books of Chronicles offer an even closer rewriting of the books of Kings. In several places narrative sections in the prophetic books overlap the versions found in the historical books.[3]

In rewriting the Bible, Kierkegaard gives it a twofold presence: he both appropriates its content and imitates its writing patterns.[4] What makes Kierkegaard's rewriting of the Bible so distinctive is that it is not merely a narrativization, but a creative reworking that produces a parallel text rather than a parallel reading of the same text. Another distinctive feature is that Kierkegaard rewrites the Bible according to the needs of the method of indirect communication, and so prepares the way for the reader's existential relation to it. Kierkegaard's practice of reinventing the biblical material in this way has immense hermeneutical implications and brings many important and interesting issues to the fore, including authority, subjective truth, reduplication, and the mechanism of appropriation.

The mere fact that Kierkegaard sees the biblical text as disclosing diverse possibilities on the textual level (not to speak of different interpretations) rather than as depicting one firmly established reality also indicates that his relation to the Bible is complex. This has especially important repercussions for the conventional distinction between the religious and the aesthetic. By looking at the biblical material in the so-called aesthetic works, one can see that this rigid distinction is "an interpretative regulative prejudice" that has often obscured and impoverished the reading of Kierkegaard's pseudonymous works.

As I said in the introduction, the prejudice works in both directions: on the one hand, when Kierkegaard is read as a theologian he is taken to be a strict, even dogmatic adherent of the traditional reading of the Bible. However, the way in which he can be shown to experiment with the Bible in *Fear and Trembling, Stages on Life's Way,* and elsewhere would not fit into the picture of this kind of religiousness at all. On the other hand, when Kierkegaard is treated as an aesthetic writer or philosopher, the role of the biblical text is neglected—or else his free and creative employment of the biblical text is used as evidence that a pseudonym does not take religiousness seriously enough.[5] A study of his fictitious stories (as I call his reinvention of biblical material) will argue for a more balanced view.[6]

From the analysis of the variations in *Fear and Trembling* we see that the treatment of biblical material is far from aesthetic, since it introduces and expresses the most important theological or philosophical concerns. In some sense this peculiar reworking of the Bible frames the whole exposition of the book, because it recreates anxiety and the possibility of choice in the reader, and, while remaining nonauthoritative (precisely because of the deviations from the "true" story), it multiplies the Bible in the same way that bread was multiplied.

In order to determine the status of Kierkegaard's experimentation with different variations of the biblical text in *Fear and Trembling* and in his pseudonymous authorship in general, we should first carefully examine each of the four variations in relation to each other and in relation to the standard translation available to Kierkegaard at that time: the Old Testament of 1740. Let us see how the same story is reworked, what is added to it and what is subtracted from it. Subsequently we will try to establish the narrative characteristics of each version in order to determine the different theological-philosophical emphases. Apart from the four most explicit and well-known variations in the "Exordium," there are several other variations woven into the rest of the text; we will also examine these. It is not my intention to give an overall interpretation of the story of Abraham, but only to draw attention to several interpretative moments resulting from the reworking of the biblical material.

I will then move to the examples of fictitious stories in *Stages on Life's Way*. I shall try to show how what seem to be mere literary inserts serve to communicate—again by virtue of their deviation from the "source" story—some of the most important issues in "Quidam's Diary." Having done that, I shall emphasize the employment of "possibility" as the only ethically effective form of communication. I shall then relate the reinvented stories to recent discussions (Ferreira, Gouwens, Polk) about the role of imagination in Kierkegaard's authorship. I shall further suggest that the treatment of the Bible that results in alternative variations rather than interpretations can be linked to a presence of negative theology in Kierkegaard's works, which in its turn is related to the negative method of indirect communication.

Prelude

The idea of drawing different stories out of the one initial text is introduced in the "Attunement" (*Stemning*) by saying that there was once a man who had first heard the story of Abraham as a child. The "Attunement" suggests an evolution in our understanding of the story, an evolution related to our age.[7] The possibility of reinventing biblical stories is then introduced, by suggesting that interpretation changes in time and that from the reader's point of view, it is a different story every time. However, usually this concerns only the interpretation, not the formal properties of the text itself. What makes the four variations of Abraham special is that the text itself changes in them. It is not so much reread as rewritten.

As a child the man heard "that beautiful story of how God tempted Abraham" (FT 9); later he read the story with an even greater surprise. Why surprise? Because "life had fractured what had been united in the pious simplicity of a child" (FT 9). We can hardly fail to notice that unity and pious simplicity are related to a very important theme for Kierkegaard, that of "the purity of heart." The pure heart is most open to the words of God precisely because by willing only one thing (unity), it necessarily wills the good;[8] the good being also the true, this leads us to the "true" reading.

Kierkegaard says that the older the man grew the more *enthusiastic* he became, but he could *understand* the story less and less. This distinction identifies the separation that occurs in life as the separation of spirit and thought, and also hints at the fact that the story of Abraham cannot be read in cognitive terms. When understanding has emancipated itself from the original pious unity of spirit and understanding, the story cannot be understood. But this does not therefore mean that the story cannot be approached at all. Indeed, another mode of approach is suggested. It is said that in the end, the man's only desire was "to be the witness of the event," that is to say, to be a contemporary of this event.

What kind of contemporaneity is wished for? It might seem to be a wish to share the experience of the actual historical event, or to be a spectator.[9] However, the man does not wish to identify with external circumstances, because it is said that he did not mind the event taking place "on a barren heath"—in the middle of Jutland rather than on Mount Moriah (FT 9). Kierkegaard's characteristic idea of contemporaneity is that of contemporaneity of spirit and not an immediate participation in the historical fact.[10] Contemporaneity is indeed of a crucial importance for the whole of *Fear and Trembling* and, as I will argue later, for all the biblical quotations in his pseudonymous works. To become contemporary, one needs to appropriate. The relation between contemporaneity and appropriation is reflective and mutual. We cannot learn to make a movement of faith by reading the story of Abraham; the only thing we can do is learn "to be horrified by the prodigious paradox" (FT 52). But in order to do that, we must make ourselves contemporary with Abraham (and with God, or his command), since unless we make it into a present, the whole story is meaningless, "for what is the value of going to the trouble of remembering the past which cannot become a present" (FT 30). I will contend later that the only way to become contemporary is to relate to Abraham through possibility.

The man in the story was not a thinker, and he did not want to go further than faith (FT 9). The man was preoccupied not so much by the thought of Abraham as by the *horror* of that thought (FT 9, "shudder at the idea," Danish *Tankens Gysen*), and precisely in this sense he was not a thinker, since for the "thinker" there is no "horror" or "doubt." This relates to the theme of doubt and anxiety introduced in the preface.[11] There faith is interestingly compared to doubt in one important sense—that it is a difficult, perhaps a lifelong task. Faith is both embracing and suspending doubt: embracing insofar as its element is uncertainty, suspending insofar as it overcomes doubt. Anxiety and doubt as being-in-between mark Johannes de silentio's reading of Abraham's story, and they are continuously stressed in order to render reading more difficult.

Toward the end of "Attunement," we find some perplexing words: "The man was not a learned exegete, he did not know Hebrew; if he had known Hebrew, he perhaps would easily have understood the story and Abraham" (FT 9). This comment leads us to reflect on the translated nature of the Bible (see my section on this in Chapter 5); but it can also be interpreted ironically, as another form of contemporaneity, one that postulates some kind of immediate access to the biblical message. Yet, as we have seen, the contemporaneity and transparency of a biblical story on the grounds of external circumstance would, in Kierkegaard's terms, be an illusion.

Before moving to the analysis of the "Exordium" stories, I would like to draw attention to an interesting parallel: there are four different stories, just as there are four Gospels in the New Testament. It may be a coincidence, or it may be a clue that we are to read Abraham's story as the prefiguration of the New Testament's sacrifice of Jesus. Alternatively, it may remind us that even in the New Testament there is no one truth, and the believer is faced with uncertainty and individual decision of appropriation—in other words, with "fear and trembling."

First Story

The starting point for all the four variations is Genesis 22.1–2, given in Kierkegaard's text in quotation marks: "And it came to pass after these things, that God did tempt Abraham, and said unto him, Abraham: and he said, Behold, here I am. And he said, Take now thy son, thine only son Isaac, whom thou lovest, and get thee into the land of Moriah; and offer him there for a burnt offering upon one of the mountains which I will tell you of."[12] When Kierkegaard quotes these verses in *Fear and Trembling,* he does not quote absolutely exactly. The most significant change is that the word of address— "Abraham"—and the response, "Behold, here I am," are missing in Kierkegaard's text, so there is no dialogue between God and Abraham (which seems strange, given Kierkegaard's usual readiness to create a dialogue).

The omission of Abraham's response may also be significant in view of the emphasis on Abraham's silence, despite the fact that he actually speaks; it could also emphasize the indirect communication in *Fear and Trembling* on two levels: first between Abraham and God, since there is no transparent command or univocal obedience; and then, second, for readers. The lack of such transparency is precisely what makes the story relevant to us, and what makes it possible to be appropriated. Even though in the Old Testament it is not unusual to hear God's voice directly, it is not so in Kierkegaard's vision, or in his creative reworking of the biblical material in *Fear and Trembling,* or in many other places in his authorship; no immediate, direct relation is given.[13] We notice also, for example, that although it is said in the Old Testament that "God did tempt Abraham," Kierkegaard (particularly in *The Concept of Anxiety*) insists that God tempts no one, but that every individual tempts himself.

It is worth noting that even the apparently direct communication from God in the Old Testament is not a direct *intervention* and leaves space both for indirectness and subjectivity. In the logic of the Old Testament, God could easily turn the knife into something inoffensive or make a river appear between Abraham and Isaac; in short, he could "intervene" by making it "impossible" for Abraham to sacrifice his son and showing that he is not demanding human sacrifice. Instead, God leaves the outcome dependent on Abraham's active interpretation and responsibility. Even the seemingly objective substitution "ram" for "Isaac" is subject to Abraham's listening to God's Word.

In Genesis 22.13 the ram is behind Abraham (and we do not know whether it has been there all the time), but it becomes visible for Abraham only *after* he has "heard" Genesis 22.12, "Lay not thine hand upon the lad." This moment of subjectivity, which, as I say, is present in the Old Testament in a very rudimentary way, is something that Kierkegaard explores and stretches to its extreme. Abraham is in-between the two commands given by God, that is, in-between two Words (and, as some may suggest, two testaments), and in this acoustical space he needs to learn to listen and to act in the tension of these words. In fact we could say that in Abraham's story, God is silent in very much the same way as Abraham was silent when he said, "God will himself provide a lamb for a burnt offering." In this way, God's communication prefigures Abraham's "communication," or the lack of it.

Let us have a look at the first of the four variations. The longest one, it features three textual peculiarities. First, the tent is not mentioned in Genesis. Such an insertion is an example of an organic infiltration (discussed in Chapter 5). Second, a much more interesting change is an example of Kierkegaard's splicing various citations from the Bible: the Sara mentioned in this version (FT 10) is not Sara but Judith (Jdt 10.10).[14] There is no mention in the Bible of Sara looking through a window. In his journals Kierkegaard quotes as an example of romanticism, "When Judith went, accompanied by her maid, the men of the town kept staring after her until she had gone down the hill and crossed the valley, where they lost sight of her"[15] (Pap. III A 197). But even that does not exhaust the compilation, since we must note the subversion: now it is Sara who looks at men.[16]

And yet the splicing is not arbitrary, because there is a certain parallelism. Sara does not know what Abraham is going to do, and neither do the elders of the council know what Judith is going to do—as she herself says, "But you must not inquire into the affair, for I will not tell you what I am going to do until it is accomplished" (Jdt 8.34). There are two potential murders and two tests of faith.[17] The inversion of the story is perfect: Judith risks her own life in order to save the faith of her people and to prove to them that their God is almighty and loving, since he can act through the hand of a single woman. The murder is committed for the sake of the universal. Abraham is tested himself, but he also proves that God is almighty and loving. In his readiness to sacrifice Isaac, Abraham transgresses the universal; he is an individual in all its isolation, and no murder is committed. Of course, it is possible that Kierkegaard did not design the story with these similarities in mind, but even the unconscious rationality of the text is too eloquent to be ignored.

Third, "He clasped Abraham's knees, he pleaded at his feet" (FT 10) represents an interesting intertwining with the Greek heritage. Embracing the knees is the ancient Greek way of expressing respect and humility (in *Ulysses* VI, Song 1142, Ulysses addresses princess Nausika in this way), but here it is attributed to Isaac.[18]

Far more drastic changes than these have been made to the texture of this story. Most notable is the fact that in this version, Abraham *speaks* to Isaac and is capable of sharing God's command. This is a very important break with the tradition of Abraham's silence. Of course, in the Bible Abraham also speaks. He says, "God will provide himself a lamb for a burnt offering," but Johannes de silentio has considered his speech to be silence, since Abraham is speaking but not saying anything. There is the question, of course, whether de silentio does not contradict himself when he says, "So Abraham did not speak. Just one word from him has been preserved, his only reply to Isaac, ample evidence that he had not said anything before" (FT 115), particularly given that he adds, "Without these words, the whole event would lack something" (116).

These words are held to be crucial and yet somehow "silent." In a footnote, de silentio gives an "analogy" to these words that emphasizes and consummates the silence: "If there is any analogy at all, it is one such provided by the death scene of Pythagoras, for in his final moment he had to consummate the silence he had always maintained, and for that reason he *said:* it is better to be killed than to speak. See Diogenes, VIII, para. 39" (FT 118). De silentio argues that Abraham cannot speak because language translates an individual into the universal, but Abraham as individual enters into an absolute relation to the absolute and transgresses the universal; otherwise he is a murderer.

However, in the first variation in *Fear and Trembling,* Abraham attempts to speak "admonishingly" (*formanende*; imploring, encouraging), while it is impossible for Isaac to understand what is said. Thus the emphasis is on the impossibility of understanding and not of language (this is not, however, developed further in *Fear and Trembling* with regard to Isaac, but strangely finds an echo in Kierkegaard's insistence on the impossibility for the reader to understand Abraham's situation). The communication takes place, but Isaac "could not understand him" (FT 10). By repeating several times that Isaac could not understand, Kierkegaard thus makes a shift from a theological emphasis on the absolute incommunicability of God's message to Abraham to the responsibility of an individual (that is to say, a deficiency on Isaac's part). This is particularly clear, for example, when he writes, "His soul could not be uplifted" (FT 10). Isaac begs for mercy.

The words "Then Abraham turned away from him" (FT 10) mark a break in the story. Realizing the impossibility of understanding and the risk of offense (since Isaac would be offended by God's command), Abraham changes his tactics. He changes his *look* (literally): "When Isaac saw Abraham's face [*Aasyn*] again, it had changed: his gaze was wild, his whole being was sheer terror [*Skikkelse var Raedsel*]" (FT 10). Abraham becomes violent: "He seized Isaac by the chest, threw him to ground" (FT 10). Calling himself an idolator,[19] Abraham says that it is his own wish[20] to sacrifice him. The consequence of the change in Abraham is that instead of taking offense, Isaac turns to God and chooses the father in heaven over the earthly father (which frames and occasions the refrain about weaning). Abraham's move is perhaps the quintessence of the method of indirect communication: a holy lie, or act of violence.[21]

In the story as it is told in the first variation, we are not dealing with the sacrifice of Isaac but with the sacrifice of Abraham. Abraham sacrifices himself: "Lord God in heaven, I thank you; it is better that he believes me a monster [*Umenneske*] than that he should lose faith in you" (FT 11).[22] Perhaps, then, *Fear and Trembling* is not about the suspension of ethics, but about suspension of truth: God suspends truth from Abraham, Abraham from Isaac, and then Kierkegaard—perhaps—suspends it from us.[23] This suspension creates a chain of possibilities, echoes, and anxiety.

All four versions end with a short refrain that acts as a kind of moral. The refrains also build upon what is essentially the same pattern, but they differ in their respective developments. It can be noted that the theme of weaning in each of these refrains echoes Genesis 21.8: "And the child grew, and was weaned: and Abraham made a great feast the same day that Isaac was weaned."[24]

Second Story

The second story is considerably shorter than the first. In the opening lines, the depiction of Abraham's departure concentrates on creating a gentle, even sentimental, family mood, first by mentioning that Abraham embraces his bride, and then by showing Sara kiss Isaac and say that he is her pride and hope (FT 12).[25] In this second variation, Abraham is silent. In fact, his silence is emphasized. The story is very laconic: one has a feeling of suspended drama that for the moment takes the form of a matter of fact. Abraham performs the actions but he is not really present; his eyes are fixed on earth (later his despair is described as, "Abraham's eyes were darkened [*fordunklet*]").

Even the most dramatic moment of the story is suppressed on the narrative level: Abraham takes the knife, sees the lamb, offers it, and goes home, as if nothing happened (and in fact we are not told what exactly has happened). But the emotions unfold later. It is said that from that day Abraham becomes old, because he cannot forget that God demanded this from him. Later in the text (FT 18), we are told that faith kept Abraham young enough to desire a child despite his actual age, and that he who keeps faith is eternally young. Thus, not being able to forget that God demanded the sacrifice of Isaac means that Abraham has lost faith.

Not being able to forget here seems to mean not being able to forgive (which is an important theme for Kierkegaard and is taken up again in, for example, "A Leper's Self-Contemplation"). It is a silent fight between God and Abraham, in which we glimpse obedience without acceptance and law without love; throughout *Fear and Trembling*, Kierkegaard traces the difference between obedience, belief, and love, an issue to which we shall return.

The second variant has an echo later in the text, when it is said (FT 35) that what sets Abraham's faith apart is that he can keep Isaac in joy, that he can forgive God. This is precisely what Abraham is incapable of doing in the second variation. As Edward Mooney observes, the joy of getting Isaac back is what sets the knight of faith apart from the knight of resignation.[26] The knight of faith is able to renounce the finite, but also to make a movement back (thus constituting a double movement), and the joy witnesses his ability to embrace the finite a second time. Abraham's joy is also a sign that he does not succumb to resentment of God.

Later in the text (FT 36), we find one more possibility (variant eight), which is related to the second variant—what if Abraham had resigned? We are told that if Abraham had resigned, he may have thought that he could just as well offer Isaac without going all the way to Mount Moriah—that is, without his journey of anxiety. But without anxiety the whole trial would have been meaningless. Kierkegaard says the fact that Abraham did not resign himself to losing Isaac is proved by his being able to receive Isaac in joy (FT 37). Thus, in the dialectics of the reduplication, the second movement confirms the validity of the first.

Third Story

The third story picks up the sentimentality of the first lines of the second, with small changes: instead of embracing Sara Abraham kisses her, and Isaac is not Sara's pride and hope but her "delight" and "joy" (FT 13). Then Abraham becomes thoughtful. What does he think of? He thinks of Hagar and her son, whom he sent to the desert.[27] Why? He thinks of them as something that is still left for him, as a hope for future.

But that means that he has resigned himself and does not believe that God will keep his promise about Isaac. Thinking about alternative future possibilities, Abraham climbs Mount Moriah and draws the knife. That is the end of the "biblical" story. It is told very concisely, with the emphasis on the other son. The original story is therefore deprived of its absolute character. What makes Abraham's trial doubly difficult is that Isaac is not only his son, but also his promise.

But then Kierkegaard adds a sequel: Abraham rides to Moriah again, this time alone, and begs God for forgiveness for having been ready to sacrifice Isaac and neglecting a father's duty toward his son. In the first instance it seems that Abraham defends the ethical and understands the trial negatively: that is, as a trial in which he was expected to resist rather than to accept the divine command. Abraham has never regained peace; he is in doubt as to whether his readiness to sacrifice Isaac was a sin or not. And if it was a sin, he cannot understand how it could be forgiven. Which sin is the more terrible one?

This question of the sin is brought up again later in the book (FT 62), in relation to the question of whether it is a sin for an individual to exist opposed to the universal. Abraham's doubt establishes a link with the problematic of doubt in "Prelude." In the "main" story Abraham has never doubted, and has always believed against all reason that God will keep the promise to bless him through Isaac (in the "Eulogy" and also explicitly in FT 20: "But Abraham had faith and did not doubt; he believed the preposterous [*det Urimelige*]"). At the same time, by emphasizing the element of anxiety in Abraham's story Kierkegaard introduces an ambiguity into the idea of doubt: doubt is necessary as an expression of the element of uncertainty in faith, which is different from doubt about faith itself.

In this variant, then, Abraham puzzles over exactly the same question as generations of Bible readers, one that generations of readers of *Fear and Trembling* have also faced. One could say that in this reflexive variation of the story of Abraham is also inscribed the whole history of its reception.

Fourth Story

In the fourth story a new character, Eliezer the faithful servant, is mentioned (in Genesis there are several servants). He rides part of the way to Mount Moriah with Abraham and Isaac. Abraham prepares himself "calmly and gently" (FT 14), but then when he draws the knife, his left hand clasps in despair and his body shivers—and Isaac sees it. They return home, *Isaac has lost his faith* (FT 14), but Abraham does not know that his reaction has been seen. Presumably Isaac loses his faith because of the scandal of God demanding such a thing from his father, which he guesses having seen Abraham's despair and apparent readiness to obey (he was saved from just such a scenario in the first story, when Abraham suddenly "changed his look").

Now Abraham fulfills his duty but without faith, that is, he is resigned. What gives meaning to the story is precisely not blind obedience, but faith that God will keep his promise in spite of all indications to the contrary. It is emphasized that nobody speaks about this. Isaac never tells anybody, and Abraham does not know that Isaac saw something.

Other Variations

After these four stories, we are told that the man thought about the event "thus and in many similar ways" (FT 14). Indeed the subjunctive retelling of the Bible in *Fear and Trembling* is not exhausted by the first four variations. We have already mentioned some, but there are others, even such a radical variation as this: "Or if Abraham perhaps did not do at all what the story tells, if perhaps because of the local conditions of that day it was something entirely different" (FT 30).[28] Let us have a look at these variations, since by diffusing Abraham's story they also illuminate it. They are scattered around the text; it is useful to bring them together in order to show how multilayered are both Kierkegaard's reading of the Bible and his own writing. I will not be able here to examine these variations in detail and will merely draw attention to them.

For example, later in *Fear and Trembling* we read, "If Abraham had doubted" (FT 20–21). Here one finds what could be called variant five, even though it is not as explicitly marked as the first four versions. It tells us that if Abraham had doubted, he would have offered to sacrifice himself instead of Isaac, and this thus relates to the first variation in "Exordium." Self-sacrifice (a humanist option, as it were) is seen as an expression of doubt. This suggests a total suspension of the ethical, and neither a sacrifice of oneself in order to save the other, nor even a spiritual self-sacrifice (by which Abraham could consciously prefer to be punished by God for disobedience, consciously prefer "to lack faith" and refuse to sacrifice Isaac) is acceptable or can replace the trial.

Kierkegaard tells us that Abraham did not doubt and did not offer himself instead, because "Abraham had faith. He did not pray for himself . . . it was only when righteous punishment fell upon Sodom and Gomorrah that Abraham came forth with his prayers" (FT 21).[29] At first glance it may strike the reader as strange that Abraham "did not pray for himself" by not offering himself instead of Isaac, but there are several possible explanations. Isaac embodies God's promise about the future, and Abraham's life will be extended through his—so in this sense to ask for Isaac, even if it involves his own death, is to ask for himself. Also, by sacrificing himself instead of Isaac, Abraham would avoid anxiety, and thus he would still be asking for himself. Another reason is indirectly given later in the text, in relation to the transgression of the universal by being willing to kill his son. "Why, then, does Abraham do it? For God's sake and—the two are wholly identical—for his own sake" (FT 59).

It is a unity of an absolute egoism and an absolute self-annihilation that is expressed by temptation or trial (*Fristelse*). This is also one reason why Abraham cannot give any other answer than that it is a temptation/trial: "To the question 'Why?' Abraham has no other answer than that it is an ordeal, a temptation [*Fristelse*] that, as noted above, is a synthesis of its being for the sake of God and for his own sake" (FT 71), which leads to the problem of silence. The coincidence of "for the sake of God and for his own sake" confirms that Abraham, as an individual, enters into an absolute relation to the absolute and thus cannot be mediated through the universal, through language.

Yet another possibility is presented in *Fear and Trembling* (version six): "If Abraham had doubted as he stood there on Mount Moriah, if irresolute he had looked around, if he had happened to spot the ram before drawing the knife, if God had allowed him to sacrifice it instead of Isaac—then he would have gone home, everything would have been the same, he would have had Sara, he would have kept Isaac, and yet how changed" (FT 22). Abraham would not then have testified to his faith in God's grace.

Of course, this leads us to the question of whether Abraham believed that God would not in the end demand the sacrifice of Isaac. Kierkegaard says that all the time, Abraham believed God would not demand the sacrifice of Isaac, but that at the same time he was ready to perform the sacrifice if it was demanded of him (FT 35). But how are we to understand this? Did he believe that God's command was different from what it seemed? One can also legitimately ask whether Abraham "understood" God's command.

As we have seen in Chapter 3, Kierkegaard seems to think that in relation to God's Word, understanding is of a rather different nature, and that it could be said that we act in some kind of "immediate reflection" and not because we understand (in the normal sense of the word). We have seen earlier that action itself defines the meaning, and that "meaning" can be divided and extracted without first realizing its totality. In this respect it is interesting to note that in *Fear and Trembling,* Abraham acts upon what can be understood: he goes to Mount Moriah, he even lifts the knife, and then—we never actually get to the really incomprehensible part, namely the killing itself. We do not know whether Abraham understood God's command, but we know that he took it upon himself and did the little that he understood of it. This *a priori* responsibility is an important part of Kierkegaard's vision of ethical and religious action.[30]

We are told that by virtue of the "double movement" Abraham was surprised at the outcome (FT 36), which is a condition of his having received Isaac back with joy. And if he had obeyed but had not been able to make the double movement, he would perhaps have loved God but would not have believed: "If it had been otherwise with Abraham, he perhaps would have loved God but would not have had faith, for he who loves God without faith reflects upon himself; he who loves God in faith reflects upon God" (FT 37). The difference between love of God without faith and love of God in faith is an interesting one. Strangely enough, it appears that obedience is a domain of love: love is blind and makes acting easy; in its euphorical sublimation it is resolute but not responsible.

But the domain of faith is not obedience; it is the double movement of resignation and joy, the tension in anxiety.[31] Faith is not blind: it does not close its eyes and jump, no, it always keeps eyes wide open—or, echoing Caputo, one could say that it stares the impossible in the eye—therefore faith does not make things easy, but makes them difficult. This difficulty is repeatedly emphasized in *Fear and Trembling.* Abraham is not the father of faith because it is easy for him: "he heard and he did," but only because—and insofar as—it was so infinitely difficult for him.

In the light of the difference between love and faith, the claim that Abraham did it "for God's sake and—the two are wholly identical—for his own sake" (FT 59) connects to what is said of Abraham in the "Eulogy" that he is "great by the love that is hatred to oneself" (FT 17), both literally and as related to Luke 14.26 (which is brought into the text later on), since self-hatred is expressed through his love to Isaac, which appears as hatred. The two moments "for God's sake" and "for his own sake" express a unity of an absolute self(ish)ness and an absolute self-annihilation, which is called temptation/trial (*Fristelse*), since in the Kierkegaardian perspective it is not God who tempts Abraham, but Abraham who tempts himself. Perhaps, then, *Fear and Trembling* is about the sacrifice of anxiety, about a surrender, learning to do this double movement of unification "for one's own sake" and "for God's sake."

We should also recall Kierkegaard's critical remark that one all too easily identifies Isaac as "the best" that Abraham can sacrifice (FT 28). This leads us to reconsider what exactly Abraham's offering to God is. Might it not be the case that Abraham's offering is his *Angest,* that "the best" is his anxiety as the expression of his faith, of his love, and of his inmost subjectivity? The story as it can be relevant for us is not about Abraham sacrificing "another," something other than himself, but rather about an offer that comes from himself.[32]

Kierkegaard introduces yet another version (variation seven) with the words "let us go further" (FT 36). Let us assume that Isaac is in fact sacrificed. Then God would give a new Isaac, because Abraham does not believe in some eternal glory, but that he will be blessed in this life. The difference between the hope for eternal and the blessedness in this life is very important, because the fact that Abraham believes in the fulfilment of promise in this life makes his trial much more difficult. In some sense it could be said that Abraham is also required to become contemporaneous, contemporaneous with his trial and his promise. Likewise, the only way to approach this story for readers is to become contemporaneous with Abraham and with God's Word.

One becomes contemporary only by listening to God's Word (and one can hear it only when one is contemporary with God). In the Christian context, God is for us through his Word, so naturally our mode of relation to it is "listening." Abraham's story explicitly features an encounter with God's voice, or rather with its echo. I think that, in the view of the emphasis on the subjective, the subjunctive, and the indirectness in Kierkegaard's version, we should make this fundamental shift from voice to echo.

It is often said that Abraham heard the voice of God and obeyed. This is quite misleading. As I have said, it seems that Abraham did not hear the voice, but listened to its echo. What does it mean, to hear an echo? I use "echo" to reflect several important components of indirect communication: both distance and overcoming the distance, the distortion and the possibility to "correct" the distortion with the help of the art of perspective, the subjectivity faced with the "objective" grain of the message, the tension of illusion of truth and truth itself. The echo in *Fear and Trembling* resonates on two levels: both for Abraham and for us. The text itself is constructed as an echo: there are the four principal variations in "Exordium," but, as we have seen, the subjunctive retelling of the Bible is not exhausted by the first four variations. These variations are scattered around in the text and witness both Kierkegaard's multilayered reading of the Bible and his own luxuriant writing. I take these variations also to be an expression of this echo; a response to each is a slightly different hearing of God depending on the perspective, on where exactly you are in the mountains on your way to Mount Moriah.

Due to the peculiar acoustics of faith, when you are close to the Word you do not hear it in an immediate sense. You hear it, but you do not know where it comes from, it multiplies itself by its echo and causes dizziness. Contemporaneity is possible only in and through anxiety, and when by appropriating the Word in repetition, in endless successions of echo, you make it resonate in yourself. Abraham's story could be understood as a parable of what it means to listen to God's Word. Kierkegaard's emphasis on reading aloud would allow us to assert that listening and reading are interchangeable and extend the meaning of Abraham's story, by saying that for us it is a metaphor of the difficulty of reading the Bible.

Stages on Life's Way

I shall now analyze several examples from *Stages on Life's Way* that further illustrate how Kierkegaard reworks the biblical material. As has been said, the dramatization or narrativization of the Bible, or the practice of creating analogous stories, are not unique to Kierkegaard, and in fact these techniques have been employed in the Bible itself. Green observes: "The Bible itself offers some images of imaginative proclamation. One of the most vivid examples is the sermon delivered by the prophet Nathan to King David, who had misused the power of his office to commit murder and adultery (2 Sm 12.1 ff.). Nathan appeals to the imagination of the king by telling him a story."[33] What makes Kierkegaard's fictitious stories special is the way in which he changes the stories and makes use of analogy by disclosing that in fact it is disanalogy. Another remarkable feature is presentation in the form of possibility, which, if it is to become "real," requires subjective appropriation.

In "Quidam's Diary" there are several entries devoted entirely to fictitious stories, loosely based on the biblical material. Their status is problematic, in relation to both the Bible and the rest of the diary. As concerns the latter, they seem to disrupt the usual flow of the discourse with no obvious purpose. And yet surely they must perform some function, whether that is literary, philosophical, psychological, or religious, or a combination. The pseudobiblical inserts may be one of the ways to bind together "Quidam's Diary." Their analysis allows us to see that underneath the surface of a rather monotonous text, there is a complicated writing structure.[34]

A Leper's Self-Contemplation

The first story is found in the 5 February midnight entry: "A Leper's Self-Contemplation" (SLW 232–234). The basis for it is the mention, in Matthew 26.6, of Jesus staying in the house of Simon. In Matthew we read: "Now when Jesus was in Bethany, in the house of Simon, the leper." However, no more is said about this Simon in the Bible. In fact there is no such a thing as a "story" of Simon the leper in the Bible—we do not know why Jesus is staying in his house, what kind of person Simon is, or anything about his attitude to his leprosy. Based on a very sparse and laconic scriptural reference, Kierkegaard invents a whole story.[35]

Not surprisingly—it is a "biblical" story, after all—the retelling features five different biblical references (even though four are not related to the leper): Matthew 26.6, Mark 14.3, and Luke 17.12; Genesis 2.18; Luke 16.22; Matthew 8.11; and Titus 2.14. The presence of so many references in a relatively short text contributes to the illusion that the text is very closely related to the biblical story, whereas in fact there is no such story at all. In this way, Kierkegaard weaves together the fictional and the authentic biblical material so that they become difficult to separate. As will be seen throughout the book, one of the features of Kierkegaard's use of biblical quotations is just this kind of "organic" synthesis.[36]

"A Leper's Self-Contemplation" is centred around one event—the concoction of a salve. It is curious to note that event. As has been observed, there is no story about the leper in the Bible, but clearly the salve relates to the ointment mentioned in Matthew 26.7: when Jesus was staying in the house of Simon the leper, "there came unto him a woman having an alabaster box of very precious ointment" (Mt 26.7).

In the isolation and loneliness caused by the external manifestation of his condition, Simon concocts the salve in anger and hatred. Manasse, the other leper, makes use of it, becomes invisibly leprous, and goes to the town "to breathe poison on the people, turning them visibly leprous." It is important to observe a sinister turn toward inwardness: "I concocted a salve by which all the mutilation turns inward so that no one can see it, and the priest must pronounce us healthy" (SLW 233). Given Kierkegaard's continuous emphasis on internalization this is particularly remarkable. It raises the problem of appearance, of possible ambiguity of inwardness, and it focuses the story on the discrepancy between the internal and external. Awoken from sleep (both literally and metaphorically), in the course of his contemplation Simon gradually attains a higher level of consciousness, in respect to both the monstrous thing he has done and his physical state.

In his internal development he starts off by reproaching God ("I ask the one who himself said that it is not good for a person to be without companionship"),[37] then moves on to repentance. However, he is still unable fully to appreciate what he has done and therefore needs some external help to get out of his crime ("Let me forget how it is prepared"), before he is finally able to say, "I thank you God of Abraham, that you allowed me to concoct this salve; I thank you that you helped to renounce the use of it." This concise story of conversion marks several important points for Kierkegaard, such as the relation between forgetting and forgiving or the gratitude for the trial.

In order to repent genuinely, you must first of all forgive yourself, but forgiving involves forgetting. However, this forgetting is not a denial of the past, but—paradoxically—a movement orientated to the future; it is the hope of future.[38] The self-contemplation of the leper leads ultimately to self-acceptance. The main issues in the leper's story—the change or transformation, the discrepancy between the internal and external, the deception of appearance—are echoed thematically throughout "Quidam's Diary" but are also related to the immediately surrounding entries, and thus add a new dimension to them. A couple of entries before the leper's contemplation, Quidam is concerned with the change: "Should I change myself and my opinion of her because she changed toward me?" (SLW 228) In the entry after the leper's contemplation, he says, "It is true, my outer being is entirely different from my inner being" (SLW 234). And in the story, the leper describes himself as "one who offers his life to save others," which corresponds adequately to Quidam's self-understanding.

Thus instead of being disconnected from the rest of "Quidam's Diary," the leper's contemplation is in fact like a symbol or a concentrated parable of the issues addressed in the diary. As we shall see from many other examples throughout the book, it is often the case that many fundamental concerns are expressed through the employment or reworking of biblical material. One cannot say that there are no biblical quotations that are merely ornamental, but many seemingly "casual" or literal references are loaded with meaning as well as strategic importance.

Solomon's Dream

Solomon's dream (SLW 251) is the second fictitious story in "Quidam's Diary" based on a biblical source. Its status is more ambiguous than "A Leper's Self-Contemplation," because there is such a thing as Solomon's dream in I Kings 3.5–15, so it would seem that it has a clear prototype. The problem is that neither in its setting nor in its content is the biblical dream the same as the one told in *Stages on Life's Way*. One could, of course, suggest that the latter is not meant to relate directly to the biblical Solomon's dream, and thus is neither a reference nor a quotation, but altogether imagined. However, the introductory sentence points toward the "real" dream and thus establishes a relationship between the dream in I Kings 3.5–15 and the one told in *Stages on Life's Way:* "Solomon's verdict is quite familiar; it was able to separate truth from deception and to make the judge famous as the wise prince. His dream is less familiar" (SLW 250). In the Bible, the example of Solomon's wise verdict is given immediately after his dream.

As in "A Leper's Self-Contemplation," there are five biblical quotations in Solomon's dream, taken from three different books. This, as it was pointed out earlier, contributes to the creation of a pseudo-biblical mode of discourse, as the boundaries between the original "factual" material, interpretation, and sheer fiction are blurred.[39]

The setting of the biblical dream is this: when Solomon goes to Gibeon to sacrifice there, God appears to him in a dream at night and asks him what he wants from his Lord. Solomon asks for "an understanding heart to judge thy people, that I may discern between good and bad" (1 Kgs 3.9). Solomon starts his entreaty to God by referring to his father as the righteous one, but the relation to his father is not given any significance in the biblical text itself. In Kierkegaard's text, however, the father-son relationship becomes central and is dealt with in a manner that is almost too Freudian.[40]

In "Quidam's Diary," the differences from the biblical account of Solomon's dream are immediately striking. The beginning of the story depicts the relationship between King David and Solomon, father and son, as a relation between the hero and his poet (which suggests a very interesting link to *Fear and Trembling*, where Abraham is said to be the "hero" of the "poet" Johannes de silentio). King

David has exhausted the possibilities of great achievements, and there is nothing left for Solomon but to admire his father's great deeds. The admiration makes him a poet. There is also a hint of tension in this relationship, because of Solomon's double role as a poet and son: "But if a poet was almost envious of his hero, the son was blissful in his devotion to the father" (SLW 251).

There is in fact a good reason for Solomon to be envious of his father, since "[Solomon's] heart was not perfect with the Lord his God, as was the heart of David his father" (1 Kgs 11.4). One night Solomon pays a visit to his royal father, awakened by noise coming from his father's sleeping room. First he is seized with horror and fears murder, but when he approaches the room he sees David crushed in spirit and crying in despair. Solomon goes back to his bed, falls asleep, and has a dream (apart from other differences, in the biblical story King David is already dead).

This version of Solomon's dream is also very different from that in I Kings in that he dreams of his father as an ungodly man condemned to rule, because "to be singled out by God one has to be an ungodly person." This is the main focus of the dream. In the view of the poet/hero relationship, the events in the dream seem very much like the classical psychoanalytic scenario of attempting to annihilate your rival, your enemy, and especially your father.

Solomon is awakened—"He approaches stealthily—he sees David crushed in spirit, he hears the cry of despair from the penitent's soul." We note the resemblance to the fourth version of "Exordium" in *Fear and Trembling*, where Isaac sees Abraham tremble, sees the secret of his father, just as Solomon imagines seeing the secret guilt of his father.[41] Isaac loses his faith, and Solomon likewise goes back to bed but does not rest, for his mind is crushed. As in "A Leper's Self-Contemplation," we are confronted with the discrepancy between the exterior and interior: David's seeming blessedness is in fact his punishment.

Another interesting point to observe in relation to the differences between the two dreams is the perception of election. In the version in *Stages on Life's Way*, Solomon talks about his father, the king, being singled out, whereas in I Kings 3.8, Solomon—a king himself already—refers to himself as the servant who is in the midst of the chosen people. Solomon's mind is crushed by the horror of what it means to be chosen by God, by the contradiction that to be singled out, one has to be an ungodly person (once again this relates to Abraham's story). Hence his despair and his tragedy: "He became a preacher, but did not become a believer" (just as he is a poet and not a hero). There is a split in his being.

All this again symbolically expresses Quidam's situation—"He became crushed, but not raised up again" (SLW 252)—like Quidam, Solomon in this version is unable to perform the double movement necessary for the renunciation. Solomon is old despite his young age.[42]This again accurately describes Quidam, who writes about this in an entry immediately before Solomon's dream—saying that if only he could always be as young as he actually is (SLW 250), the whole torment would be over. Another suggestive phrase is the description of Solomon as "womanly weak in the bold infatuations of the imagination and in amazing fabrications," that could as well be applied to Quidam himself and the whole construction of his diary. It seems thus that Quidam identifies himself with Solomon, with a newly concocted Solomon who is a blend of the biblical Solomon and of Quidam's fictitious one.

This identification would clarify the strong presence in "Quidam's Diary" of the Book of Ecclesiastes. There are a number of quotations from this and other sources, such as Isaiah, Psalms, and I Corinthians, which carry a thematic connotation of—broadly speaking—vanity. The Hebrew word for vanity *hebel* literally means "breath" or "vapor," and it designates what is transient and lacking in substance. The biblical quotations provide a frame for the exposition of reflections on several existential issues: the perception of temporality and nothingness, the conflict between the world of possibilities and that of actuality, the relationship between faith and despair.

Given the marked differences between Solomon's so-called dream and the biblical material, we could ask why this beautiful story masquerades as Solomon's dream. Why is it important for Kierkegaard to use the biblical reference, however much he deviates from it, rather than write a completely original story?

Nebuchadnezzar

The third fictitious story (SLW 360) is a "reconstruction" and supplement to an actual biblical story. It imitates the biblical discourse by numbering the statements as if they were verses. Some of the utterances by Nebuchadnezzar in *Stages on Life's Way* are very close to their biblical counterparts: statements 2 and 3 are very much like Daniel 4.30; statement 9, "A voice was suddenly heard, and I was transformed," is taken from Daniel 4.31–33, but the rest of the same sentence, "as swiftly as a woman changes color," is not taken from the Book of Daniel even though its stylistic appearance resembles some biblical phrases.

That is, indeed, one of the features of Kierkegaard's use of biblical quotations. There are quite a few instances in which he starts off with an authentic biblical quotation and then adds something that could be taken for another one but actually is not. This pattern forms part of what I will call pseudo-biblical language (see Chapter 5). In the majority of cases it is achieved by giving the quotations a particular stylistic value, but there are instances of specific thematic turns instead. The interaction between the biblical quotations and their contextual surroundings is so intense that the boundaries blur.

The opening sentence tells us that what follows are Nebuchadnezzar's recollections from his life when he was a beast of the field. In fact he starts by telling how he became a beast, and then recollects his life as a beast. This means that Nebuchadnezzar retained his full consciousness and identity throughout the transformation and after the reversion back into a human body (which is subsequently important with regard to whether or not this was a dream). Before the meditation on God's nature, Nebuchadnezzar exclaims that his thoughts terrify him.[43] What follows is a meditation on God and his ways. This is not an abstract meditation, but one prompted by Nebuchadnezzar's status as a beast. As Nebuchadnezzar says, "One does not know whether he [God] exists before it has *happened*" (my emphasis).

He attributes the following characteristics to the Mighty One: "his wisdom is like a dream that he alone controls," "no one knows where he resides," "neither does he reside in his temple," "no one knows anything about him," "he does not say 'tomorrow' but says 'today,'" "he says 'Be done,' and it is done." They seem to be marked by the Christian theological tradition and differ significantly from those given in the Old Testament: "All whose works are truth, and his ways judgement: and those that walk in pride he is able to abase" (Dn 4.37). It is not the first instance in Kierkegaard's writings where the Old Testament is reworked in the light of the New.[44]

According to Quidam, Nebuchadnezzar summons wise men when seven years have passed (this is not mentioned in the Bible), and asks them to explain why he has become a beast of the field. What the wise men answer is interesting: "This is a fantasy, an evil dream; who would be capable of doing this to you?" However, in the biblical story it is not a dream but a fulfillment of a dream. The wise men's answer—unless it is motivated by fear—opens up the possibility of a discussion about how literally we should take Nebuchadnezzar's transformation into "a beast of the field." Is it an inner reality or an external fact?[45] Nebuchadnezzar seems to have little doubt about its being very real and not figurative at all.

However, we should remember Kierkegaard's specific understanding of literal meaning, as discussed in Chapter 3. The pessimism of statement 32, "Babylon is no longer the renowned Babylon; I, I Nebuchadnezzar, am no longer Nebuchadnezzar," is also Quidam's interpretation, for in the Bible it is said that after those seven years, "I was established in my kingdom, and excellent majesty was added unto me" (Dn 4.36). That is, in the Bible Nebuchadnezzar is capable of making the double movement and regaining his status as a king with joy, whereas in "Quidam's Diary"—like Solomon, like Quidam—he is unable to "raise up" again. We also note the degree to which Kierkegaard's famous double movement is not so much based on interpretation of the biblical material as directly imitated: the double movement is quite unambiguously stressed in the Bible (for example, in Abraham's and Nebuchadnezzar's cases) by the joy after the trial.

The striking similarities (despite their original differences) in the three "biblical" stories give the impression that they rewrite not only their biblical correlatives but one another as well, creating a continual spiral movement of repetition in which the same is never exactly the same.

Possibility, Imagination, Imitation

I hope I have succeeded in showing that, at least in the case of *Fear and Trembling* and *Stages on Life's Way*, the use of biblical material is not just a narrativization of the biblical story but a peculiar textual strategy that has its grounds in Kierkegaard's understanding of essential communication and the existential dimension of reading. The reading of the Bible transmitted in this way is part of his indirect communication.

Kierkegaard draws our attention to the fact that even in the New Testament, one can find places that endorse the view that subjectivity is higher than reality and that accept irony when it is used teleologically. As an essential element of indirect communication, such irony can hide and suspend "the best."

Even the New Testament would acknowledge such a silence. There are even places in the New Testament that praise irony, provided that it is not used to conceal the better part. But this moment is just as much one of irony as in everything else that is based on the premise that subjectivity is higher than actuality . . . In the Sermon on the Mount, it says: When you fast, anoint your head and wash your face, that your fasting may not be seen by men. This passage shows clearly that subjectivity is incommensurable with actuality, indeed, that it has the right to deceive (FT 118).

Thus Kierkegaard finds the justification for the method of indirect communication (and one of its components: deception, the teleological suspension of truth) in the New Testament itself, which allows deception because subjectivity and reality are incommensurable. The analysis of these biblical "inserts" shows that the domain in which the Bible becomes the object of appropriation is that of possibility and not of a normative reality. Kierkegaard tells the biblical stories in a subjunctive mood, allowing an individual reader to turn them into his own reality through reduplication and infinite passion. In *Fear and Trembling*, Kierkegaard says that speaking about a past event, however great it may have been, is vain if this past cannot become present for you (FT 30). Or, as he says elsewhere, "To take an example, that Job believed should be presented in such a way that for me it comes to mean whether I, too, will have faith" (CUP 359).

I have hinted, and will further develop later on, that reading the Bible is meaningful only in an attempt to become contemporary with God's Word. But in order that the reality of Job or Abraham may become present and that we may test, distill, and condense our own faith through it, it must be represented in the form of possibility. According to Kierkegaard, it is possible to understand or relate to alien actuality only in the form of possibility. Ethically there are no direct relations between subjects. Every actuality outside myself I can grasp only in thinking, and in thinking I turn it into a possibility (CUP 321), thus the other's actuality turns into a possibility for me.

Interestingly, Kierkegaard "corrects" the Bible in this respect, saying that one person cannot judge another because he understands him only as a possibility. Referring to Matthew 7.1, "Judge not, that you be not judged," Kierkegaard says that although it is said as an admonition and warning, it is also an impossibility (CUP 322).

Thus, according to Kierkegaard essential communication can take place only in the form of possibility: "A production in the form of possibility places existing in it as close to the recipient as it is possible between one human being and another" (CUP 358).[46] In the relation between author and reader, telling a reader that a biblical character actually has done this and that only leads the reader to imagine that he understands the story, but even such understanding does not mean that he is able to relate to it. Presentation in the form of actuality excludes the reader from participation, by turning him into a passive spectator who admires the hero or skeptically doubts whether what is told has actually happened. The fact that something has happened to somebody else is the "indifferent," in which an individual cannot be interested.

On the other hand, when somebody else's actuality is presented as a possibility, the reader can understand the other's actuality as possibility and appropriate it through his interest in his own actuality (it is interesting to observe how in this framework, the "realism" of the Bible becomes irrelevant). A human being can really be interested only in his own actuality, since, according to Kierkegaard, to be interested in the actuality of another is possible only in the faith-relation (CUP 323) to the God-man, perhaps precisely because it is the only actuality that cannot become a possibility for a human being. The fact that one can only understand another's actuality as possibility is also an expression of hope and openness: everybody is invited, and everybody can do it equally well—that is why nobody is excluded from responsibility either.

"Possibility operates with the ideal human being (not with regard to difference but with regard to the universal), who is related to every human being as a requirement" (CUP 359). In presentation as possibility, the greatest freedom of interpretation and respect for the individual are combined with a requirement, that is, an ethical demand and a responsibility to fulfill it precisely because it is possible for everyone.[47]

What is particularly important in relation to *Fear and Trembling* is that possibility relates to an individual as a requirement. The story is ethically challenging and interesting for an individual only if it is presented in a form of possibility that can and, moreover, should become actuality. We notice an ambiguity here, however. On the one hand it is said that Abraham is an example; on the other hand that one should not attempt to imitate what Abraham does. The reason for which we should not literally imitate the example is that nobody is like

Abraham, by which Kierkegaard really means "as" Abraham, not "like" Abraham. What is most individualizing, unique about Abraham? It is his exceptional fatherhood. The reading should indeed be so literal that it turns against itself.[48] Nobody is "as" Abraham in the sense of being the father of Isaac, so the story would not be ethically challenging or interesting to us in an existential sense if it were about the sacrifice of the historical Isaac, the sacrifice of the other.

Indeed, Kierkegaard emphasizes exception as a paradigm.[49] In *Repetition,* for example, it is repeated that Job is exceptional (R 207–10, 226–28), and that if anybody were to utter Job's words, it would be as inappropriate as for a child to put on his father's clothes (R 206). Of course, Christ is the ultimate example of the singular that has to be followed. What sense does it make to give as an example somebody who is essentially different from us? Kierkegaard says that the religious paradigm is different from the ethical one because

> the religious paradigm is the irregularity and yet is supposed to be the paradigm (which is like God's omnipresence as invisibility and revelation as a mystery), or because the religious paradigm does not express the universal but the singular (the particular, for example by appealing to visions, dreams, etc.), and yet is supposed to be the paradigm. But to be the paradigm means to be for all, yet one can be the prototype for all only by being what all are or ought to be, that is, the universal, and yet the *religious paradigm* is the very opposite (the irregular and the particular)(CUP 259).

Everyone faces a collision in which the ethical becomes the temptation, if in no other way than by having to relate to the religious paradigm. The way Kierkegaard presents religious paradigms can help us to discover what imitation really means.

It is hardly accidental that in relation to the story of Abraham, Kierkegaard brings in Luke 14.26: "If any man come to me, and hate not his father, and mother, and wife, and children, and brethren, and sisters, yea, and his own life also, he cannot be my disciple." In its extreme position, Luke 14.26 is the counterpart of the Akedah in the New Testament. It is a significant change, of course, that the "killing" of the Old Testament has been replaced by "hating" in the New, but hating is no less shocking when it is commanded in the context of the religion of love, so that hating is the highest possible spiritual sacrifice. And yet Kierkegaard speaks about the need to understand Luke

14.26 literally (FT 72), and derides the attempts of theology students to mitigate the meaning of *misô*.[50]

We remember that in the "Eulogy," Kierkegaard says Abraham was "great by the love that is hatred to oneself" (FT 17). Precisely because the story is told as a possibility and is meant to be an ethically valid paradigm, we must look for another sacrifice. We have already considered the anxiety and the sacrifice of one's self in order to regain it in the unity of "for one's own self" and "for God's sake."

The analysis of the different variations of Abraham's story, as well as of the three quasi-biblical stories in "Quidam's Diary," suggests that Kierkegaard reads the biblical story by means of a double movement: he illuminates different "invented" possibilities of its narrative structure, and at the same time he eliminates them so as to reveal what is most unique in the "source" story. In this way he, as it were, multiplies the meaning of the source story and draws attention to the smallest details and possible ways of reading it.[51] Different retellings of the story, as well as the parallel but not analogous stories of Iphigenia and others in *Fear and Trembling*, resemble the technique of negative theology as they show the implicit tautology of the matter in question and the impossibility of grasping it by approaching from the outside.[52]

Kierkegaard seems to share the position of Nicolas of Cusa: "Every enquiry . . . consists in a relation of comparison that is easy or difficult to draw; for this reason the infinite as infinite is unknown, since it is away and above all comparison."[53] In this spirit, Kierkegaard's analogies are often disanalogies (for examples, see Chapter 5). Gouwens has remarked that Kierkegaard employs "the imagination of disanalogy as a *via negativa* in apprehending (not comprehending) Christ."[54] But the *via negativa* in Kierkegaard's works stretches much further, so that it could be argued that the whole project of indirect communication is a negative communication.[55] Toward the end of *Fear and Trembling*, Kierkegaard says, "It was also pointed out that none of the stages described contains an analogy to Abraham; they were explained, while being demonstrated each within its own sphere, only in order that in their moment of deviation [*Misvisningen*] they could, as it were, indicate the boundary of the unknown territory" (FT 112).

There is a continual attempt to approach the meaning of something not by looking at the thing itself but by looking at what it is not, or by raising such questions as "What if it were not so?" The "negative" approach is made possible by imaginative narratives, since, of course, looking at what is not pertains to the domain of imagination.

However, this imagination in Kierkegaard is paired with irony and, in its negative approach, has something positive: it brings us to the boundary and opens a possibility of crossing it. Thus, though it is impossible to tell the biblical story in other than its own words, there is a possibility of appropriating those words and repeating them as your own. This relation is not only a remote representation but also a real presence.

Theologians and philosophers have widely discussed imagination over the past decades,[56] and those who have focused most prominently on the role of imagination in Kierkegaard are Gouwens, Polk, and Ferreira. In her interesting discussion of the transition to faith, Ferreira says, "Despite his clear sensitivity to the many ways imagination can mislead and be prejudicial to self-development, an undeniable commitment to the value and necessity of imaginative activity is integral to Kierkegaard's various accounts of genuine selfhood."[57] Ferreira also argues that imagination for Kierkegaard involves the "other."[58]

I fully share her emphasis on imagining "otherness" and the role of the genuinely separate "other" in Kierkegaard's ethical imagination — and, I would add, the divine Other in his religious imagination. In the indirect use of biblical quotations, this acknowledgement of otherness is apparent in Kierkegaard's relation both to his reader and to God's Word. The imagination is also central for Kierkegaard's vision of faith, inasmuch as it keeps the active (will, reason) and passive (grace, passion) in constant tension.

This tension is naturally also reflected in the way in which we are invited to read the Bible. It is most perceptible in Kierkegaard's emphasis on keeping literal and nonliteral meaning in a close tension of mutual corrective (as discussed in Chapter 3). Ferreira's discussion of the role of imagination in the transition to faith is very relevant for my study, insofar as I try to trace a transition from reading to redoubling of the reading in action, and I also claim that imagination and possibility are essential in this process. Gouwens observes:

> In the Christian sphere, the imagination is indeed redeemed, and the artistry of existence continues with new vigor. Thus while Kierkegaard uniformly criticizes the possibility that any capacity can comprehend the divine, he is willing, once the defensive measures are secure, to outline a necessary place for the imagination within Religion B, in both faith and discipleship. We may call this further dialectic an "imagination of

repetition through reversal." Both aspects—repetition and reversal—are crucial.[59]

We note the important connection between imagination, possibility, and repetition, which has been already touched upon in the beginning of this chapter and will be elaborated in the final chapter.

It seems that in speaking about Kierkegaard's imagination, Gouwens and Polk have in mind the interpretative imagination, that is, imagination in the service of understanding. I prefer to emphasize the presence of imagination in Kierkegaard as recreation, which, though related to interpretation, is not interpretation in the immediate sense. That is to say, I would like to claim that imagination for Kierkegaard has first and foremost to do with the power of imagination to emphasize differences rather than similarities. For Kierkegaard, it is only by means of such deviations from the primary narrative that we can approach the story to be comprehended.[60]

However, this circling around the subject cannot be reduced to a kind of hyperbole that in the end will bring us to "the" story. Rather, it demonstrates that the biblical word is not approachable through the other, but always remains in some sense self-enclosed and tautological, and also in a certain respect "absent." The revealed truth is still hidden (or sealed) and needs to be revealed as if it were anew in each individual. We could thus say that imagination for Kierkegaard is indeed an extension of the Kantian concept of imagination, because it is quite literally a "means of expressing or communicating the absent" (hence the link with negative theology)—only in a more radical sense, that is, not as temporarily absent but as essentially absent, which is not graspable in its essence but can become present for us in our relation to it.

Despite the prominent role that imagination plays in his authorship and in his approach to the Bible in particular, Kierkegaard's views on imagination are ambiguous in that according to him, if imagination is allowed to rule alone, it dissolves moral tension.[61] As a supplement (and corrective) to imagination, Kierkegaard speaks about the need to understand the Bible literally, that is to say, ethically/literally. One could say that imagination in Kierkegaard is employed not to make interpretation easier, but on the contrary to bring forward all the difficulty and uncertainty (*skandalon*, the subjective, the choice).

For Kierkegaard, the crucial point in Abraham's story is that his trial is rendered even more difficult by his faith (not easier, as is often assumed), "the faith that makes it difficult" (FT 30). It is important for Kierkegaard to stress that the one who tells Abraham's story in a worthy manner is rare (FT 22), that in the story of Abraham one forgets the anxiety (FT 28) and that in order to speak about Abraham properly, one should emphasize the time that his journey takes (FT 52)—which Kierkegaard himself does masterfully by "multiplying" Abraham's story—and bring out all the anxiety (FT 53). Imagination serves a double dialectical goal: we are given the imagined stories so that we will read *the* story literally, but—it is important to note—not as somebody else's actuality. Rather, as a possibility for us. (On the other hand, it is difficult to deny that *the* story is deconstructed.) Once again we need to stress that "literal reading" in Kierkegaard does not mean "factual" but "concrete," as discussed in Chapter 3.

The point here is not about realism, but about the way in which God's Word molds its meaning upon each individual existence. The lesson of Abraham's story is not "sacrifice Isaac when demanded," but "listen to God's Word and be the doer of it" in fear and trembling. That God's voice is said to have spoken to Abraham (or that Abraham has heard its echo) introduces a dimension of contemporaneity that we should take literally, namely, that it is possible for us to hear if we listen.

Deviations

Do not say that these are quibbling comments about words, anything but upbuilding. Believe me, it is very important for a person that his language be precise and true, because that means his thinking is that also (PC 158).

In one of the first books written on Kierkegaard in English, Francis Fulford remarks: "One weakness of Kierkegaard in relation to Bible study—his neglect of the original text and contempt for all criticism—has already been mentioned. There remain the defects that he is sometimes careless in quotation and fanciful in interpretation."[1] Whether the neglect of the original text (understood as a standard translation) is a weakness or a deliberate choice remains to be discovered, but what is interesting is that Fulford notices a "carelessness in quotation," a subject that was not taken up by other commentators.

Many, perhaps even the majority of the biblical quotations in Kierkegaard's pseudonymous works, do in fact deviate from the "standard" text, some slightly, some radically. The purpose of this chapter is to explore these deviations and ask the question whether at least some of them are deliberate, and, if so, what their purpose and function might be. The question is: Are they simple, "careless" misquotations or a reflective choice, a kind of appropriation in which deviations form an integral part of Kierkegaard's attitude to the Bible and writing?

Why can we not put all of Kierkegaard's free, creative use of biblical quotations in the pseudonymous works down to purely stylistic concerns or to insignificant memory failings? There are numerous reasons. The first is simply the evidence of his intense attention to words (particularly witnessed by his preoccupation with translation), his "literal" side. But second, there is the "literal" element in the Bible itself. The Bible is not just any book, it is a Book of a divine Word and of letter, and the letter is sacred (even though we bear in mind 2 Corinthians 3.6).[2] Kierkegaard himself speaks about the biblical discourse as being different from all human discourse, because the Bible consists in revealed truth. Third, there is substantial evidence that some of the "misquotations" play a vital role in Kierkegaard's arguments. In relation to what, though, can so many of Kierkegaard's biblical quotations be said to be "misquotations"?

The tradition of translation of the Bible in Kierkegaard's time in Denmark was rather fluid. There was no single established and authorized version. The main versions in use were the 1819 translation of the New Testament and the 1740 translation of the Old Testament. Kierkegaard employed various translations, including his own, and translations from Luther's into German (for more about these issues, see the last section of this chapter). In light of this complexity, the possibility that some "deviations" actually are not deviations at all, but faithful quotations taken from an unidentified source, cannot always be excluded. However, this does not affect the overall picture of the alterations in Kierkegaard's quotations from the Bible.

Various types of deviations will be dealt with here. Some are more like "mistakes," for example, the replacement of words or adaptations prompted by the context. Others are deviations in a loose sense, that is to say, they deviate from usual understanding and employment of the biblical text, as, for example, when Kierkegaard inverses the original meaning or makes a humorous employment of biblical quotations.

It is important to make it clear that the seemingly "negative" phenomena of "misquotations" is being dealt with here from a hermeneutical point of view, and that from this point of view the deviations are not only interesting, but also fruitful. Even if they are referred to as "misquotations," this is more to draw attention to the phenomenon and its consequences than to judge or introduce any notion of abuse of the text. The issue is not that Kierkegaard does not conform to modern standards of academic quoting, with exact and full references to his sources. Neither is it an occasional lapse such as the one found in *Stages on Life's Way:* "Is this the way to be a mother?

wailed Rachel when the twins' struggle began in her womb, and many a person presumably has said this to himself when he obtained what he craved: Is this the way it is?" (SLW 215). It is, of course, not Rachel, but Rebecca whom he means: "And the children struggled together within her; and she said, If it be so, why am I thus? And she went to inquire of the Lord" (Gn 25.22).

On the other hand, if the emphasis is on the positive function of deviations, this is certainly not in order to defend Kierkegaard. On the contrary, in order to appreciate the hermeneutical function of biblical quotations in his pseudonymous works and their role in indirect communication, I think it is necessary fully to acknowledge Kierkegaard's seemingly free and casual, and, as conservative readers may—and do—say, "disrespectful" way of treating the Bible. Deviations and "mistakes" are one of the most differentiating features that disclose the particularity of a thinker, and consequently "misquotations" are interesting in this respect also. They provide us with the tangible traces of Kierkegaard's subjectivity and indirectness.

Regarding biblical misquotations in Kierkegaard's pseudonymous works, there has also been debate about the differences between his aesthetic and his religious writings. Some scholars have used biblical "misquotations" to support the thesis that Kierkegaard's pseudonyms are aesthetic authors: their supposed abuse of the Bible is held to confirm the view that the pseudonyms do not take religious matters seriously. This interpretation was introduced by Hirsch, and quite a few scholars subsequently took it up. Of course, it belongs to the tradition of reading Kierkegaard's pseudonymous writings as exclusively aesthetic: "Kierkegaard, writing as the consummate aesthete, restricted his use of Scripture to an aesthetic appropriation of the Bible."[3] So too Holmes Hartshorne says: *"Fear and Trembling* is ironic to the core. It pretends to be a serious analysis of faith, but it carries the reader very persuasively, very artfully and insightfully, from one absurdity to another. The irony is pervasive; for example, Johannes quotes from the New Testament and gets it wrong."[4] One of the aims of this chapter is to show that this line of argument is false.

A study of Kierkegaard's biblical "misquotations" can draw attention to the sensitivity needed in reconstructing his theological and philosophical views. A case of "misquoting" is helpful in making us aware that quotations are segments of text that need careful treatment, and that in many cases, very complex hermeneutical issues lurk behind their employment. It is often easy to overlook the alterations inflicted on the quotations and, by reading them as if they had not been changed, to destroy some of the texture of Kierkegaard's writing (a point that is particularly important for translators).

A good example of the awareness that is needed when one reads Kierkegaard is his disanalogous use of the Bible. Kierkegaard enters into a dialogue with the Bible, modifies its sense, and adds a new dimension, which appears only in the view of a certain deviation.[5] For example, in *Philosophical Fragments* he varies Philippians 3.13–14, "But this one thing I do, forgetting those things which are behind, and reaching forth unto those things which are before, I press toward the mark for the prize of the high calling of God in Christ Jesus," and writes instead: "Let us call such a sorrow *repentance* [*Anger*], for what else is repentance, which does indeed look back, but nevertheless in such a way that precisely thereby it quickens its pace toward what lies ahead!" (PF 19). This is a "twisted" quotation: the reference is obvious (only as regards the movement—not the context of the movement, since there is no mention of repentance in Philippians 3.13–14), but it is less obvious that Kierkegaard subverts it. Kierkegaard describes a different and even an opposite movement when he stresses the dialectical nature of repentance. It is not by forgetting but by remembering, precisely by virtue of looking back, that one moves forward.

We see how a barely perceptible change reveals Kierkegaard's peculiar understanding of the time structure of the God-man relationship. At the same time, one could say that although there is disanalogy on a surface level, it may be that this is a legitimate reading of the New Testament, in light of St. Paul speaking about freedom as hope and freedom for the future (Kierkegaard often used cross-reading of various parts of the Bible and reinterpreted these in the light of other passages). However, even though the change that Kierkegaard makes might seem to be an immaterial emendation, this biblical quotation and the way in which it is used (namely, subverted) touches upon a recurring theme in Kierkegaard's authorship: that of movement. Movement back and forth, and the mutual dependence of the movements, is a major issue throughout Kierkegaard's writings. This movement has to do with repetition and temporality of self, a key element in Kierkegaard's influence on twentieth-century thought, especially through Bultmann and Heidegger, for whom this issue was of utmost importance.

There are many examples of the changes in quotations that cannot be dismissed as unimportant, since they disclose deeper structures lurking behind their use in terms of either the meaning of the immediate argument or Kierkegaard's strategy of communication as such.[6]

Tradition of Alterations

Kierkegaard is not unique in altering quotations. The Bible itself presents us with many examples. The biblical narrative is full of repetitions of phrases and sentences that can be considered as "quotations" and not simply recurring motives or themes, and in which the exact original wording is rare. Most notable, of course, are the instances where the New Testament quotes the Old. Two opposing positions have been taken in respect to this: (1) it is insignificant, because even though the wording is changed, the meaning has been preserved; (2) each word has its own precise meaning in combination with other words, and therefore it is vital to take the changes seriously. The obvious middle position is to claim that some changes are meaningful, while others are not.[7] One example that has provoked many debates is St. Paul's free use of biblical quotations. Some scholars have suggested that we should not make much of it, because in fact it is consistent with the absolute freedom of the Holy Spirit.

> Finally at other times we need look no farther than the absolute Freedom and good Pleasure of the Holy Ghost, according to which he thought proper to substitute one Word in place of another; which ought so much less be wondered at or blamed, as it is a very common Thing in Quotations of this Kind, whether sacred or profane, sometimes only to give the Sense in different and fewer Words; sometimes to repeat the very same Words, but turn'd a little to our Design and Purpose, and accommodated to the Connexion, yet without incurring the Charge of Corruption.[8]

Others have sought explanations, of which two main types have presented themselves: the theological and the sociological. The theological reasons for St. Paul's reshaping the wording of the biblical text include the following: (1) the Spirit led him to the true "Christian" meaning of the passages cited, thus the phenomenon was described as "charismatic exegesis"[9]; (2) he lived in an era when all individual pronouncements of Scripture would be fulfilled, so his "eschatological conviction explains the remarkable 'freedom' in relation to the text."[10]

Those who take a sociological rather than a theological position argue that there are ample parallels to this "free" approach in the rabbinical sources and in Greco-Roman heritage. Thus St. Paul was not unique in this practice, but was merely following the literary conventions of his day. This tradition of freely altering the text continued. The translator of Pascal's *Provincial Letters* observed: "It is important to realise in this connection that in the seventeenth century neither translation (most of the original texts were in Latin) nor quotation was expected to be literal or accurate; even quoting his own words, or the Bible, where accuracy might seem essential, Pascal seldom takes the trouble to reproduce the precise words."[11]

A free use of biblical quotations, including "misquotations," was not therefore something peculiar to Kierkegaard, but rather a general tendency that included Kierkegaard's contemporary theological context.[12] But this context of a free use of biblical quotations does not account for all cases of alterations and, given Kierkegaard's own hermeneutics and his view on issues of reading and writing, his "misquotations" are still curious and intriguing. What makes Kierkegaard's case special, in this respect, is the sheer variety of the different ways he finds to incorporate the Bible in his works, his conscious reflection on the problems related to quoting the Bible (cf. Chapter 6), and the role that deviations play in his indirect communication.

The nature of the topic requires numerous examples and, as a result, some parts of the present chapter might seem like little more than a long list.[13] However, I hope that in this course of the chapter I shall succeed in revealing something of the underlying structure and main implications of the phenomena of altered quotations. It should be made clear that my objective is not so much the interpretation, but rather the interpretative action that is implicit in the act of reading the Bible.

Memory and Scrutiny

First of all, we should bear in mind two aspects of Kierkegaard's approach: the meticulous and scrupulous reading of the Bible on the one hand; and on the other, quoting it by heart and thereby quite often "losing" the fruit of such a thorough reading.[14] Kierkegaard read the Bible with a pencil in hand (we will also see this extreme attention in our discussion of his preoccupation with translation issues). Bradley Rau Dewey observes that there are 131 notes, underlinings, and marks scattered over the pages of a New Testament from Kierkegaard's personal library.[15] If Kierkegaard worked on the Bible in this manner while preparing the manuscripts of his pseudonymous works, as Dewey suggests he probably did with *Edifying Discourses in Various Spirits*, then it would be clear that at least not all misquotations are due to slips of memory (though some of them surely are).[16]

Kierkegaard's theological education required him to pay close attention to the biblical text.[17] Apart from this, he never ceased to reflect on various texts in the Bible and write his reflections in the journals. For example, in December 1833 he concentrated on Galatians 3.19–4.8. The numerous markings in the New Testament that supplemented Kierkegaard's theological education indicate that some "misquotations" may be intentional alterations with an interpretative emphasis.

Dewey notes that Kierkegaard disputed and corrected the Bible in his markings. "At one point, he seems to chide Matthew for some injudicious Messianic proof-texting. Referring to Jesus, Matthew cites Second Isaiah's passage about "the servant . . . who will not wrangle or cry aloud, nor will any one hear his voice in the streets" (Is 42.2 as cited in Mt 12.19). In a marginal note, Kierkegaard gently corrects: "Yet he certainly did talk in the streets; but, to be sure, with an entirely different purpose" (Pap. VIII 2 C 3,7).[18]

One can see that Kierkegaard is engaged not only in the interpretation of the Bible, but also in the critique of its textual composition, which once again reminds us that he was very attentive to the texture of the text and to the interaction of different elements in its construction. In his close reading of the Bible, Kierkegaard engaged in a dialogue with it and dared to discuss its details.[19] This kind of close and attentive reading proves the importance of the actual biblical wording for Kierkegaard, and thus also confirms the relevance of our interest in the case of misquotations. We note that these are examples taken from the journals. However, the possibility of a different treatment of biblical quotations in the journals and in the pseudonymous works would only confirm the suggestion that instead of being "careless" mistakes, alterations perform a certain function.

As has been said, Kierkegaard's extensive use of biblical quotations relies, as a rule, on memory. In other words, the majority of the biblical quotations scattered throughout his texts are quoted by heart. We are, thus, dealing with reading as remembering. Kierkegaard's ability to store such an incredible number of biblical quotations has often been praised and exalted as a proof of his careful reading of the Bible. Few commentators, however, have paid attention to the potential complications with respect to authority and exactness of his relying on the "inner" Bible, which seems to have become almost independent of its original external source of reference. Kierkegaard's own position with respect to quoting by heart can be illustrated by the following entry in his journals:

> All is over. Plato has already expressed this very beautifully somewhere when he lets Epimetheus ask Jupiter whether he will bestow the ability [*evne*] for good and evil in the same way as the ability for poetry, music etc., so that some become poets, others speakers, etc. Jupiter answers no, for this ability belongs equally to each human being.
>
> *May the reader forgive me for quoting like this. The idea* [Tanken] *has always been my major concern, and as I never used any other means but my memory, I would not be able to find the quotation without a lot of effort, which would not be worth it* (Pap. V B 56, 7; my translation and my emphasis).

This comment very accurately describes how Kierkegaard appropriates the Bible and other sources in an "approximate manner." In contrast to the scientific or scholarly method, he quotes by heart and thinks that it is not worthwhile verifying whether these are the exact words. However, we note that this "approximation" does not replace an in-depth knowledge or mask its lack, but rather fulfills it. This approximation is also very different from the one Kierkegaard attacks in the historical scientific method—the latter is necessarily only approximate in its attempt to be exhaustive, while this approximation has, as it were, overcome "exactness," has appropriated it and liberated itself.

This entry in the journals also testifies to the fact that Kierkegaard was conscious of his inaccuracies. Sometimes, as we shall see, alterations perform a very concrete function in the given context. However, more broadly speaking, they also reflect his view of truth as subjectivity, which he puts forward in *Concluding Unscientific Postscript*. That is to say, the truth is a matter of subjective appropriations and not objective "fact."

But memory is also required on the part of the reader. Kierkegaard weaves into his works many complicated comparisons where a biblical passage serves as a pattern. For example, in *Either/Or* the young man puts himself in front of Cordelia for her observation just as Jacob put rods before the cattle (E/O I 391; Gn 30.31–42). Even though this type of simile does not have theological implications it is not inconsequential, since it makes meaning dependent on the biblical context; indeed, the passage is virtually incomprehensible without knowledge of the original meaning. Kierkegaard's reader would have had a much greater familiarity with the Bible than would be expected of today's readers, but it is also clear that Kierkegaard requires from his reader this ability to juggle biblical images and semantic fields.

Misrepresentations?

Kierkegaard's thorough familiarity with the Bible allows us to take seriously the possibility that some misquotations are intentional, but we still need to establish the purpose and functional value of conscious alterations. As we have said, attempts have been made to suggest that the use of the Bible in Kierkegaard's pseudonymous works confirms the aesthetic nature of the works. The implication of this line of argument is that misquotations are designed to show that an aesthete misreads, misinterprets, and misrepresents the Bible.

One obvious way to see whether this hypothesis holds is to examine some veronymous texts to see whether inaccuracies occur there as well. Let us take as an example "Love Hides the Multitude of Sins" from "Three Upbuilding Discourses 1843," a discourse published on the same day as *Fear and Trembling*. In it is said: "[He] loved in such a way that his eye 'did not begrudge the gift'" (EUD 58) (elskede saaledes at "hans øje ikke førtrød Tilgivelsen") (SKS 5, 68). This refers to Tobit 4.8, in which Tobit says to his son: "Giør Almisse af det du haver, og dit øie fortryde ikke, naar du giør Almisse; vend ikke dit ansigt fra nogen Fattig, og Guds Ansigt skal jo ikke vendes fra dig" (Danish 1740 edition of the Bible). Kierkegaard substitutes *Almisse* with *Tilgivelsen*, and thus the wording is changed even though it is inserted in quotation marks.[20]

We also note the shift from active to passive meaning. In *Works of Love* (another veronymous work), we find further inaccuracies in quoting. Even while quoting such a well-known passage as 1 Corinthians 2.9, Kierkegaard varies the verb and says, "det ikke oprandt i noget Menneskes Hjerte" (in the New Testament [NT] 1819 edition, the verb used is not "oprandt" but "opkommet"), "which did not arise in any human being's heart" (WL 25). At other times he varies while quoting in quotation marks: "*bedrøver Aanden*" (in NT 1819 Ephesians

4.30: "bedrøver ikke Guds hellige Aand"), "grieve the spirit" (WL 10). There are many other examples of this.

Thus even if various other aspects of Kierkegaard's use of the biblical quotations may differ in the pseudonymous and veronymous works, it seems that we can safely conclude that misquotations are not deliberate misrepresentations designed to show that aesthetic authors distort the biblical text, whereas religious authors are always very careful and reverential, including in formal aspects. This is an important point, which could contribute to the process of undermining the customary chasm between the aesthetic and religious in Kierkegaard's works. There is sufficient evidence to suggest that this misunderstanding has been based exclusively on what could be called a "regulative prejudice" in Kierkegaard's scholarship, concerning a supposedly insoluble formal distinction between the religious and the aesthetic.

Humor

One type of the use of biblical quotations that could be easily misunderstood and interpreted as an aesthetic abuse is the humorous one. The comical play on "body" in *Repetition* is a good example of the interplay between biblical quotations and their immediate context in Kierkegaard's pseudonymous works. A description of the journey to Berlin by Shnellpost features a humorous juxtaposition of the problem of space in an express coach and corpus Christi. Fearing to be jounced together with those sitting next to him, the young man chooses to sit in the forward compartment: "Hoping at least to remain a limb on a lesser body, I chose a seat in the forward compartment" (R 151). However, "During those thirty-six hours, we six people sitting inside the carriage were so worked together into one body" (R 151) that "God knows if . . . you will ever be human again, able to disengage yourself in the singleness of isolation, or if you will carry a memory of your being a limb on a larger body" (R 151).[21]

This refers to Ephesians 5.30 (or 1 Corinthians 12.12–31): "For we are members of his body, of his flesh, and of his bones." The passage is not only witty and amusing, but also linked to some fundamental issues for Kierkegaard, namely, being individual and being individual in a community. Such a humorous use can be considered as a kind of deviation because of the way in which it affects the register, the connotation, and the mood of the quotation. Given the role that

Kierkegaard ascribes to humor, as a boundary between the ethical and the religious, it is not surprising that humor marks some of the biblical quotations.[22]

Humor serves as an expression of subjectivity. It could also be related to the potential offensiveness of religion, to the *skandalon*, because such a use brings forth and highlights the paradox and "hard sayings." The emphasis on *skandalon* indicates, of course, that the Bible is treated not merely aesthetically. Humor is not a form of evasion but, on the contrary, a possibility to face certain aspects of religious reality that could not be affronted in an immediate, direct way. Humor and parody share some common characteristics with the method of indirect communication, such as maintaining distance in proximity (or familiarity), inverse presentation, displacement, exaggeration (as in "corrective"), and the art of perspective. The humorous employment of biblical references reveals the dependence of meaning on the perspective within which the quotation is set.

It also nicely illustrates the relation between the "how" and "what" in Kierkegaard's understanding of the nature of language and of perception in general. For example, in his journals he asks "to what extent the humorous appears in Christ's own expressions, see *The Lily in the Field*" (Pap. II A 84 p. 53; JP 1686). He says that the words about Solomon, who in all his splendor was not dressed as well as one of the lilies, and some other expressions could easily become humoristic, but uttered by Christ they are redeeming. In his journals Kierkegaard recalls that in the Middle Ages parody prospered in Christianity, adding that he should digest this idea in an essay (Pap. II A 85). In several places in his pseudonymous writings, Kierkegaard approaches this kind of rough medieval humor with respect to biblical texts, which particularly accentuates the picturesque, the "down to earth" side of it. For example, in *Concluding Postscript* we read: "When a German-Danish pastor declares in the pulpit, 'The Word became pork (*Fleisch*),' this is comic" (CUP 518; Jn 1.14). And in *Either/Or*: "If I wanted to be clever [*aandrig*—witty], I could say here that the individual knows himself in a way similar to the way Adam knew Eve, as it says in the Old Testament. Through the individual's intercourse with himself, the individual is made pregnant by himself and gives birth to himself" (E/O II 259). Or: "Of these sophists I am one, and even if I were capable of devouring the others I would still not become fatter—which is not inexplicable, as in the case of the lean cows in Egypt, for with respect to the religious, the sophists are not fat cows but skinny herring" (SLW 485; Gn 41.1–4, 17–21, 26–31).

All these examples demonstrate Kierkegaard's original approach to the Bible, and his eagerness to emphasize those aspects of it that do not let us treat it as a "cozy" book.

Double Context

In order to determine the current value of the quotation — regardless of fidelity to the original wording — a careful consideration of both contexts is necessary. But this is even more important when the quotation has been altered. In order to appreciate the significance of any adaptations, we should become aware of the extent to which close interaction between the two texts, the play with double context, is present in Kierkegaard's writings.

It is through alteration and adaptation that biblical discourse enters into dialogue with the pseudonymous works. In a sense, an inner appropriation is perhaps only possible when the original boundaries of a textual unit have been loosened, as is the case with so many biblical quotations in Kierkegaard's pseudonymous works. Seen like this, alterations would not be a deficiency but a natural consequence of a genuine appropriation, where what is "mine" and what is "yours" blend in a creative way.

I should like to draw attention to the way in which biblical quotations interact with Kierkegaard's text so as to reveal their constructive power. That is to say, there are cases where the biblical quotation dictates the direction of the discourse, whereas at other times it is Kierkegaard's text that determines the form and meaning of the quotations. This influence does not primarily concern the meaning of the text, but rather the choice of subject or the range of associations. It literally determines the construction of the discourse. But given the degree to which Kierkegaard's thought is rhetorically self-reflective (in the sense of an interdependance of form and content), this can hardly be just a matter of a literary quality.

There are several examples of the invisible yet constructive presence of the Bible, where the text is illuminated by full reference to the biblical text, or rather by the deciphered presence of the Bible. Let us look at an example. In *Either/Or* I, Kierkegaard speaks about his doubt concerning the correctness of the well-known philosophical statement that the external is internal and the internal external: "A doubt such as this comes and goes, and no one knows whence it comes or whither it goes" (E/O I 3). The allusion is to John 3.8: "The wind bloweth where it listeth, and though hearest the sound thereof, but canst not tell whence it cometh, and whither it goeth: so is every one that is born of the Spirit." At first glance this may seem to be a purely associative use that has no effect on the context. The quotation is not given in full: the second part, where "sound" is mentioned, is omitted. Nonetheless it is inscribed in Kierkegaard's text a few lines later. This connection illuminates an otherwise hardly understandable focus on the sense of hearing in this opening page of *Either/Or*: "Gradually, then, hearing became my most cherished sense, for just as the voice is the disclosure of inwardness incommensurable with the exterior, so the ear is the instrument that apprehends this inwardness, hearing the sense by which it is appropriated" (E/O I 3).[23]

It is only with the help of the biblical reference that we can understand Kierkegaard's fundamental challenge to Hegel here, namely, that spirit is free.

Splicing

Another important and interesting phenomenon consists of the compilation or intertwining of several biblical quotations and sometimes incorrect attribution. Sometimes lines from different books of the Bible (but more often from the same passage) are brought together to form a unity that they do not immediately form in the Bible.

A complicated case of compilation can be found in *Preface (s)*: "There you sit and stare off into space like a ghost or like King Nebuchadnezzar reading the invisible writing" (P 9). Two separate dreams, both interpreted by Daniel (Dn 2 and 4), are mentioned. In Daniel 2 we read that King Nebuchadnezzar has a dream that troubles his spirit, but that when he wakes up he forgets the dream. He summons all the wise men to show him his dream and give its interpretation. The king, atypically, demands that they tell him his own dream. The wise men are helpless, because dreams are known only to gods. Nebuchadnezzar is furious and orders them all to be killed. Daniel asks for mercy from God and is blessed—the contents of the dream are revealed to him in a night vision. Thus Daniel is able to give the king his dream back and to give an interpretation of the dream.

On the one hand, "reads the invisible writing" can be understood as referring to the fact that Nebuchadnezzar is troubled by a dream that he does not remember; on the other hand, the words can be understood to refer to Nebuchadnezzar's "reading" of Daniel's interpretation of the dream that still remains invisible to him (in Daniel 4, Nebuchadnezzar has another dream, but this time he remembers it and merely asks for interpretation). But more important, in Daniel 5 there is a much more concrete reference to a reading of invisible writing. Here, however, it is Nebuchadnezzar's son, Belshazar, who hosts a banquet at which: "In the same hour came forth fingers of the man's hand, and wrote over against the candlestick upon the plaster of the wall of the king's palace: and the king saw the part of the hand that wrote (5.5). Then the king's countenance was changed, and his thoughts troubled him, so that the joints of his loins were loosed, and his knees smote one against another" (Dn 5.6).

The writing is invisible/unreadable. It is again Daniel who reads it (although this time no vision is needed) and interprets it. The episode clearly echoes Nebuchadnezzar's "invisible" dream. Is this blurring of lines and chapters, this confusing of images insignificant, or is the ambiguity intended? Could it be used to stress the harmony in the Bible despite the discoveries of the historical-critical method?[24]

Again, splicing is not an unprecedented practice. For example, it appears that St. Paul also spliced biblical quotations.[25] Researchers seem to think that it cannot be accidental.

> Careful examination of Paul's "combined" and "conflated" citations has demonstrated further that far from upholding the "memory quotation" explanation, the passages in question actually support the opposite view. The skill with which these composite units have been knit together and adapted for their present use shows that it was no careless lapse of memory, but rather a conscious editorial hand that produced such sophisticated pieces of literary and rhetorical artistry.[26]

Indeed Kierkegaard's "combined" quotations are too elaborate to be accidental.[27] We have already considered the intertwining of the *Book of Judith* with Abraham's story in *Fear and Trembling*. Another good example can be found in *Philosophical Fragments*: "If he cherished every instructive word that came from his mouth more than his daily bread, if he had a hundred others to catch every syllable [*bogstave*] so that nothing would be lost" (PF 60): "dersom hvært lærende Ord der udgik af hans Mund havde vaeret ham vigtigere end det daglige Brød dersom han holdt hundrede Andre, der opfangede ethvert Bogstav, for at Intet skulde spildes" (SKS 4, 262).

The quotation sounds so familiar that it is difficult to spot the splicing. The biblical passages are: Deuteronomy 8.3 or Matthew 4.4:

"Man shall not live by bread alone, but by every word that pro-
ceedeth out of the mouth of God," and John 6.12, where, after having
fed five thousand people with five barley loaves and two small fish,
"he said unto his disciples, Gather up the fragments that remain, that
nothing be lost." The two references are joined in a way that the effect
of an echo is produced. First bread is mentioned and then it is inscribed
in the second quotation, although bread crumbs are substituted with
letters.[28] This quotation deals with the issue of contemporaneity, and
this peculiar splicing shows both the importance of every word that
comes from God and the fact that contemporaneity is a matter not of
historical proximity but of spiritual kinship.

Style and Pseudolanguage

Apart from those alterations that seem to be deliberate, whether due
to a conscious interpretative emphasis or to disagreement with the
standard translations of Kierkegaard's time, there is, of course, a
large number of alterations that serve stylistic purposes. Such
changes are "insignificant" in the sense that it is difficult to see what
theological or philosophical purpose they could serve. For example,
Kierkegaard uses "world" instead of "city" in *Fear and Trembling*: "He
that is slow to anger is better than the mighty; and he that ruleth his
spirit than he who taketh a city" (FT 113; Prv 16.32). In *Repetition* he
writes, "The forest ass does not bray when it has grass" (R 209). The
Hongs translate this as "wild ass" ("Skov-Aeslet ikke skryder over
Graesset," SKS 4, 76). In Job 6.5 it is: "Doth the wild ass bray when
he hath grass?" ("Mon et vildt Aesel skryde over Graesset").
Although Kierkegaard gives the quotation in quotation marks, he has
turned "wild" into "forest." Unless we assume that "forest" is the
Danish equivalent of "wilderness," this type of synonymous substitution probably does not affect the meaning of the text. But it still
remains interesting, as it illustrates the freedom of Kierkegaard's
relation to the Bible and his way of incorporating it into his writing.
Some of the alterations embellish the text, making it more picturesque.

This does not contradict my claim that the use of biblical quotations
is not merely aesthetic. On the contrary, it shows that the aesthetic,
stylistic employment is only one of many ways of deviating. An example of such a picturesque use can be found in *Either/Or*, when "For
charity shall cover the multitude of sins" (1 Pt 4.8), "kaerligheden
skjuler mange synder" in Kierkegaard's text, becomes: "She loves
him—maybe so, but her love, broad and copious, nevertheless flut-

ters loosely about him. She still possesses the cloak of love that can cover a multitude" (E/O I 357). The author does not finish the biblical reference and omits "sins"; the phrase "cloak of love" used instead of "love" not only has its internal logic as an image, but also interacts closely with the description of a young woman and the preceding mention of her hat ribbons and dress. A similar case can be found in *Repetition* in the quotation from the Book of Proverbs 19.13, "The contentions of a wife are a continual dropping." Here Kierkegaard replaces "continual dropping" (*idelig Drøb*) with *tagdryp*, dropping from the roof.

Many alterations can be explained by the processes of stylistic adjustments, mainly in the form of substitutions.[29] Following his stylistic and rhetorical concerns, Kierkegaard aims at creating a closer verbal link between the text and interpretation, or at accentuating what is most relevant in the new context.[30] However, there are examples of "whimsical" changes, which can hardly serve a clear stylistic point. For example, in *Fear and Trembling* we read: "But Abraham was the greatest of all, great by that power whose strength is powerlessness" (FT 16), "men Abraham var større end Alle, stor ved den kraft, hvis styrke er Afmagt" (SKS 4 113, 29). The corresponding biblical quotation is 2 Corinthians 12.9: "My grace is sufficient for thee: for my strength is made perfect in weakness." In the Danish New Testament it is said: "min magt udøves i magteløshed," which contains a beautiful play of words between "power" (*magt*) and powerlessness (*magtløshed*). Strangely enough, Kierkegaard changes it to the less playful "ved den Kraft, hvis styrke er Afmagt," while he could have said "magt, hvis styrke er Afmagt." It may be an indication that *kraft* is given a special semantic nuance in the context and is not the same as *magt*. Indeed, it seems that Kierkegaard uses *kraft* as "power," speaking for example about the constitution of a self, while he uses *magt* for "force," something external and violent.

Quite a few alterations, even the significant ones, are difficult to identify, because Kierkegaard creates a kind of a pseudo-biblical language that allows an invisible and unobtrusive manipulation of his subject.[31] As has been said, the creation of this kind of pseudo-language was not unheard of in Kierkegaard's time, particularly among theology students or those otherwise linked to contemporary theological discussion. To give just one example, in *Repetition* we read: "No, you who in your prime were the sword of the oppressed, the stave of the old, and the staff of the broken-hearted, you did not disappoint men when everything went to pieces—then you became the voice of the suffering, the cry of the grief-stricken, the shriek of the terrified, and a relief to all who bore their torment in silence" (R 197; Jb 29.12–17). Kierkegaard summarizes and gives names to what is referred to in the Bible, but none of the particular descriptions that he uses actually occur in the biblical text, even though they sound astonishingly biblical.

Translation and Play with Originals

In any discussion about the Bible, we immediately stumble upon the question of translation. The whole tradition of reception is thoroughly permeated by issues of translation. It can justly be said that even an immediate (literally literal) reading of the Bible is often problematic, since one may question the standard translation, and it is important to have the "right" translation precisely because of its status for the believer.

Kierkegaard engages in a lively way with issues of translation of the Bible.[32] In an entry in his journals, he criticizes Scriver's translation: "Scriver somewhere (pt. 1, p. 40) translates Job 13.15 thus: Even if he (God) slays me, I nevertheless hope in him.[33] *A beautiful translation, but not correct*" (Pap. X 4 A 199; JP 2327, my emphasis). From this remark about Scriver's translation, we see just how much words do matter to Kierkegaard, since in this case he seems to make a distinction between "hope" and "trust."[34]

As a part of his theological studies in 1833–1834, Kierkegaard began translating the Bible, the Acts from Greek (G. C. Knapp's edition) into Latin by means of Breitschneider's *Lexicon Manuale Graeco-Latinum* in *Libros Novi Testamenti*.[35] He made use of the Vulgate (although it is not known which edition) and consulted the Latin translations of Erasmus of Rotterdam, Sebastian Castello, and Theodor Beza. However, he was not dependent on these translations or the lexicon, and used them creatively as he tried to find new solutions for various issues of translation. In 1834–1835, Kierkegaard made a complete Latin translation of the Epistle to the Philippians, the Epistle to the Colossians, and the Epistle to the Thessalonians (see Pap. I C 36). In 1835 he translated 1 and 2 Epistles to Timotheus, Titus, and the Epistle to Philemon; during the winter term 1835–1836 he translated the Epistle to the Hebrews and some parts of James 1–3.

Kierkegaard, therefore, had considerable experience in translating the Bible, though it is curious to note that he mostly translated the epistles. It is also worth observing that he translated into Latin, whereas later in his works he quoted in Danish (we can therefore presume that some inaccuracies could be due to this process of a double translation—to Latin and then Danish). The translations are performed with a full awareness of ambiguities and the importance of wording (a fact that recalls the tension between literal and nonliteral).[36] Thus, commenting on his own translation of the Acts 3.20–21, he said: "You may say either that he must conquer heaven . . . heaven must receive him—which seems to have a dogmatic implication, as Christ's duties were not fulfilled until his return, and insofar as heaven received him—or: he returned to where he came from in order to conquer heaven" (Pap. I C 11, cf. I C 12).

The commentators of the new Danish edition of Kierkegaard's works observe that although normally he follows the Greek text from Knapp very carefully and exactly, in a couple of cases he constitutes his own text, as it were, because he takes up the possibility of a certain reading from the critical apparatus.[37] They further note that sometimes he forgets a half or a whole verse, quite often omits a less significant word, and occasionally inserts a word.

A preoccupation with issues of translation is incorporated into Kierkegaard's writings. This takes several basic forms: a quotation is given in Greek or the translation is modified; which in turn can be Kierkegaard's own translation, an older Danish translation, or Kierkegaard's translation influenced by a German translation by Luther.[38] One of the best known and obvious examples is Kierkegaard's preference for *pæl* rather than *torn* for "thorn," choosing the older (1740) Danish translation of 2 Corinthians 12.7, "en pæl i kødet," while in the 1819 version it says, "en torn i kiodet." One can also find cases of combined translation, where part has been taken from the 1647 translation of the New Testament, and part from that of 1819. For example, in *The Concept of Anxiety* Kierkegaard says, "men ogsaa i Frygt og megen Baevelse" (but also with fear and lot of trembling) (1 Cor 2.3, cf. Phil 2.12). This is a combination of the 1819 New Testament's "og jeg var hos Eder med ydmyghed og med Frygt, og med meget *Baeven*" and the 1647 New Testament version, "med Fryct oc med stor *Befvelse*" (my emphasis).

All such cases bear witness to the fact that Kierkegaard was by no means passive in his relation to the Bible, but actively and creatively sought the most adequate rendering. Throughout his works Kierkegaard continued translating the Bible for himself, both in a literal and in a metaphorical sense. The literal and the metaphorical senses became inseparable inasmuch as his interpretation of the Bible depended on the reading he chose.

It needs to be remarked that this ongoing attempt to find the "right" translation can be found in both his pseudonymous and signed writings. In a veronymous text, *Love Hides the Multitude of Sins*, Kierkegaard says: "A rascal looks down and listens with his rascal's ear" (EUD 60), "thi en Skalk slaaer øiet ned og lytter med sine Skalkeren (Sirach 19.24)" (SKS 5, 70). The changes are not significant, and Kierkegaard's translation is probably influenced by Luther's translation of Sirach 19.24.[39] There is an analogous expression in Sirach 19.27: "Bowing down his face, and making as if he were deaf by one ear."[40] The fact that alterations in translations occur in both the pseudonymous and veronymous texts once again proves that whatever the reason may be for changes to the biblical quotations in the pseudonymous works, it is not simply to make them more "aesthetic" by showing disrespect for the Bible.[41] Alterations form an integral part of Kierkegaard's use of the Bible and of his method of indirect communication.

With these comments in mind, let us examine some other examples of Kierkegaard's concern with the question of translation. The very first biblical quotation in *Stages on Life's Way* is found in the preface and thus sets the tone: "If someone thinks that a secret is transferable as a matter of course, that it can belong to the bearer, he is mistaken, for the [riddle] 'Out of the eater comes something to eat' is valid here" (SLW 9). Kierkegaard makes a direct translation from Hebrew in order to retain the play on "eat" and "eating," which is lost in the Danish translation of his time. The quotation is from Judges 14.14: "Out of the eater came forth meat, and out of the strong came forth sweetness," which refers to the story of Samson taking honey out of the carcass of the lion that he himself had killed.

Why is it important to retain the play of words? There is a double secret in the short biblical narrative. First, Samson does not tell his parents that he met a young lion whom he killed with his bare hands; second, after some time he finds honey in the carcass of the lion, eats it and gives some to his parents, but does not tell them where he found the honey. The background of the story in Judges 14.14 is that it is God's will that Samson should pick a fight with the Philistines. He marries one and gives a riddle to her people. They cannot solve the riddle but make Samson's wife get the answer from Samson. The riddle is solved by betrayal. As regards form, the riddle's charm is partly the unexpected combination of strongest and sweetest, partly the paradox that "out of the eater came something to eat."

In what sense does it help to understand that a secret does not belong to the bearer? Once you decipher the biblical riddle (that is, if you remember the original answer but also the story pertaining to it, and bear in mind the play of words in the original), you also have a key to understanding the author's textual strategy.

Sometimes Kierkegaard's explicit concern with translation and etymology is woven into the text, as in *Preface(s)*: "Why do you not send forth one of your lovers who not only has thoughts in his head but wrath in his nostrils to consume the hypocritical worshipers?" (P 64). The commentary in the new Danish edition tells us that the Hebrew expression *ruah afo* (used, for example, in Job 4.9, and rendered in Danish as *hans vredes pust*, "his anger's breath") means "breath of his nostrils" or "hiss of his nostrils" (SKS K4 524). Indeed, in the English Job 4.9, it is translated literally: "By the blast of God they perish, and by the breath of his nostrils are they consumed." This shows the degree to which Kierkegaard is preoccupied with the etymology, and it also proves that he is often keen on stressing the more picturesque, tangible image of the original (related to the issue of humor and strong expressions). One can also note that although there is no record of Kierkegaard's translating from Hebrew, these two examples confirm that he was equally concerned with the Greek and with the texture of the Hebrew original.

As has been mentioned, a separate case of concern with translation issues is reflected in the quotations in Greek. In *Preface(s)*, Kierkegaard quotes in Greek: "He is convinced that to be able *'sympathesai tais astheneiais tôn anthropôn'* ('to sympathize with the weakness of human beings') is the true principle of knowledge" (P 41).[42] The quotation is not exact: instead of Kierkegaard's *tôn anthropôn*, in the Bible it is *emôn*. The significance of this change is that "ours" becomes "human," making the meaning more abstract (interestingly, the movement usually is the opposite one—from general to more personalized). In this case, the issue of translation and that of inaccuracies become inseparable.

The Concept of Anxiety is particularly rich in examples of quotations from the Greek New Testament.[43] A special case of play with the Greek in *The Concept of Anxiety* is the following: "Spiritlessness is the stagnation of spirit and the caricature of ideality. Spiritlessness, therefore, is not dumb when it comes to repetition by rote, but it is *dumb [dum]* in the sense in which salt is said to be so. If salt becomes dumb, with what shall it be salted?" (CA 95).[44] This might be called a latent quotation, and it is impossible to understand the play without knowledge of the relevant passage in Greek. In Matthew 5.13 we have: "Ye are the salt of the earth: but if the salt have lost his savor, wherewith shall it be salted?" The meaning of Kierkegaard's passage relies on a sophisticated word play. As the commentators in the new Danish edition explain, Kierkegaard plays with the literal meaning of the Greek verb *moranthe* (first person, passive voice): to become insipid, flavorless, to lose taste or flavor, which comes from *moraino* (is stupid, acts or speaks stupidly; in the passive, to become stupid and, in a metaphorical sense, to be made insipid). The word play here is taken to a deeper than stylistic level.

What is behind this concern with translation? Among other things it is, of course, a concern with the "true" and correct text, but at the same time it shows an awareness of multiple possibilities. This tension between the search for an exact nuance and the dialectical elasticity of meaning takes us once more to the issue of the literal and nonliteral, and to Kierkegaard's specific understanding of epistemology. Kierkegaard's attention to translation also confirms that the tiniest differences are of great importance to him, and that indeed sometimes it is those details that make all the difference.

Perspective

We have seen that the alterations Kierkegaard makes in quoting the Bible in his pseudonymous works are of various kinds and perform different functions, but all play a part in his complex attitude toward the Bible as he attempts to appropriate it. We have shown that "misquotations" do not mean that the pseudonymous authors do not take the Bible seriously. On the contrary, the Bible is central to their works. Some of the deviations are indeed insignificant stylistic adaptations (but even these could be considered appropriation in a very pragmatic way), but others demonstrate the art of perspective in indirect communication.

One of the ways to regard Kierkegaard's misquotations is to look at them as a kind of anamorphosis. "Anamorphosis—a word that makes its appearance in the seventeenth century but for a device already known—plays havoc with elements and principles; instead of reducing forms to their visible limits, it projects them outside themselves and distorts them so that when viewed from a certain point they return to normal."[45] The art of perspective is analogous to indirect communication: it involves obtaining equality by inequality, and stability through instability. Thus the Bible is inscribed, but not in a direct way—it is either hidden or "broken," so that the individual reader has to find the right point of view that allows restoration of the text to its fullness. Its fullness is only attained by subjective appropriation.

This perspective-conscious way of inscribing the Bible is what makes it possible for it to be omnipresent without being authoritative, and without ever eliminating uncertainty. It creates a much deeper individual choice and freedom than mere interpretative freedom, because here one needs to find a point from which a picture becomes visible and makes sense at all, but in order to do that one must first become conscious that there is something more than more or less distorted and dispersed forms, that actually there is a unity. Kierkegaard was quite interested in the phenomenon of reconstituting perspective and appearance.

For example, he speaks about the image of the stick that, when immersed in water, seems broken but actually is not; or about the blurred idea of Christianity that needs to be stilled with the right mirror. We remember also the supplement in *Philosophical Fragments* with subtitle "An Acoustical Illusion." However, the most helpful description of the need for perspective in essential communication can be found in *The Concept of Irony*.

Kierkegaard's well-known emphasis on the many points of similarity between Socrates and Christ concerning the art of communication allows us to apply what he says about Socrates to his own indirect communication of the Bible. In *The Concept of Irony*, Kierkegaard criticizes Xenophon's depiction of Socrates, saying that it is as "a straight line" and that such a portrayal does not do justice to Socrates, whose perception was profound and multilayered. For Socrates, the true center was not fixed but *ubique et nusquam* (everywhere and nowhere). Contrasting his thought to those whose "discussions often end and begin in a stagnating village pond" (CI 17), in a footnote Kierkegaard says: "For Socrates nothing was static in this sense; what we read in the Gospel story about the water in the pool of Bethesda also holds true for his view of knowledge—it was healing only when it was agitated" (CI 17). We note the reference to John 5.2–4. In John 2.4 it says: "For an angel went down at a certain season into the pool, and troubled the water: whosoever then first after the troubling of the water stepped in was made whole of whatsoever disease he had." The image of the troubled water is threefold: it applies to Socrates, to the New Testament, and also to Kierkegaard himself. The troubled water stands for a "movement," an essential category in indirect communication. It may seem far-fetched, but one could say that in some sense, deviations express this very concretely through their attempt to reverse, disturb, extend the meaning or make a humorous use.

Kierkegaard does not see the Bible as a static reality, but as a mirror in movement. The mirror has a healing power if one is ready to see oneself in its ripples. He draws a parallel with Socratic discrete communication:

> Allow me to illustrate what I mean by a picture. There is a work that represents Napoleon's grave. Two tall trees shade the grave. There is nothing else to see in the work, and the unsophisticated observer sees nothing else. Between the two trees there is an empty space; as the eye follows the outline, suddenly Napoleon himself emerges from this nothing, and now it is impossible to have him disappear again. Once the eye has seen him, it goes on seeing him with an almost alarming necessity (CI 19).

This very precisely describes the presence of the Bible in the pseudonymous works. It is, as I have already called it, an invisible omnipresence. It is introduced in between other things, but it forms an outline that keeps those other things in shape. It can be easily ignored, but if one follows carefully the line, "it emerges and it is impossible to have it disappear again." This is exactly what Kierkegaard's indirect communication (and specifically his use of biblical quotations) is about: The reader is free to make his choices, but he has already been deceived into seeing "it."

Stealing a Gift

God hath spoken once; twice have I heard this; that power belongeth unto God (Psalms 62.11).

Kierkegaard is an extremely self-reflective author in that he is constantly performing an internal criticism of his own writing techniques, of his own hermeneutical positions, and of the possible interpretations of his works.[1] This reflection applies also to the use of biblical quotations in his authorship. Kierkegaard's concern with the legitimation of quoting and the hermeneutical procedures that this involves is best illustrated by the use of biblical quotations in *Philosophical Fragments*, because it is here that he discusses these issues in the most explicit and concrete manner. The most striking presence of the Bible in *Philosophical Fragments* takes place in the hypothetical dialogues at the end of every chapter. These dialogues present us with a hermeneutical program *in nuce.* In themselves they constitute a curious metatext, interwoven into the main text and yet opening up a totally new dimension.[2]

The dialogues in question consist of a hypothetical accusation by somebody I shall name the Probable Accuser, and then a response by the author of *Philosophical Fragments.* It is instructive to focus on these dialogues because they bring up the issue of the use of quotation (understood here very broadly as the use of others' words or ideas) and demonstrate the remarkable degree to which the author himself is conscious of the problems involved. Here one finds both quotations and reflections on quotations. From these passages, we can see that the use of quotations involves a complex web of attitudes and positions on the author's part: the relation to tradition, textuality, readers, and authority; his views on issues of legitimation, attribution, and more. Specifically, the dialogues in *Philosophical Fragments* problematize the use of the Bible (and at the same time the identification with Christian tradition of the text's meaning), and they also challenge the "hypothetical" status of Kierkegaard's book because of the extensive biblical use in what purports to be an independent philosophical project.[3]

The use of the Bible is, then, questioned first of all with regard to its place in a philosophical discourse, but also in more general terms. One of the crucial questions that emerge is whether there is another way of speaking about God than by becoming his plagiarist. What is the appropriate language in which to speak about God? Is it not ultimately bound to be a tautology (for reasons that will become clearer as we proceed)? This critical concern, or metaconcern, therefore betrays or bears witness to Kierkegaard's thoroughly reflective usage of the Bible.

The other reason for looking at these dialogues in particular is that although they are largely overlooked in the secondary literature, in them the key problems of *Philosophical Fragments* are most explicitly considered.[4] And since the dialogues are clearly preoccupied with the presence of the Bible in the text, we see once again how central biblical quotation is in the construction of the pseudonymous works. The biblical quotations are not used in a merely instrumental or ornamental way, but form the very core of the structure of Kierkegaard's writings. One could say that they shape his discourse into a kind of a spiral: Kierkegaard takes them as a source (or occasion) for the presentation of almost all the major philosophical problems with which he deals in his pseudonymous works, but he often does so by deviations from the "original" reference. It seems, however, that the deviations (in the multiplicity of forms they can take: subjunctive use, alterations, disanalogy, etc.) are teleological: the text turns so as to repeat the biblical words in a way that enables the reader to incorporate them in his subjectivity.

I will proceed by giving a detailed account and analysis of each dialogue in *Philosophical Fragments*. This concrete analysis will bring up several important aspects of Kierkegaard's use of biblical quotations, thus in the last part of the chapter I will concentrate on the issues of tautology, repetition, redoubling/reduplication, appropriation, and the logic of the gift. In this discussion I will move from questions that are specific to *Philosophical Fragments* to a discussion that embraces issues relevant to the use of biblical quotations in all pseudonymous works.

I

In the first dialogue (PF 21–22), the Probable Accuser speaks about the model that Johannes Climacus "invents" in opposition to the Socratic model of truth: teaching and learning. He asserts that everything Climacus says is ridiculous, because there is nothing serious and true about his project, not even its authorship. The argument for something being ridiculous and not serious is drawn from its being inauthentic, in the sense that the author's self does not genuinely participate in it. This is a typical textual move—one may think that it is just a very casual remark, but in fact it discloses or leads to quite a central preoccupation of Kierkegaard's: the question of authenticity. The issue is about the self that expresses itself as it is, but also as it is concerned with what is essentially the self's. As we have said earlier, the etymology of *auctor* reveals that authenticity is in fact related to authority.[5] Thus the Probable Accuser charges the author of *Philosophical Fragments* with being an author without authority. But, as we shall see later, the author is himself conscious of being without authority while invoking the words of authority, hence his peculiar employment of biblical quotations.

The Probable Accuser continues: "You are behaving like a vagabond who charges a fee for showing an area that everyone can see" (PF 21). This is a particularly interesting accusation. What exactly is this common knowledge that is supposedly so obvious and on which proof is wasted, because it does not need proving? The matters discussed in the preceding text are highly complex and controversial: birth and rebirth, the conditions of learning the truth, the decisive role of the moment, and so on. The author himself constantly expresses his insecurity in the face of such questions by asking: "Is the developed idea conceived legitimately?" That is to say, "Is what has been elaborated here thinkable" (PF 20)?[6] There is a cunning move in the accusation. The Probable Accuser not only criticizes the author, but he also performs a positive task: by granting certain truths the status of something obvious, he confirms them as more than possible—as absolutely true, to the point of being hackneyed. Thus the accusation in fact negates the conflict, the doubt, and the hypothetical status of the investigation itself, which is also negated by the specific and extensive use or "appropriation" of the Bible.[7]

The response to this initial accusation is a reconstruction and a deconstruction of the accusation, which eventually leads to its being reformulated as follows: "You are not angry with me because I falsely attribute to myself something that belongs to another human being, you are angry with me because I falsely attribute to myself something that belongs to no human being" (PF 22). The problem transcends the question of "authorship" and leads to one of authority.[8] According to Climacus, the nonhuman nature of his discourse can be demonstrated from the content of his message, because one of its key elements is rebirth, conceived as a transition from nonexistence to existence, which cannot be thought by the one nonexisting. At the same time, the nonhuman origin proves the truth of the hypothesis.

Climacus then goes on to discuss the nature of a "text" that has no human author. The paradox is this: There is a property that is shared by everybody but does not belong to anybody: "Is it not curious that something like this exists, about which everyone who knows it also knows that he has not invented it" (PF 22). Where does it come from? There is only one way to break the circularity — through the transcendent.[9] In order to trace the original owner of the words, it therefore becomes necessary to posit some Other, some ultimately different reality;[10] the Other who can perceive *for* a person that he is not existing (in order to think fully the transition from "not to be" to "to be"); the one who can write the first letter. Thus the philosophical discourse merges with the theological, because the paradox cannot be thought from the premises of reason alone. The fact that the text cannot have a human author, nor can it be explained by human reason, proves that the hypothesis is correct. "Yet this oddity enthralls me exceedingly, for it tests the correctness of the hypothesis and demonstrates it" (PF 22). It is not possible humanly to conceive an idea of absolute difference (even though, as Kierkegaard says, it is the passion of reason to come to something it cannot think), and it is the absolute difference that leads to the paradox:

> If a human being is to come truly to know something about the unknown (the god), he must first come to know that it is different from, absolutely different from him. The understanding cannot come to know this by itself (since, as we have seen, this

is a contradiction); if it is going to come to know this, it must come to know this from god, and if it does come to know this it cannot understand this and consequently cannot come to know this, for how could it understand the absolutely different? (PF 46)

Toward the end of the first dialogue (PF 22), Climacus invites us to differentiate between those who want to claim the authorship of a particular idea and the idea itself; or, to put it otherwise, between the author (or in this case author-impostor) and the text. This is an important notion to bear in mind while thinking about Kierkegaard's hermeneutics. On the more immediate level, he is talking here about a concrete idea, that is to say the non-Socratic project, but the distinction seems to fit into his overall view on the relationship between the idea and its author.

Ideas, once they have been originated, belong to everybody—the question of who is the author is irrelevant, says Climacus (very much in line with the principle of ancient rhetoric that speech as public discourse is *res publica*).[11] The analogy Climacus draws is that of gunpowder—it does not matter who invented it, what matters is that we know how to use it. On the other hand, from the fact that we know how to use it does not follow that we invented it. We can also recognize the very Kierkegaardian theme of the "how" rather than "what," or, in this case, "who."

This question becomes problematic when we speak about the use of the Bible, because in the Bible there is one fixed "what"—a historical fact concerning God's incarnation. A statement about the what and the how of a text, of course, instantly problematizes the author's claims over his creation and points to tension in the following relationships: the author vs. the reader (which is in a sense analogous to teacher vs. pupil) and the author vs. other authors. This is, of course, particularly relevant with respect to quotations, which are others' ideas or texts *par excellence*.

II

In the second dialogue, Climacus is accused of plagiarism: "What you are composing is the shabbiest plagiarism ever to appear, since it is nothing more or less than what any child knows" (PF 35). It is not an accusation in relation to any concrete work or author, that is, it is not about a trespass on a copyright held by a particular author.

Rather, it is about the plagiarizing of what every child knows, that is to say, what is absolutely universal.

At the same time the charge is about tautology, about presenting the obvious as something authentic and new. Climacus answers by saying, "Every poet who steals, steals from another poet" (PF 35). Then he asks from whom he steals. "Who then is the poet?" (PF 35). If there is a poem, surely there must be a poet (unless one allows for the possibility that it is a proverb, or functions as a proverb). "Was this perhaps why you called my plagiarism the shabbiest ever, because I did not steal from any one person but robbed the human race?" (PF 35). Climacus goes on to the question of collective authorship (quite analogous to collective responsibility): if no one, taken separately, has created anything, how can it be that all together they have created something? What is the unifying power that acts in the name of humanity? Climacus points out that the matter is not so simple as it might seem: "So perhaps it is not a poem at all, or in any case is not ascribable to any human being or to the human race, either" (PF 35).[12]

Once again Climacus reformulates the original charge against himself, and explains that what enrages the Probable Accuser is that Climacus's creation is so different from all human poems that it is not a poem at all but a wonder or a miracle, and that he has stolen neither from humanity nor from any particular human being, but from the Divinity: "Robbed the deity or, so to speak, kidnapped him and, although I am only a single human being—indeed, even a shabby thief—blasphemously pretending to be god" (PF 36).

Thus it is a sacrilege, and the Accuser's anger is justified. But how is it possible to steal from God? Steven Mulhall observes: "It is not obvious that human beings can steal anything from God, let alone his words or his Word; indeed, since, Christianly speaking, the Word of God *is* God, this plagiarism would have to be what its etymology suggests—a form of kidnapping."[13] We will come back to the question of whether it is possible to steal from God in the last section of this chapter.

The reason that the project presented in *Philosophical Fragments* cannot be a human creation is this: "Presumably it could occur to a human being to poetize himself in the likeness of the god or the god in the likeness of himself, but not to *poetize* that the god *poetized* himself in the likeness of a human being, for if the god gave no indication, how could it occur to a man that the blessed god could need him?" (PF 36). The idea of Incarnation is therefore the second reason for the nonhuman origin of the hypothetical project. Why is this secondary level impossible? Climacus's answer is simply that certain ideas do not originate in human hearts, they must be given. He says, "It could not arise in him" (PF 36).

The reference to the Bible here is remarkable, since Climacus uses the Bible itself in order to explain his use of the Bible. The reference is to 1 Corinthians 2.9: "Eye hath not seen, nor ear heard, neither have entered into the heart of man, the things which God hath prepared for them that love him." This is not an entirely satisfactory answer, but it is as far as we can get, given the non-Socratic project and the idea that human beings must be given a condition for understanding such that we are dependent on God for our idea of Him as dependent on us. We notice also Climacus's statement that this creation is so different from all human creation that it is a miracle that is beyond the human fight about "mine" and "yours": "And since we both are now standing before this wonder [*Vidunderet*], whose solemn silence cannot be disturbed by human wrangling about what is mine and what is yours" (PF 36). Thus the usual critique cannot be applied to this type of creation; the question remains how this miracle can be inscribed in human writing, and what its status there is (this leads us to the issues of gift and appropriation considered later).

III

The third dialogue does not deal with plagiarism, but with the absurdity of the project (PF 46). However, it also relates to negative theology and tautology, as will be discussed later. The Probable Accuser says that in order to understand this "whim" (*grille*), one has to ignore everything else in one's consciousness (PF 46), a remark with which Climacus agrees. The problem is how to think the unknown (God) as different without confusing difference with likeness. The understanding by itself cannot come to know that the unknown is absolutely different. In order to get to know that God is different, one needs God. But if God is to be absolutely different from the human being, He must be so in some respect that man does not owe to God. The only thing we have but do not owe to God is sin:[14] "What else but sin, since the difference, the absolute difference, must have been caused by the individual himself" (PF 47). As Stephen Mulhall remarks, the absolute difference is not read as a cognitive distance but as a moral or spiritual one. "The transition of rebirth, which the thought-project in Chapter 1 presents as embodying the anti-Cartesian intellectual challenge of thinking of oneself as non-existent, is here presented as the existential challenge of thinking of oneself as spiritually non-existent, as living a life that is oriented away from the good."[15]

The insert ends with the description of the relation between paradox and understanding. In the moment of passion, both understanding and paradox will be the downfall of understanding. After giving what he himself calls an "imperfect metaphor" about self-love at the basis of love, Climacus says, "So also with the paradox's relation to understanding, except that this passion has another name, or rather we must simply try to find a name for it" (PF 48). This last phrase can be interpreted in two, perhaps interrelated, ways. First, not only God but also faith is nameless for Climacus; its "name" appears only when we relate to it. Second, the phrase can be understood as a hint that the passion, which in *Philosophical Fragments* is presented anonymously, in fact has a name, only this name is, as it were, suspended by the claim that this is a hypothetical project and a "composed story" (PF 47). When the true identity of the project becomes disclosed, the passion regains its name.

IV

Turning to the fourth dialogue (PF 53-54), we find a further elaboration on the issue of ideas, property and appropriation, and quotation. This dialogue brings in a number of human authors. We should bear in mind, though, that the accusation about the use of others' ideas refers not only to the concrete quotations employed in *Philosophical Fragments*, both as regards human and nonhuman authors, but also to quotation as a hermeneutical practice in general. The project of the dialogues is much wider than a self-orientated critique.

The Probable Accuser starts by saying, "You really are boring, for now we have the same story all over again; all the phrases you put in the mouth of the paradox do not belong to you at all" (PF 53). We notice that an accusation of this sort at the same time expresses or implies a certain agreement, since the complaint is about repetition, not about the content or controversial nature of the statements.

Climacus answers, "How could they belong to me, since they do indeed belong to the paradox?" (PF 53).

The Probable Accuser replies that it is not just that the phrases are universal and cannot be attributed to anybody in particular, as was suggested in the second dialogue, but that "everyone knows to whom they belong" (PF 53).

Climacus then gives an amusing and ironical confession: "I admit that I trembled when I wrote them down. I could not recognize myself" (PF 53), and asks to whom the sayings belong. The Probable Accuser lists the real authors: Tertullian, Hamann, Lactantius, Luther, and Shakespeare.

Quotations are thus problematic not only with respect to texts that can be traced back to the divine revelation, but also with respect to those generated by human authors. Climacus has to admit that he has indeed used other authors' ideas as if they were his own. But he also says that the author is not the beginning or the end of the chain.[16] He says that the authors he quotes spoke not only for themselves, because although they were not offended they spoke *as if* they were: "Have not all these men talked about a relation of the paradox to offense, and will you please notice that they were not the offended ones but the very ones who held firmly to the paradox and yet spoke as if they were the offended ones, and offense cannot come up with a more striking expression than that. Is it not peculiar that the paradox thus seems to be taking bread from the mouth of the offense" (PF 54).

This is a very peculiar kind of argument, as it links authenticity with authority and the latter to offense. Mulhall says: "By citing these authors' words, Climacus implies that this description of them applies to him; he therefore identifies himself as holding firmly to the paradox despite speaking as if he were offended by it, and he implies that this does the paradox the service of pointing up the difference—the paradox—more clearly."[17] Once again we see the hypothetical status of the book collapse in the dialogues.

Climacus, in other words, is suggesting that what an author says does not necessarily belong to him: it can be borrowed, in which case the author has predecessors; it can be the voice of a character and, as such, it does not belong to the author even if he has created it;[18] it can be an echo of universal ideas that by definition do not belong to anybody. In this chain of possible creators, a text appears as a lost property. But is the text of the paradox a property at all, and does it have an initial master? And if it is not a property, on what terms can it be appropriated? What is the relationship between the originator of an utterance and the "incarnator" who makes it present for us in his own text? Such questions illustrate that Kierkegaard is concerned with issues relating to the process of quoting and its legitimacy. This concern, in turn, provides a horizon for the hermeneutical study of biblical quotations in Kierkegaard's works.

I have mentioned that the form of accusation in the *Philosophical Fragments* dialogues often implies a certain level of agreement. In relation to this, we should briefly consider the issue of caricature, often brought up in Kierkegaard's scholarship with respect to the hypothetical project of *Philosophical Fragments*.[19] It is curious to observe that the Probable Accuser does not at any point so much as hint at a distortion of the ideas. In one entry he calls the project absurd (in the sense of redundant or impossible to perform by human mind without divine intervention), but that is not the same as calling it a parody. By saying that Climacus repeats only what is already known to everybody, he surely implies that the way Climacus renders these ideas is recognizable and makes sense. The only aspect of parody seems to be the claim that the project is an original one.

V

The fifth dialogue starts, as does the third, with a general polemic that continues the discussion in the preceding chapter. Here the issue is that of contemporaneity, and whether there is any advantage to be derived from being a contemporary with the God-man. Climacus suggests that one is genuinely contemporary not by immediate contemporaneity in time and space, but by virtue of something else. Only a believer can be contemporaneous with the teacher. The Probable Accuser interrupts Climacus: "You talk like a book and, what is unfortunate for you, like a very specific book" (PF 68). He has good reason to say so, because immediately before the interruption, Climacus used four biblical quotations. The Probable Accuser continues: "You have introduced words that do not belong to you" (PF 68).[20] At last the Probable Accuser names the source of Climacus's words: "The words of the Bible (for they are Bible words) are such."

What follows is very interesting, because the Probable Accuser corrects the biblical quotation that Climacus employs, but he does not quote absolutely correctly either. The text in dispute is Luke 13.26–27: "We have eaten and drunk in thy presence, and thou hast taught in our streets. In verse 27 the Lord says, "I know you not." In the Bible it says, "and you taught" (*og du lærte*), not "the teacher taught" (*hiin Lærer lærte*), as Climacus says, or "he taught" (*han lærte*), as the Probable Accuser puts it. But that is not the most important thing. The content of the Probable Accuser's allegation is that Climacus shifts from plural (employed in the Bible) to singular when he speaks about a contemporary of the incarnated God, "I have eaten," and God says, "I do not know you [*∂ig*]". The Probable Accuser says, "You [Climacus] use singular instead of the plural" (PF 68). The substitution is hardly accidental, given Kierkegaard's philosophical emphasis on the individual, on the singular, and on the personal relation to God.

After making the point about the shift from plural to singular, the Probable Accuser criticizes or at least challenges Climacus's interpretation of the Bible. He asks Climacus, "Are you not concluding too much" (PF 68), when from the fact that God says "I do not know you" (*∂ig*) Climacus concludes that the person being addressed is not contemporary with God and does not know him (this brings out two senses of contemporaneity: the historical and the spiritual, which is the only truth). All along, the biblical quotations in the pseudonymous works express and problematize the issue of contemporaneity with the Word.

Climacus ends the dialogue by saying, "I would give even more to have understood it completely, for that is of greater concern to me than who produced [*opfundet*, invented] it" (PF 69). But in order to understand, he reinvents it in his mind as a possibility, not as a necessity, thus giving it a subjunctive mode and confirming his status as an author without authority.

Tautology, Repetition, Reduplication

Analysis of the last dialogue will take us to discussion of such issues as tautology, repetition, reduplication, and finally the gift itself.[21] The questions addressed there are very complex and together weave a finely meshed net, which, I believe, covers the essential features of Kierkegaard's use of biblical quotations. Although these issues are prompted by the analysis of *Philosophical Fragments*, they extend beyond it and apply to the use of biblical quotations in all pseudonymous works. The crucial term used to describe the employment of biblical quotations, "appropriation," will hopefully emerge as a conceptual unity, which is not merely a vague expression approximating to the subjective and existential dimensions of Kierkegaard's writing.

In the final dialogue, the Probable Accuser says again, "You always mix in some little phrase that is not your own, and that *disturbs* [*forstyrrer*] by the recollection it prompts" (PF 105, my emphasis). He then locates one of the central ideas of the non-Socratic project: that it is good for the disciple that the teacher goes away: "The idea that it is to the follower's [disciple's] advantage that the god depart is in the New Testament, in the Gospel of John" (PF 105). In the corresponding text, John 16.7, we read: "Nevertheless I tell you the truth; it is expedient for you that I go away: for if I go not away, the Comforter will not come unto you; but if I depart, I will send him unto you."

The departure of the teacher is, one may infer, analogous to the disappearance of the author. The analogy may be not entirely accidental, since Jesus says the words in John 16.7 before he leaves this world to go to the Father, and Climacus likewise puts them at the end of his book. It is an interesting feature of Kierkegaard's writing that the Bible is mirrored not only by the choice of themes and problems, but also by the imitation of its writing strategy.[22] On the one hand the Bible merges with the rest of the discourse and disappears there, as it were, but on the other hand it is said to interrupt the flow of the text and to "disturb" it. It "disturbs" because while reading *Philosophical Fragments* the reader stumbles upon the biblical reference, which, by virtue of the peculiar nature of the biblical text, compels him to undertake a different kind of reading, since it engages him by means of its requirement of reduplication.

Toward the very end of the book, Climacus says: "I shall make just one more comment with respect to your many allusions, all of which aimed at my mixing of borrowed phrases in what was said. I do not deny this, nor shall I conceal the fact that I did it *deliberately* and that in the next section of this pamphlet, if I ever do write it, I intend to call the matter by its proper name" (PF 109, my emphasis). Yet, in a typically impatient manner, he immediately breaks his promise and names it Christianity. It is thus confirmed that the biblical quotations are neither merely ornamental nor accidental, but play a central role in the structure of *Philosophical Fragments*. In fact, we find that the text is written so as to inscribe the Bible in itself.

The word "inscribe" seems very appropriate with respect to Kierkegaard's use of the biblical quotations. First, it reminds us of the connection between the Bible and writing, which, because of the Latin *scribere* and *scriptura* (translated from the Greek *biblos*, "book," which has come for us to mean "the book"), has profoundly marked the Christian tradition of writing. Second, I want to convey the meaning of "to inscribe" as "to engrave, to impress, to leave a mark," and, very interestingly, "to dedicate." The biblical quotations are not ornaments or "attachments," they are carved into Kierkegaard's writings and become an integral part of them, and yet at the same time — precisely because they blend together with the rest of the text and do not point to themselves — they are an incognito that awaits personal recognition. In a sense one could say that the project of the *Philosophical Fragments*, and perhaps of the whole pseudonymous authorship, is to some degree a tautology, a writing that does not produce a new sense, but inscribes reading of the Bible in a "new" text. This reading is performed by the ubiquitous and yet unobtrusive presence of biblical quotations throughout the corpus. Kierkegaard does not aim to explain the Bible, not even to interpret it; instead he reproduces it in a kind of spiral movement of imitation through deviations and reduplications — without authority.

Kierkegaard himself has hinted at a presence of tautology in his writings. Speaking about the pseudonymous authors, he says in the *First and Last Explanation:*

> Their importance (whatever that may become *actually*) uncon-
> ditionally does not consist in making any new proposal, some
> unheard-of discovery, or in founding a new party and wanting
> to go further, but precisely in the opposite, in wanting to have
> no importance, in wanting, at a remove that is the distance of
> double-reflection, once again to read through solo, if possible in
> a more inward way, the original text of individual human exis-
> tence-relationships, the old familiar text handed down from the
> fathers (CUP 629–630).

Another aspect of tautology in Kierkegaard's writings is his insistence on the "obviousness" of certain truths and concepts, and on the
fact that certain questions are only meaningful insofar as they do not
have answers. This feature may be related to the emphasis on will,
silence (as inexpressible obviousness), and (perhaps) the autopsy of
faith.[23] Stanley Cavell has also noticed this reliance on obviousness
(although he has not expanded on it), in relation to similarities
between Wittgenstein and Kierkegaard,[24] "yet they both claim that
obviousness and silence provide *answers*, and moreover that nothing
else does, that is, not *their* questions."[25]

Before embarking on a further discussion of tautology and its cor-
relative concepts, such as repetition and reduplication, I would like to
emphasize that the kind of tautology I have in mind always expresses
tension between the same and the different (residue related to the time
structure, to the individual as being-in-becoming). "Tautology," "repetition," "reduplication" are, of course, not used here according to the
strictest analytical definition, which would not allow any difference

between the concepts. I hope that it will appear in the course of the discussion that this is not merely due to a lack of rigor, but that it is an ambiguity that forms the kernel of these concepts when they are applied to existence understood as a process of becoming.

These concepts are interesting and meaningful for Kierkegaard only in their internal dialectical tension. Their abstract rigor and identity is loosened by the double reflection. That is to say, while Kierkegaard's writing is tautological in the sense that it does not write *about* the Bible but inscribes the Bible (with the Bible), it is not tautological when it becomes reading.[26] Such a "tautological" way of writing is not redundant, and although it does not produce any new meaning in the text itself, it is designed to produce an existential sense for the reader, that is, a sense embodied by the individual's actions, which constitutes again a sort of reduplication.

As we have already observed in the case of fictitious stories and of deviations, the way in which Kierkegaard writes and, in particular, the way in which he uses the Bible often has a precedent in the Bible itself. The clearest example of tautology in the Bible is, of course, Exodus 3.14: "And God said unto Moses, I AM THAT I AM: and he said, Thus shall thou say unto the children of Israel. I Am hath sent me unto you." The tautology here arises from the fact that the existence of God is his essence itself.[27] In a remarkable journal entry, Kierkegaard describes the tautological being of God as its perfection, as opposed to a human being, who would die of anxiety if its being had to be a tautology. Moreover, a human being would not be able to achieve such a being, and the perfection of a human being is being in becoming.[28] Kierkegaard also considers tautology to be the highest principle of thinking.[29]

However, Kierkegaard draws our attention to the dialectical nature of tautology. It can be a truism, the lowest kind of communication and a meaningless evasion, as, according to him, is the case when Hegel tries to avoid the problem by saying that the actual is possible and the possible is actual.[30] Or it can be the highest form of expression, when it is the only right way to speak about certain things and when any other discourse except tautology would be chatter (*sludder*).[31] The tautological character of the project of the pseudonymous works has, therefore, grounds both in the nature of its main concern—the individual's relation to God—and in the very principle of indirect communication. Writing about the individual's relation to God involves a moment of tautology because it repeats the tautology inherent in the relation. It is tautologous in at least three aspects: first, it involves imitation; second, the Bible is God's Word, and since God's essence for us is his love for us, his communication to us, the Bible can be said to be a tautologous expression for God himself;[32] third, God's essence corresponds to his existence. Finally, the tautologous is present in all statements of faith such as "I believe that God exists," which are "self-sufficient."

A certain degree of tautology is also natural for the method of indirect communication, inasmuch as it follows the Socratic model and requires imitation and representation. "Imitation and representation are not merely a repetition, a copy, but knowledge of the essence. Because they are not merely repetition, but a 'bringing forth,' they imply a spectator as well. . . . The presentation of the essence, far from being a mere imitation, is necessarily revelatory."[33] The knowledge of essence (understanding a thing in its essence implies tautology) and imitation as a repetition (in sense similar to reduplication) are the aims of indirect communication. When it is described, the communication of the individual's relation to God becomes "fictional," however, partly because what the author describes is a possibility and partly because it is merely a reflection of the relation. The reader then needs to restore the relation to its real existential dimensions, which also means that the communication does not create a new relation for the individual but only invites him to make that relation concrete.

Another relevant feature of indirect communication is the attempt to present things negatively, that is to say, by what they are not. From I AM THAT I AM (Ex 3.14), we see that in tautology, both reduplication and absence are expressed by the fact that the tetragrammaton YHWH was not even pronounced, but was uttered as Adonai. The name remains hidden even when it is redoubled; its only presence is in relation to the moments of reduplication. The real "absence" of the Word for Kierkegaard is linked to belief in "the invisible and ineffable"[34] God, who (or his name) cannot be known in terms of ontological presence, but only as relation and in relation. This relation is for Kierkegaard inscribed by the invisible omnipresence of the Bible in his pseudonymous works.

It is in this moment of a doubling, which at the same time effects a concealment, that tautology links up with the other crucial issue, that of repetition. Consider what Kierkegaard says in *Concluding Unscientific Postscript:* "But the repetition of inwardness is the resonance in which what is said *disappears* [my emphasis], as with Mary when she *hid* the words in her heart" (CUP 260), itself a radicalization of Luke 2.19, "But Mary kept all these things, and pondered them in her heart."

This negative quality makes repetition particularly suitable for indirect communication. "Things repeat always by virtue of what they are not and do not have. We repeat because we do not hear. As Kierkegaard said, it is the repetition of the deaf, or rather for the deaf: deafness of words, deafness of nature, deafness of the unconscious. Within representation, the forces which ensure repetition—in other words, a multiplicity of things for a concept absolutely the same—can only be negatively determined."[35]

At this point we should further develop Kierkegaard's concept of repetition (discussed in Chapters 1 and 2) in order to clarify the meaning of the biblical quotations as internal repetition in appropriation. The first question, of course, is whether a repetition as such is possible, or whether it is always only a mere semblance, repetition in a very remote and derivative manner. The answer depends on how we understand the relation between repetition and difference.[36] It seems that despite the difference "which is always already there," Kierkegaard sees repetition as possible, while remaining closely related to the impossible. "So there is a repetition, after all. When does it occur? Well, it is hard to say in any human language. When did it occur for Job? When every *thinkable* human certainty and probability were impossible" (R 212).[37]

Repetition in Kierkegaard has been proposed as an alternative to recollection, as "remembering forward."[38] It would seem that the focus is on the future, but this future is actually created in the present inasmuch as it is the renewal of the old, and this encounter of the past and future takes place in the "moment of presence." Through the moment (we will see later that this is also important for the gift), repetition is further related to contemporaneity. For Kierkegaard, repetition means becoming yourself (becoming concrete), gaining yourself.[39] "I am myself again. Here I have repetition. . . . The split that was in my being is healed; I am unified again. . . . Is there not, then, a repetition? Did I not get everything double? Did I not get myself again and precisely in such a way that I might have a double sense of its meaning?" (R 220).[40] The dynamics of the same and the different, of what is the same and yet also new, dynamics that are inherent in repetition, are always held in tension and yet at the same time somehow reconciled when the act of repetition is a true appropriation. Thus it is possible to say, "Although I have read the book [Job's book] again and again, each word remains new to me. Every time I come to it, it is born anew as something original or becomes new and original in my soul" (R 205).

To justify this claim further and give meaning to the "appropriation" of biblical quotations in Kierkegaard's pseudonymous authorship, I would like to draw attention to another very important passage, which tells us how Kierkegaard understands the individual's relation to the "objective" reality of the Bible. For Kierkegaard, such reality is constituted by appropriation, that is to say interior quoting, which by repeating accepts certain things as its own and takes responsibility for them, thus they become concrete for the reader and therefore real. "If Job is a poetic character, if there never was any who spoke this way, then I make his words my own and take upon myself the responsibility" (R 205).[41]

Repetition in Kierkegaard borders on another key term: "reduplication." Indeed one could say that repetition is the first step: becoming concrete, growing together with oneself is a condition that enables the movement of reduplication. Reduplication is essentially a category of reflection and cannot take place in the immediate. It means to live in what we understand (or, as in the case of the Bible, in what we read): "To exist in what one understands is to reduplicate" (PC 134). And this is what constitutes a self through redoubling: "And what, then, is to be a self? It is to be a redoubling [*Fordoblelse*]. Therefore in this relation it means truly to draw a duplexity to itself" (PC 159). "Reduplication" is one of the terms that Kierkegaard employs to explain indirect communication; he also says that "the reduplication of the contents in the form is the artistry" (CUP 333). In this sense, the pseudonymous works can be rightly called aesthetic. Quotation (and more specifically biblical quotation) combines the elements of tautology, repetition, and reduplication, both in their rhetorical and in their philosophical-existential senses.[42]

Thus we see how several interrelated issues merge together into a complex pattern of appropriation. "Indeed, on whom did God lay his hand as on Job! But quote him—that I cannot do. That would be wanting to put in my own pittance, wanting to make his words my own in the presence of another. When I am alone I do it, appropriate [*tilegne mig*] everything" (R 204). But "quoting as my own" in some sense dissolves "quoting" as such (we will come back to this).

Kierkegaard's biblical quotations, understood as repetitions, are incorporated into his style and manner of writing. Complementing its philosophical and existential sense, repetition has also a rhetorical value, as Deleuze says: "Repetition is the power of language, and far from being explicable in negative fashion by some default on the part of normal concepts, it implies an always excessive Idea of poetry"[43]

Repetition, reduplication, and tautology are not only concepts about which Kierkegaard speaks, they are also part of the way in which he speaks.[44] One could say that they have a certain transitive quality. We see once again how the existential level is mirrored by the textual level. For example, not only is reduplication a requirement for action in the ethico-religious sphere, but the meaning of this requirement is created in the text by means of reduplication. This is a very peculiar feature of Kierkegaard's writing that somehow bridges the distance between what he writes and how he writes. This is what gives his texts a unity of form and content, and what makes it so important to look very closely at the "texture" of the text, in this case at the employment of biblical quotations.

In the light of tautology, reduplication, and repetition, we might reread and find a new sense in the famous image of Kierkegaard as copyist, an image he offers in *The Point of View*:

> I seem to hear a voice that says to me: Obtuse fellow, what does he think he is; he does not know that obedience is dearer to God than fat of rams? Do the whole thing as a work assignment. Then I become completely calm; then there is time to write every letter, almost meticulously, with my slower pen. . . . Then, when I read it through later, I find an entirely different satisfaction in it. Even though some glowing expression perhaps did elude me, what has been produced is something else—it is not the work of the poet passion or of the thinker passion, but of devotion to God, and for me a divine worship (PV 73).[45]

The emphasis on hearing and on inscribing rather than writing also corresponds to Kierkegaard's description of himself not as an author, but as a reader of his own works (PV 12). This decidedly humble idea of what it is to be a writer does not express a straightforward obedience (see also Abraham's mode of hearing in Chapter 4), nor, as some have suggested, a claim to be inspired. It rather bears witness to the fact that Kierkegaard never ceased "copying" the Bible, inscribing it in the body of his own text.[46] He never ceases to hear the Bible (note the importance Kierkegaard always attaches to reading aloud) and to embody its echo.[47] Given the proximity in so many Indo-European languages between verbs of obedience and those of listening,[48] Kierkegaard can be read as somebody who chooses to hear,[49] thus the voice that "speaks to him" is rather a figure of hearing (reading the Bible) than a claim of any direct contact, inspiration, and subsequently authority. It is important to note that he hears not the voice itself, as would be the case with inspiration, but the echo—and thus his use of the Bible is also based on this paradigm of hearing and reading, and on the deviations and uncertainty caused by the echo rather than on the security of obedience.

There remains a final qualification to add to our discussion of tautology, repetition, and reduplication as the core of appropriation. This has to do with the unique nature of the Bible as a text whose tautologous character is taken to the very extreme. Could it be that *it is not possible to quote the Bible?* It is not possible to quote because it is a gift (in which property and appropriation are suspended, or rather blend into one), because it is given to us and it is ours, and thus there is no alien element, without which there can be no quotation (we have already mentioned that "quoting as your own" dissolves "quoting" in the usual sense). With this concept in mind, the question of legitimation takes another turn: the only legitimation is through faith in fear and trembling. This reflection—that quoting the Bible is essentially different from any other quotation—is suggested in *Philosophical Fragments*, but I think it is congruent with analysis of biblical quotations in other pseudonymous works, where the same mechanism of appropriation applies.

Gift

Toward the end of the analysis of *Philosophical Fragments'* second dialogue, we considered the problem of stealing God's Word in relation to plagiarism. Stephen Mulhall suggests that stealing God's Word (incarnated in Christ) is a form of kidnapping.[50] I prefer to look at it from a slightly different angle. God's Word is there for us, yet not as something deriving from ourselves: it does and does not belong to us. It is something that we have but do not own, and thus it is a gift.[51] Therefore, the question of the hypothetical project of *Philosophical Fragments* and the employment of biblical quotations in general can be expressed by the question of whether it is possible to steal a gift.

The question of "gift" has found a place in contemporary philosophical and theological discussion.[52] It has reinterpreted the anthropological understanding of gift, as Marcel Mauss discusses in *The Gift*. Mauss's interest in the problem of gift is largely a political and social one. According to Mauss there is no such a thing as a free gift, nor should there be. If there were a "free" and "pure" gift, by breaking the system of reciprocity, return, and recompense, it would sever mutual social ties. Instead, gift happens in the framework of a threefold obligation: to give presents, to receive them, to reciprocate presents received.[53] There is no place for freedom in this scheme, not even for gods — Mauss speaks about a "contract sacrifice," that is to say that sacrifice is a gift, which God is obliged to return.[54]

Another source for the modern discussion of gift is, of course, Heidegger's treatment of the expression *es gibt* in *Being and Time*.[55] Heidegger speaks about a feast of gift in being: the sheer happening of things, the givenness of things, "without why."[56] It is to this "without why" that the modern discussion about gift owes a notion of gift as something absolute and indefinite. Indeed, the philosophical and theological discussion has moved away from anthropology and put emphasis on a pure, unconditional gesture of giving, rejecting a notion of gift as an object of exchange, one that circulates in the chain of value. Recently the question of gift has been approached in the most explicit and concentrated manner in the writings of Derrida and John D. Caputo. They speak about the *aporia* of gift, which is not simply impossible but *the* impossible.[57] "The conditions that make the gift possible simultaneously make it impossible,"[58] writes Caputo.

Apart from the condition that it be free from any economic exchange, like reciprocity or contracting a debt, a gift also has to be an unconscious happening and not an intentional act. Moreover, according to this conception gift should pass as incognito, that is to say, it should not be recognized as a gift. "The impossible gift is one in which no one acquires credit and no one contracts a debt. That in turn requires that neither the donor nor the donee would be able to perceive and recognize the gift as a gift, that the gift not appear as a gift."[59]

"Gift," in the sense used by Derrida and Caputo, is understood as an event that is unforeseen, unexpected, and that tears up time. "Il n'aurait don qu'à l'instant ou l'instant paradoxal (au sens où Kierkegaard dit de l'instant paradoxal de la décision qu'il est la folie) déchire le temps."[60] Interestingly, here Derrida evokes Kierkegaard, suggesting that we are correct in relating the gift to the Kierkegaardian moment (which in its turn is related to the "fullness of time").[61] The connection between "gift" and "moment" is also an important one, if we recall that "moment" is also crucial for repetition (as explained earlier in this chapter). It seems that this link through the moment (as well as through the impossible) may support Deleuze's interesting suggestion that repetition is related to gift: "If exchange is the criterion of generality, theft and gift are those of repetition."[62] Quotation and repetition and gift meet in the moment, thus enabling appropriation through contemporaneity.

Kierkegaard himself ponders the subject of gifts and giving, most notably in the four upbuilding discourses published in 1843, but also elsewhere, for example in *Repetition* and *Works of Love*. For Kierkegaard, gift is a "pure" gift (but not an absolute); it is not an *aporia* but an opening, since the gift is made possible by faith.[63] Kierkegaard understands the gift not as an object but as an act. However, for him it is crucial to recognize the gift as such. In the first of the four discourses, the one based on Job 1.21,[64] Kierkegaard emphasizes that faced with the loss, Job does not say "the Lord has taken away"; he first says, "the Lord gave" (EUD 115). He further adds that it is precisely at this moment of loss that Job becomes grateful for the gift and is able to see not merely what God gave, but *that* he gave, his giving itself and therefore his goodness. In other words, recognizing a gift is a moment of mature faith. In another discourse called "Every Good Gift and Every Perfect Gift Is from Above" (Jas 1.17), Kierkegaard says it is a perfect gift because in human terms, to be in need of something (such as a gift) is an imperfection, but in relation to God, to be in need of the gifts that God gives is a perfection.

God is the only giver of true gifts, since, due to our finitude, we cannot break the circle of exchange and purpose ourselves. Is there no exception? Can love, itself a gift of grace, not break this circle? Indeed, in the discourse of 1843, Kierkegaard makes an exception for love in human relations, even though he traces it back to God: "The only good and perfect gift a human being can give is love, and all human beings in all ages have confessed that love has its home in heaven and comes down from above" (EUD 157). If the receiver accepts love as gift, then the giver and the receiver become inseparable in the gift; it remains forever an unbreakable bond between them—you cannot give away a gift, neither can you cancel it. Hereby they are also made essentially and fully equal before the gift (EUD 157), and then they are both equally indebted one to another (or not indebted).

Human equality before God, which is made possible by accepting God's love as a gift, has as its corollary that everybody is equally close to God. Being equally close to God means that everybody can be his contemporary. We see that in fact the issue of gift is related to being contemporary: being contemporary is an expression of proximity, and in relation to God, given the essential difference, this is only possible through the dynamics of a gift of love.

Let us come back for a moment to the difference between Kierkegaard and Derrida/Caputo. Caputo writes: "For when a gift produces a debt of gratitude—and when does it not?—it puts the beneficiary in the debt of the benefactor, who thus, by giving, takes and so gains credit."[65] Caputo/Derrida claim that gift produces a debt of gratitude and thus implies "economics," demonstrating the impossibility of a pure gift. The first reason that Kierkegaard does not see gift as being canceled by "need" or "debt" is the abovementioned perfection of human beings to be in need of gifts from God. The other reason is that even in human relations (where even though every truly perfect gift is from above, we have seen that the gift of love is possible),[66] it is not the gift that produces gratitude, but gratitude that creates the gift.

The creation of gift is very peculiar in that it is a backward movement: the gift is fully constituted only after having caused the effect. There is no debt in gift, because the receiver trusts that it is a gift (that no exchange is expected; he trusts because it is a secret that we can never disclose); that is to say, in turn he gives a gift of trust and preempts debt.[67] As in the exchange, reciprocity is a vital element in the constitution of gift.[68] However, it is not reciprocity with regard to an object, but with regard to an attitude and commitment. Despite its "coming from above," a gift is not something that just falls to us, it is created by the giver giving it unreservedly, and by the receiver accepting it with gratitude and making it into a gift.

A gift thus involves both interaction and dialogue, because it is constituted as such only by mutual actions—giving and receiving with gratitude. The reciprocity is expressed in that the gratitude of the receiver is mirrored by the joy of the giver. In the discourses, we are invited to give unconditionally and with joy for God's sake. The receiver must seek the giver with gratefulness, and having found him and thanked him, in his gratefulness he will also find God (EUD 145).[69]

Although we speak about the giver and the receiver, there is essentially no giver nor receiver in gift and love: "Love does not seek its own, there is no *yours* and *mine*," according to *Works of Love* (WL 265). Climacus has already said the same (in the second hypothetical dialogue in *Philosophical Fragments*) about the "miracle" that is radically different from all human creation, the Bible—that it is above the human fight between "mine" and "yours." Love for God finds expression in reading the Bible and bringing it to life by blending it with what is "yours" and giving this gift to another. The way biblical quotations are incorporated into Kierkegaard's writings is really a work of love, because there is no yours and mine, and what is given by the Bible is given on to the reader.

Quotation is an act of generosity; it is that by means of which one author makes place for another, withdraws himself, and makes possible the other's tête-à-tête with the reader. Quotations as such are a gift, but biblical quotations are also a gift in the specific sense that passing the Bible to others is a gift, when I do not give what I have but what I have not (Mk 12.41–44), what I have been given myself and can "have" only as gift.

Throughout this book, I have often used the word "appropriation" to describe the way Kierkegaard uses biblical quotations in his pseudonymous works and also the purpose this should serve for the reader. I hope that "appropriation" has now been enriched by my discussion of quotation as a repetition, reduplication, and a gift. The ambiguity that exists in the term, namely its capacity to denote both theft and a legitimate coming into possession of certain property, has been transformed by the gift, since in such appropriation there is no yours and mine (we note, however, that this merging never allows a total vanishing of "you" and "me," because a gift creates a relation).[70]

The gift of the Word can neither be stolen nor possessed. To appropriate the gift is thus to become passionately interested in it, and to accept it with gratitude. Appropriation is not identification,[71] but it is imitation, and uncertainty is never absent and the process never finished. Appropriation is not an integration but incorporation, or — incarnation. It is different from integration because it bridges the distance by a double movement: by adapting something to one's own reality, but also by forthcoming and approaching it oneself. It is an invitation and a responsible engagement. Appropriation as incorporation is an act of communion. Perhaps in appropriation, I take to myself what is most proper to me.

Concluding Remarks

I hope that the outlined hermeneutical pattern of the use of biblical quotations will contribute to an emergence of a more delicate reading of Kierkegaard, where greater attention is given to the fine grain of his writing and argument.

In my analysis of the biblical quotations, I have attempted to show that the presence of the Bible in *Philosophical Fragments* and in other pseudonymous works cannot be ignored nor reduced to dogmatic issues or abstract philosophical ideas. Neither can it be used as a tool to support the claim about the aesthetic nature of these works. The biblical quotations are not an ornament but a constructive power behind almost all the major issues discussed in Kierkegaard's work.

This strong presence of the religious in the philosophical or aesthetical means that the overarching scheme of the religious *versus* the aesthetic in Kierkegaard's authorship needs to be reconsidered. I have mentioned earlier that this binary scheme serves only as an interpretative prejudice, which obscures our reading by imposing a one-sided viewpoint. The pseudonymous, philosophical works are deeply concerned with an individual's relation to God, and this is expressed not only by the choice of problems and questions but also in the very texture of Kierkegaard's writing, which never ceases to inscribe the Bible within itself. Kierkegaard's texts speak to us about imitation of the Bible, reduplication, and becoming contemporary to God's Word — and they also embody this requirement.

The invisible omnipresence of the Bible in the pseudonymous works indicates that the employment of biblical quotations forms a crucial part of Kierkegaard's indirect communication and is its example *par excellence*, indeed perhaps the only tangible proof of such communication. The dissemination of the Bible through deviations, which can be restored to their "true" form when viewed from a certain subjective perspective, the ever-veiled dimension of meaning that becomes apparent and perceptible only when all presuppositions are locked out of one's consciousness (PF 46), the humorous as the boundary between ethical and religious, the teleological emphasis on "hard sayings" such as hatred and scandal — these and other features of the use of biblical quotations instantiate indirect communication. Furthermore, the reality of the Bible is presented not in a normative way but in a subjunctive mode and in the form of possibility, since it is the only representation that can stir up instead of inviting to be a mere spectator. This stirring, the movement, is further expressed in that God's Word is inscribed not as voice but as echo, with all alteration, disfiguration, and distance that this can involve, and thus with fear and trembling.[72] Kierkegaard's dialectical imagination keeps the meaning of the Bible in tension between its literal sense and its spiritual sense (forming a kind of oxymoron: spiritual literalness), and this tension assures a transition to action.

Kierkegaard's reading of the Bible has been compared (as he himself compared it) with looking in the mirror. I think my work shows that this image has to be qualified: this mirror does not have a hard surface but a shimmering, liquid surface. Better yet, one could employ a metaphor already used by Meister Eckhart—the mirror is in the bottom of the well. In this double reflection, transparency is combined with uncertainty, the given content with the content we give ourselves.

Speaking of God's Word as a gift raises several fundamental questions, such as whether we are heterogeneous in relation to God—that is to say, whether we can have something that is exclusively ours. Kierkegaard's writings, of course, were in a vivid dialogue with the problems raised by the Enlightenment project, and perhaps particularly with the claim of autonomy.[73] Kant argued that earlier attempts to ground obligation in, for example, the will of God led to "heteronomy of the will," because these attempts subjected rational agents to an authority external to reason. Kant's proposition was an alternative to earlier conceptions of morality that were grounded in obedience. Obedience was required partly because as created beings we were in debt to our Creator and thus bound by gratitude to carry out all his commands, and partly because of the deficiency of our moral abilities: weak will, insufficient reflection skills, and so on. Kant thought, however, that the autonomy of rational agents was consistent with moral objectivity; for him, "Morality is identified with objective necessity, which cannot rest on any advantages that act brings about. Neither can it rest on the will of God."[74] In *Concluding Unscientific Postscript* Kierkegaard attacks this notion, saying:

> Indeed, in a desperately ironic way he is as if exempted (in *the same sense* as Scripture speaks of being free from God's law) by becoming heterogeneous with it, and the more profoundly its requirement is proclaimed to him, the more clear his dreadful exemption becomes to him. The dreadful exemption from doing the ethical, the individual's heterogeneity with the ethical, this suspension from the ethical, is *sin* as a state in human being (CUP 267, my emphasis).[75]

But, as I have suggested, Kierkegaard is closer to the notion of hearing than to blind obedience: he never denies the need for thinking and reflection—indeed, he thinks that the task of contemporaneity can only be achieved by uniting imagination, thinking, and feeling in *existing* (CUP 348). Kierkegaard's idea of the individual's relation to God is not purely heteronomous, it is not absolute dependence, but neither is it a detached autonomy, and perhaps understanding God's Word as gift can square this circle.

We have mentioned that the individual's relation to God is what interests Kierkegaard most, but in this relation, the individual's relation to another individual, his love for neighbor is of paramount importance for him too. An author's first ethical relation is to his reader — and Kierkegaard embodies this by giving his reader a gift of God's Word in the most discrete way, so that only the one who wants to be grateful will receive it. I think that what he says in a preface to one upbuilding discourse is also true of his pseudonymous works:

> And yet a book is a gift, and it is the reader, if he is "favorably disposed" and capable of receiving it, who is the blessed one: "May 'that single individual' whom I with joy and gratitude call my reader" receive this gift. It is true that to give is more blessed than to receive, but if it is so, in one sense the giver is indeed the needy one, needing the blessedness of giving; and if that is so, then the greatest benefaction is indeed that of the one who receives — and thus it is really more blessed to receive than to give (WA 113, SV3 14, 169).

I wish to end by suggesting the final metaphor of prayer: it is inscription of quotation in one's proper life, as contemporaneity through saying *Du* to God. Prayer is an emblem of tautology and repetition. It entails a constant renovation of the meaning through its confirmation, which corresponds, as we have said earlier, to the dynamics of quotation as always different according to the value one gives to it in the moment of reduplication, where the same is never the same. Prayer as quotation expresses the ambiguity and dialectical elasticity inherent in the Bible, which is only resolved by an individual's existential attitude: "These words, like all sacred words, at various times can be milk for children and strong food for adult, even though the words remain the same" (EUD 129).[76]

In speaking about the problem of negativity, Kierkegaard says, "Praying is incommensurate with every external expression" (CUP 90),[77] and indeed its apparent expression can be misleading, but it can nevertheless be a true repetition. This allows me to suggest that the so-called aesthetic works are a form of anointing one's head and washing one's face when fasting.

"Moreover when ye fast, be not, as the hypocrites, of a sad countenance: for they disfigure their faces, that they may appear unto men to fast. Verily I say unto you, They have their reward. But thou, when thou fastest, anoint thine head, and wash thy face" (Mt 6.16–17).

Notes

Introduction

1. It is not my aim to prove that only those readers who are thoroughly familiar with the Bible can understand Kierkegaard's texts. On the contrary, it will be my suggestion that even those who perhaps have never read the Bible read it through Kierkegaard.

2. Only Chapter 5 focuses on language and translation issues. However, the material discussed in this chapter is also put in the framework of indirect communication.

3. The term "deviation" is not used negatively, but as an indication that Kierkegaard does not so much *trans*scribe the Bible as *rein*scribe it. See Chapter 5.

4. Sylvia Walsh, *Living Poetically: Kierkegaard's Existential Aesthetics* (University Park, Pa.: Pennsylvania State University Press, 1994), 1.

5. For a useful overview of different approaches, see the introduction to David Gouwens's *Kierkegaard as Religious Thinker* (Cambridge: Cambridge University Press, 1996).

6. The conflict between religious and philosophical is very poorly staged by his commentators. As a rule, it relies on the opposition of direct and indirect communication, an opposition that itself has led to quite a few non sequiturs. For example, if the pseudonymous "aesthetic" writings are indirect communication and edifying discourses are direct communication, then how does it come about that the religious can only be communicated indirectly? This is true of both Kierkegaard's writings and the Bible itself. We will see that one of the important features of Kierkegaard's use of biblical quotations is that it mirrors the hermeneutics of the Bible, and of the New Testament

in particular. Indeed in the Gospels, for example, before the crucifixion Jesus tells his disciples that he has so far communicated only indirectly: "These things have I spoken unto you in proverbs: but the time cometh, when I shall no more speak unto you in proverbs, but I shall show you plainly of the Father" (Jn 16.25).

7. Here and elsewhere I will refer to the works signed by Kierkegaard's own name as "veronymous."

8. Steven M. Emmanuel, *Kierkegaard and the Concept of Revelation* (Albany: State University of New York Press, 1996).

9. Arnold B. Come, *Kierkegaard as Theologian: Recovering Myself* (Montreal: McGill-Queen's University Press, 1997), 4.

10. M. Plekon, "Kierkegaard as Theologian: The Roots of his Theology in *Works of Love*," in *Foundations of Kierkegaard's Vision of Community: Religion, Ethics, and Politics in Kierkegaard*, ed. G. B. Connell and C. S. Evans (New Jersey and London: Humanities Press, 1992), 2–18 (4). According to Plekon, "Kierkegaard's theology is paschal, eucharistic, and ecclesial" (14).

11. See Stephen Prickett, *Origins of Narrative: The Romantic Appropriation of the Bible* (Cambridge: Cambridge University Press, 1996), 15. The story in Genesis 27.28 is this: Isaac is old and cannot see very well anymore, so he asks Esau, his firstborn, to make him his favorite savory dish so that he can bless him before death. Esau goes hunting, and Rebekah—who overhears Isaac's words—wants Jacob to pretend to be Esau and go to his father with the meat so that he will be blessed instead of Esau. Rebekah prepares the dish; she then puts the skins of the kids of the goats upon Jacob's hands, chin, and neck, so that Isaac can feel him and think it is his hairy son Esau. Jacob goes to his father; Isaac is deceived by the appearance and blesses Jacob. Later, when Esau comes back with the venison and asks to be blessed, Isaac and Esau realize the mischief, but the blessing has been given to Jacob and nothing can be changed. The "appropriation" is even more ambiguous given that earlier on, Esau has sold his birthright to Jacob for the pottage of lentils, thus it is not clear whether the blessing is stolen or justly appropriated.

12. Kierkegaard introduces key distinctions by means of redefinition or extenuation of the biblical meaning. For example, the important distinction between the selfish and the sensual is formulated with reference to the Bible: "Yes, indeed the Christian God is spirit and Christianity is spirit, and there is discord [*Splid*] between the flesh [*Kjød*] and the spirit [*Aand*], but the flesh is not the sensuous [*sandselig*]—it is the selfish. In this sense, even the spiritual can become sensuous—for example, if a person took his spiritual gifts in vain, he would then be carnal [*kjødelig*]" (E/O II 49; Gn 3.15, Gal 5.16–17, Rom 8.7; Rom 7.18–20; Eph 2. 3). Sometimes Kierkegaard arrives at crucial definitions by sharpening the focus of the biblical text. For example, in *The Concept of Anxiety* he says: "The narrative in Genesis also gives the correct explanation of innocence. Innocence is ignorance. It is by no means the pure

being of the immediate, but it *is* ignorance . . . Innocence is something (whereas the most correct expression for immediacy is that which Hegel uses about pure being: it is nothing)" (CA 37).

13. "Troen troer saaledes hvad den ikke seer; den troer ikke, at Stjernen er til, thi det sees, men den troer, at Stjernen er bleven til" (SKS 4, 281; Heb 11.1).

14. In an unpublished paper, Mark Heidman gives a survey of the scholarship pertaining to Kierkegaard's understanding and use of the Bible. One could mention Paul S. Minear and Paul S. Morimoto, *Kierkegaard and the Bible* (Princeton: Princeton Theological Seminary, 1953); Timothy H. Polk, *The Biblical Kierkegaard: Reading by the Rule of Faith* (Macon, Ga.: Mercer University Press, 1997); to some extent Gouwens (1996); as well as the articles by W. von Kloeden, "Biblestudy," *Kierkegaardiana* 1 (1978: 16–39); J. Pedersen, "Kierkegaard's View of Scripture," in *Bibliotheca Kierkegaardiana*, ed. N. Thulstrup and M. Mikulova Thulstrup (Copenhagen: Reitzel, 1978), 27–57; and Niels Thulstrup, *Kierkegaard og Kirken i Danmark* (Copenhagen: Reitzel, 1985).

15. Joseph L. Rosas III, *Scripture in the Thought of Søren Kierkegaard* (Nashville, Tn.: Broadman and Holman Publishers, 1994).

16. Ibid., 22.

17. Ibid., 46.

18. Jas 1.13–14: "Let no man say when he is tempted, I am tempted of God: for God cannot be tempted with evil, neither tempteth he any man: But every man is tempted, when he is drawn away of his own lust, and enticed."

19. Rosas says, for example, "Also, the Scripture passages and phrases S. K. appropriated are on the order of allusions and serve as literary devices rather than as the exposition of biblical teaching" (Rosas, 61).

20. Rosas, 61. It should be noted that I will only partly refute Rosas's claim that the treatment of biblical quotations differs markedly and meaningfully between the pseudonymous and veronymous books, since I have not performed a systematic comparative treatment of the whole authorship. I will, however, establish that inaccuracy of quotation *per se* is not simply an aesthetic ploy.

21. Rosas, 145.

22. Ibid., 154.

23. Gianni Vattimo, *Beyond Interpretation: The Meaning of Hermeneutics for Philosophy*, trans. D. Webb (Stanford: Stanford University Press, 1997), preface.

24. "Paradoxically in fact, hermeneutics, whose Enlightenment origins are demythologizing and rationalistic in inspiration, leads in contemporary thinking to the dissolution of the very myth of objectivity and to the 'rehabilitation' of myth and religion" (Vattimo, 52).

25. Vattimo, 33.

26. For elaborated arguments, see Chapter 2.

27. For an introduction to the history and theory of quotation, see Chapter 1.

28. Excluded are *Practice in Christianity* and the three smaller works *A Cursory Observation Concerning a Detail in Don Giovanni, The Crisis and a Crisis in the Life of an Actress*, and *Two Ethical-Religious Essays*. The reason I did not take *Practice in Christianity* into account is that the use of biblical quotations there resembles Kierkegaard's veronymous works: its sections are opened by quotations that then become the direct object of deliberation, and the discussion is interlaced with prayers. The use of biblical quotations in this book is no doubt also noteworthy, but since the mode of employing the biblical text is quite markedly different from other pseudonymous works, it would need to be the subject of a separate study.

29. It is also likely to be the case that some "types" of quotation are more present in one book than in another, but I did not engage in a comparative study and do not think it would give any fruitful results.

30. I have in mind the commentators who worked on the new Danish edition of Kierkegaard's works; in cases where it was not yet available, my source was the footnotes that Howard and Edna Hong prepared for their translations, as well as commentators who worked on earlier Danish editions. I have also relied on Minear and Morimoto and on Parkov indices.

31. I refer to the problem that several quotations considerably differ from their correlatives in the Bible, so that one can legitimately ask whether they are quotations or references at all. As regards the possibility that there are more quotations than have been pointed out, it is unlikely that there would be a significant number—the combined efforts of scholars have already led to a rather exhaustive index.

Chapter 1

1. In more complicated cases between three and more texts, for example, quotation involves a quotation from a previous source.

2. In the historical overview, I will rely heavily on the work done by Antoine Compagnon in his *La Seconde Main, ou le travail de la citation* (Paris: Seuil, 1979). However, my reading of this only comprehensive study of the history of quotation remains critical and selective.

3. For a description of various functions, see S. Morawski, "The Basic Functions of Quotation," in *Sign, Language, Culture*, ed. A. J. Greimas and R. Jakobson (The Hague: Mouton, 1970), 690–705.

4. In *Republic*, speaking about whether or not to admit tragedy and comedy into the city, Socrates says that Homer and other poets effect their narration through imitation: "When he delivers a speech as if he were someone else, shall we not say that he then assimilates thereby as his own diction as far as possible to that of the person whom he announces as about to speak?" (*Republic*, 393).

5. Quintilian, *Institutio Oratoria*, trans. H. E. Butler (London: William Heinemann, 1958) X. I.19.

6. This is relevant for Kierkegaard given his understanding of himself primarily as a reader; see Chapter 2.

7. *Rhetoric* II, 21, 1394 a21.

8. See also, for example, *Rhetorica ad Herenium* (III, 16–26) for the difference between *memoria verborum* and *memoria rerum*.

9. Compagnon, 158.

10. This is, of course, related to typology.

11. One could say that this subsequently leads to yet another function of quotation, that of representing the totality of the author's views by one or several examples.

12. See Compagnon, 205. The decree was passed in a document dated 13 February 1905. The biblical commission answered the question about the implicit quotations in the following manner: "Negative, excepto in casu in quo, salvis sensu ac judicio Ecclesiae, solidis argumentis probetur: 1 hagiographum alterius dicta vel documenta revera citare et 2 eadem nec probare nec sua facere, ita ut jure censeatur non proprio nomine loqui" See R. P. F. Prat, *La Bible et l'histoire* (Paris: Bloud, 1904).

13. We should also bear in mind the intricate net of translation. For example, Aquinas quotes the Latin translations of Arabic translations of Greek versions of Aristotle, which themselves depended on a history of transmission.

14. It is only with print that quotation becomes marked and acquires a modern sense, that is to say, it becomes a specific category in the textual practice. It is also in this period that one started to employ quotation marks, first in 1580–1590 in France, with different signs of indication. Quotation marks as we know them today were invented in the seventeenth century by a printer named Guillaume, thus in French they are called *guillemets*.

15. Compagnon, 282.

16. Seneca, *Letters to Lucilius* IV, 33.

17. Yet in the same period we still find authors such as Baltasar Gracien, in his treatise on baroque eloquence *Agudeza y Arte de ingenio*, advocating taking liberties with quotations. The notion of intellectual property was developed in the larger context of new legal definitions of property as such.

18. Immanuel Kant, *The Metaphysics of Morals*, trans. M. Gregor (Cambridge: Cambridge University Press, 1996), part 1, *Metaphysical First Principles of the Doctrine of Right*, § 31.

19. England is often given the credit for having the first copyright statute, *The Act of Anne* of 1709; the specific law regulating literary property in France, for example, dates from 1793. However, even earlier there existed in many European countries a complex system of royal decrees and privileges that regulated the circulation of books and art objects.

20. Georg Wilhelm Friedrich Hegel, *Elements of the Philosophy of Right*, trans. H. B. Nisbet (Cambridge: Cambridge University Press, 1991), 74, § 43.

21. Ibid., 100.

22. There have, of course, already been periods when it was customary to quote very carefully. Meyer refers to pedantic quoting in countless works of Renaissance and Baroque poetry, a tendency that was challenged by Cervantes. Herman Meyer, *The Poetics of Quotation in the European Novel*, trans. T. and Y. Ziolkowski (Princeton: Princeton University Press, 1968), 58.

23. One thinks particularly here of Flaubert's *Bouvard et Pecuchet* as a turning point, because of the extent to which the words of the two main characters are quotations. Bouvard and Pecuchet read books on different subjects and completely identify themselves with respective discourses, so that their words are always a reproduction of the absorbed literature.

24. Jacqueline T. Miller, *Poetic License: Authority and Authorship in Medieval and Renaissance Context* (New York: Oxford University Press, 1986), 6. By contrast, see Harold Bloom, *Anxiety of Influence* (New York: Oxford University Press, 1997); and Edward W. Said, *Beginnings: Intention and Method* (New York: Basics, 1975).

25. Meyer (1968), 58.

26. Levi-Strauss called serial quotation "a creature of whim."

27. Compagnon, 391.

28. Ibid., 17.

29. Contemporary linguists pay attention to quotation mainly insofar as it is an essential element in "reported," "direct" speech (Tuomarla, Authier-Revuz). Emphasis is typically placed on detachment and the dissociation of responsibility. A considerable discussion on the issues of quotation has taken place in German linguistic studies. German scholars have discussed quotation with much technical scrutiny, in a very concrete and yet at the same time abstract mathematical way; there are labels for every tiny aspect or rare function, but since such analysis does not lead to a reflection on the broader textual issues, the utility of such an exercise is rather limited (see, for example, Harweg, Mieder, Wills).

30. In literary studies, Meyer's *Poetics of Quotation in the European Novel* (previously cited) stands out. Meyer acknowledges that: "As we read certain novels, of whose typological nature we shall still have to speak, it strikes again and again that the effect of the employed quotations is not limited to their statement of substance. They are put into overarching contexts of a formal nature and fulfill an essential function within them" (Meyer [1968], 5). Nonetheless, the majority of other studies of the use of quotation in literary works speak about ornamental function or about the invocation of association, and then impose a rather crude analysis of comparison.

31. Donald Davidson, "Quotation," in *Inquiries into Truth and Interpretation*, ed. D. Davidson (Oxford: Clarendon Press, 1984), 79–92 (79).

32. Davidson says: "The connection between quotation on the one hand and the use-mention on the other is obvious, for an expression that would be used if one of its tokens appeared in normal context is mentioned if one

of its tokens appears in quotation marks (or in some contrivance for quotation)" (Davidson, 79). For a long time it has been maintained that the quoted expressions in quotation are mentioned and not used.

The classical account of the view that a quotation is the mention rather than the use of an expression can be found in Church's *Introduction to Mathematical Logic:* "We may distinguish between *use* and *mention* of a word or symbol. In 'Man is a rational animal' the word 'man' is used but not mentioned. In 'The English translation of the French word *homme* has three letters' the word 'man' is mentioned but not used. In 'Man is a monosyllable' the word 'man' is both mentioned and used, though used in an anomalous manner, namely autonomously." Alphonso Church, *Introduction to Mathematical Logic* (Princeton: Princeton University Press, 1964), 61).

Closely related to this is the proper-name theory, according to which a quotation, consisting of an expression flanked by quotation marks, is like a single word and is to be regarded as logically simple. See Alfred Tarski, *Logic, Semantics, Mathematics* (Oxford: Clarendon Press, 1956). A remarkable point in the discussion about whether quotation is to be considered as mention or as use is the debate between Derrida and John R. Searle. See Jacques Derrida, *Limited Inc.* (Evanston, Ill.: Northwestern University Press, 1988). It is interesting to note that, arguing against Searle, Derrida— piece by piece—quotes Searle's text almost entirely, thus making it not only the object of discussion but also its example. In it, among other things, Searle accuses Derrida of having confused citationality with parasitic discourse, as well as iterability (the latter is Derrida's word for the repeatability of the same expressions in different contexts, which always involves transformation), while Derrida denies the charges. Austin and Searle advance the distinction between use and mention, while Derrida does not believe that it is possible to draw such a rigorous distinction. Thus Derrida disagrees with Austin when the latter seems to exclude the possibility of performative utterances being quoted, insisting that this possibility remains abnormal and parasitic.

Apart from the "mention" theory, there are two other influential theories in the philosophy of language: demonstration theory and dramaturgical theory. According to the first, quotation is a species of demonstration (Davidson, 79–92.). The demonstration theory, in its turn, is divided into those scholars (such as Davidson) who think that quotation is a type of indication and those who disagree. The latter view is best expressed by Clark and Gerrig. They describe quotations as nonserious actions and selective depictions and claim that demonstrations are different from descriptions (H. H. Clark and R. J. Gerrig, "Quotation as demonstration," *Language* 66, no. 4 (1990): 764–802 (764). Clark and Gerrig further claim that this difference can be traced back to Aristotle's notion of *mimesis* and *diegesis*. According to the dramaturgical theory, represented by Wierzbicka, quotations are imaginary speech performances: the person temporarily assumes the role of another person. See A. Wierzbicka, "The Semantics of Direct and Indirect Discourse," *Papers in Liguistics*, no. 7 (1974): 267–307.

33. Clark and Gerrig, 791.

34. Compagnon, 32–34.

35. Ibid., 56.

36. Ibid., 113.

37. Kierkegaard discusses the manipulation of quotations in his response to Heiberg's critique of *Repetition*. According to Kierkegaard, Heiberg quotes only to page 40 and ignores the second part of the book. However, the concept of "repetition" can only be understood in the light of the second part. Kierkegaard analyzes a quotation that in Heiberg's review is quoted in relation to natural phenomena, whereas in *Repetition* it is used speaking about freedom. The quotation thus becomes meaningless. See Pap. VI B 111.

38. Meyer (1968), 44.

39. Compagnon, 27.

40. See, for example, PV 12.

41. Meyer (1968), 17.

42. John D. Caputo, *The Prayers and Tears of Jacques Derrida: Religion without Religion* (Bloomington: Indiana University Press, 1997), 184.

43. In ancient Greece, there existed an old ludic tradition of quotation. For example, during festivals contests of quotation were organized. Whittaker also claims that "The identification of quotations and allusions, both in and out of context, has been a sort of literary sport or intellectual exercise in many societies with strong literary tradition." J. Whittaker, "The Value of Indirect Tradition in the Establishment of Greek Philosophical Texts or the Art of Misquotation," in *Editing Greek and Latin Texts*, ed. J. N. Grant (New York: AMS Press, 1989), 66.

44. Gilles Deleuze, *Difference and Repetition*, trans. P. Patton (London: Athlone Press, 1994), 286.

45. Pierre Menard wanted to write not another Quixote, but *the* Quixote. He wanted not to transcribe mechanically, not copy, but produce an already existing book.

46. Jorge Luis Borges, *Fictions* (London: John Calder, 1985), 49.

47. Prickett, 34.

Chapter 2

1. Friedrich D. E. Schleiermacher, *Hermeneutics and Criticism*, ed. A. Bowie (Cambridge: Cambridge University Press, 1998), 7. For an attempt to throw light on the link between rhetoric and hermeneutics, see W. Jost and M. J. Hyde, eds., *Rhetoric and Hermeneutics in Our Time: A Reader* (New Haven: Yale University Press, 1997).

2. Rudolf Bultmann, "Das Problem der Hermeneutik," *Glauben und Verstehen* (Tubingen, 1961), II, 211–235.

3. Hans-Georg Gadamer, *Truth and Method*, trans. J. Weinsheimer and D. G. Marshall (London: Sheed and Ward, 1999), 165.

4. Ibid.

5. Ibid., 167.

6. Georg Wilhelm Friedrich Hegel, *Phenomenologie des Geistes*, ed. J. Hoffmeister (Hamburg: Felix Meiner, 1952), 524.

7. W. Dilthey, "The Rise of Hermeneutics," trans. Frederic Jameson, in *The Hermeneutic Tradition: From Ast to Ricoeur*, ed. Gayle L. Ormiston and Alan B. Shrift (Albany: State University of New York Press, 1990), 101–114.

8. Gadamer (1999), 179.

9. For specifically biblical hermeneutics, see Chapter 3.

10. Gadamer (1999), 179.

11. Charles Altieri, "Toward a Hermeneutics Responsive to Rhetorical Theory," in Jost and Hyde, 90–105 (93).

12. Gianni Vattimo, *Ethique de l'interpretation*, trans. Jacques Rolland (Paris: Editions la Découvertes, 1991), 212.

13. Ibid., 213.

14. Paul Ricoeur, *Le Conflit des interpretations: Essais d'herméneutique* (Paris: Seuil, 1969), 10.

15. John D. Caputo, *Radical Hermeneutics: Repetition, Deconstruction, and the Hermeneutical Project* (Bloomington: Indiana University Press, 1987), 2. If we agree that the new hermeneutical thinking, so-called radical hermeneutics, set out to "restore" the difficulty of things and to disrupt the "coziness" of metaphysics, we need only remember Kierkegaard's clearly expressed wishes to make things difficult, to be a "corrective," to remind us of the difficulty of being and of faith, of offense and of paradox.

16. Jean Greisch, *Herméneutique et grammatologie* (Paris: Editions du CNRS, 1977), 33.

17. Caputo (1987), 61.

18. Ibid., 38.

19. Ibid., 39.

20. Martin Heidegger, *Being and Time*, trans. John Macquarrie and Edward Robinson (New York: Harper and Row, 1962), §32.

21. Caputo (1987), 71.

22. Ibid., 81.

23. Charles Taylor, *Philosophy and the Human Sciences: Philosophical Papers* (Cambridge: Cambridge University Press, 1985), 18.

24. Greisch, 35.

25. Caputo (1987), 53.

26. Ibid., 32.

27. I will develop Kierkegaard's concept of repetition in Chapter 6.

28. Kierkegaard makes the difference between memory (*hukommelse*) and recollection (*erindring*). Recollection and memory are distinct but also inter-dependent: "To recollect [*erindre*] is by no means the same as to remember

[*huske*]. For example, one can remember very well every single detail of an event without thereby recollecting it" (SLW, 9). One can have a memory of something without having a recollection of it, but not a recollection without at least once having had memory of it. That is, memory is a condition of recollection. The distinction between recollection and memory is not Kierkegaard's invention. We can refer, for example, to the discussion in Plato's *Philebus* 34 a–c. "Do we not call it 'recollection' when the soul recalls as much as possible by itself, without the aid of the body, what she had once experienced together with the body?" (*Philebus* 34 b).

29. For a study of self and temporality, see Mark C. Taylor, *Kierkegaard's Pseudonymous Authorship: A Study of Time and the Self* (Princeton: Princeton University Press, 1975).

30. Caputo (1987), 91.

31. "Possibility" for Kierkegaard can acquire two different senses: it can be "a possible actuality," but also "actuality as possibility," that is to say that it sometimes belongs to the past, but often to the future. In *Works of Love*, Kierkegaard says that "the past is actuality; the future is possibility. Eternally the eternal is the eternal; in time the eternal is possibility, the future" (WL, 234). This future mode of possibility is further related to faith, in the light of "With God everything is possible" (Mt 19.26).

32. Caputo (1987), 66.

33. Ibid., 68.

34. Gerald Bruns, *Hermeneutics Ancient and Modern* (New Haven: Yale University Press, 1992), 9.

35. Hans-Georg Gadamer, "Rhetoric, Hermeneutics, and the Critique of Ideology: Metacritical Comments on 'Truth and Method,'" in *The Hermeneutics Reader*, ed. K. Mueller-Vollmer (New York: Continuum, 1994), 274–292 (277).

36. Gadamer (1999), 292.

37. Ibid., 268.

38. Ibid., 301.

39. Gadamer speaks, for example, of "constantly self-renewing contemporaneity" (1999), 302; see also Gadamer (1994), 275.

40. Gadamer (1999), 295.

41. Ibid., 291.

42. Ibid., 296.

43. Ibid., 311.

44. We note the significant play on *Being and Time* in one of Ricoeur's major works, *Temps et récit* (Time and Narrative, Paris: Seuil, 1983)

45. Greisch, 38.

46. Ricoeur (1969), 13.

47. Ibid., 14.

48. Ibid., 16.

49. Ibid., 22.

50. Ibid., 328.

51. Ibid., 325.

52. Ibid., 296.

53. Ibid., 321.

54. Ibid., 20.

55. Ibid., 294.

56. Richard E. Palmer, "What Hermeneutics Can Offer Rhetoric," in Jost and Hyde, 127.

57. Richard Rorty, *Philosophy and the Mirror of Nature* (Princeton: Princeton University Press, 1979), 315.

58. Rorty, 359.

59. Hans Robert Jauss, *Pour une Herméneutique littéraire*, trans. Maurice Jacob (Paris: Gallimard, 1982), 15.

60. Jauss, 29.

61. Gadamer (1994), 280.

62. In introduction to Jost and Hyde, 5.

63. Heidegger (1962), 178.

64. Altieri, 94.

65. Louis Mackey, *Points of View: Readings of Kierkegaard* (Tallahassee: Florida State University Press, 1986), 188. The latter claim will interestingly resonate in the discussion of tautology in Kierkegaard's writings in Chapter 6.

66. Gerard Genette, *Paratexts: Thresholds of Interpretation*, trans. J. E. Lewin (Cambridge: Cambridge University Press, 1997), 51. Genette also notes that "the pseudonym habit is very much like the drug habit, quickly leading to increased use, abuse, even overdose" (52).

67. I first encountered this term in Stephen Evans's book *Passionate Reason: Making Sense of Kierkegaard's Philosophical Fragments* (Bloomington: Indiana University Press, 1992). "In this book I intend to follow the policy of Roberts and Nielsen and the precedent of my own Kierkegaard's *Fragments* and *Postscript*, by taking the Johannes Climacus pseudonym as a genuine pseudonym" (6). Evans might have borrowed the term from Niels Thulstrup. Of course, Kierkegaard himself, in *The Point of View*, has drawn the difference between lower pseudonymity (all except Anti-Climacus) and higher pseudonymity (Anti-Climacus), but this has hardly anything to do with pseudonyms being more or less "genuine."

68. This is a well-established interpretation, ranging from researchers as different as Walter Lowrie to Roger Poole.

69. There is a further complication, since sometimes aesthetic is equated to philosophical and sometimes it is said to exclude it.

70. Mark C. Taylor, *Journeys to Selfhood: Hegel and Kierkegaard* (Berkeley and Los Angeles: University of California Press, 1980), 92.

71. Roger Poole, "'My Wish, My Prayer': Keeping the Pseudonyms Apart, Preliminary Considerations," in *Kierkegaard Revisited* (Berlin: Walter de Gruyter, 1997), 156–176 (162).

72. This is not to reduce the pseudomyms to the level of characters, but merely to indicate that there is "the author of authors."

73. M. Holmes Hartshorne, *Kierkegaard, Godly Deceiver: The Nature and Meaning of His Pseudonymous Writings* (New York: Columbia University Press, 1990), 1.

74. Ibid., 76.

75. Likewise, in spite of his constant reminder to keep the pseudonyms apart and not to attribute their works to Kierkegaard, Roger Poole nevertheless talks about the relation between Kierkegaard's biography and his pseudonymous works. For example, "Kierkegaard wrote book after book under a series of easily distorted pseudonyms, which referred to, while occluding or distorting significant information, the broken engagement to Regine and the ever-renewed puzzle of his relationship to his father." Roger Poole, *Kierkegaard: The Indirect Communication* (Charlottesville: University Press of Virginia, 1993), 4.

76. For example, "The First and Last Declaration" (which is neither the first nor the last) has been often contrasted with *The Point of View*, in which Kierkegaard claimed to give an account of his authorship and of himself as an author, to explain "once and for all" what kind of author he really was. In fact these two texts convey very similar messages employing similar terms: in both Kierkegaard makes normative declarations about authorship and gives directions how to read his works; in both he defines himself as the third person, as a reader, as the author of authors, and he acknowledges the role of Providence in the whole of authorship.

77. See also: "When I understand a thinker, then, precisely to the same degree to which I understand him, his actuality (that he himself exists as an individual human being, that he *actually* has understood this in such a way, etc., or that he himself has *actually* carried it out, etc.) is a matter of complete indifference" (CUP 325).

78. It is, of course, true that many "modern" notions are merely rediscoveries of the old ones. For example, in his *Essais* Montaigne says: "Je n'ay pas plus faict mon livre que mon livre m'a faict, livre consubstansiel a son autheur." Michel de Montaigne, *Essais* (Paris: Garnier-Flammarion, 1969), II 18, 648c.

79. One can, of course, speculate whether the subtle change in his name (Kjerkegaard instead of Kierkegaard) does not make it into an (ephemeric) pseudonym. Notable also is the title of the book, which is most likely inspired by the book of a pseudonymous Tutti Frutti (Furst von Pückler-Muskau) *Aus den Papiren des Verstorbenen*, see Pap. I A 41.

80. The most elaborate and explicit examples of an "unknown author" in Kierkegaard's oeuvre are found in *Stages on Life's Way* and *Either/Or*. But does not the same thing, even if on a smaller scale, happen in *Fear and Trembling* or *Philosophical Fragments?* After all, in the preface to the latter one reads, "But what is my opinion? . . . Do not ask me about that" (PF 7). Could it not be that such dissimulation of authorship is less noticeable simply

because some books have less obvious literary qualities than others, at least on the structural level?

81. At this point, one should ask oneself how reasonable is the insistence of some scholars to refer to the pseudonym of the book and never to Kierkegaard. It is dubious what is gained by that, since within pseudonyms there are other authors. Saying that it is a position of, for example, Climacus is in fact as complicated as saying that it is Kierkegaard's position.

82. This is a very interesting quotation, taken from Jn 19.22. Its context is this: 21: "Then said the chief priest of the Jews to Pilate, Write not The King of the Jews; but he said, I am King of the Jews." 22: "Pilate answered, What I have written I have written."

83. Although Kierkegaard can be justly called a forerunner of the contemporary obsession with the problematics of writing, his relationship to the current theories of textuality remains ambiguous.

84. An interesting example of Kierkegaard's concern with reading can be found in *Either/Or:* "In this book you will find something you perhaps should not know, something else from which you will presumably benefit by coming to know it. Read, then, the something in such a way that, having read it, you may be as one who has not read it; read the something else in such a way that having read it you may be as one who has not forgotten what has been read" (E/O I 15). It refers to 1 Cor 7.29–31: "But this I say, brethren, the time is short: remaineth, that both that have wives be as though they had none; [30] And they that weep, as though they wept not; and they that rejoice, as though they rejoiced not; and they that buy, as though they possessed not; [31] And they that use this world, as not abusing it: for the fashion of this world passeth away." Kierkegaard replaces the original meaning with the problematics of reading.

85. "Hovedsagen er den Inderlighed, med hvilken han læser . . . Om alle Mennesker vilde læse Bogen engang flygtigt igjennem: saa er jeg misforstaaet; paa en anden Side, naar blot een Eneste vilde læse Bogen saaledes, at han tilegner sig den i den væsentlige Inderlighed, saa det tildsidst er tilfaeldigt, at det er mig, der har skrevet den, fordi han selv producerer den—saa er jeg forstaaet og er glad" (Pap. VII 1 B 86, 281).

86. The peculiar nature of *The Point of View* has aroused very different opinions among Kierkegaard scholars. The most radically opposed positions are held by Lowrie and Fenger. In Lowrie's opinion, *Point of View* is a sincere confession and we must take every word of it at its face value: "*The Point of View for My Work as an Author* is an intimate and sincere revelation of Søren Kierkegaard." Walter Lowrie, *Kierkegaard* (New York: Oxford University Press, 1938), 437. By way of contrast, Fenger seeks to prove that nothing in *The Point of View* should be taken at face value, that everything in it is consciously counterfeited and fabricated.

Between these two there is another radical, though not extreme position represented by scholars such as Norris, Mackey, Garff, etc. The *summa summarum* of this latter view is that the problem is that of writing as such, and that *the* point of view is not possible. Therefore, if a project claims to offer the correct point of view, we must doubt the project itself. As Mackey says: "This book is not *the* point of view for his work as an author. It is only a point of view . . . A plurality of wholes and no totality." Mackey (1986), 190.

87. This is ironically true to the extent that it is a posthumous work.

88. It needs to be remarked, though, that what Kierkegaard writes in *The Point of View* is at the same time a utopian attempt to describe writing as it takes place *now* (and not a year ago, and not a moment ago).

89. The role of Providence should also be placed in the context of indirect communication, since, as I will argue later, it is not a question of revelation but of an echo. "The voice of the one speaking comes from me but it is not my voice; the hand is mine, but it is not my handwriting" (Pap. VII 1 B 75; JP 5964).

90. Oxford Latin Dictionary (1968). *S.v. auctoritas, auctor*.

91. Unless we take it to be related to the problematic of exchange, as discussed in Chapter 6.

92. "According to medieval grammarians, the term [*auctor*] derived its meaning from four main sources: *auctor* was supposed to be related to the Latin verbs *agere* 'to act or perform,' *augere* 'to grow,' and *auieo* 'to tie,' and to the Greek noun *autentim* 'authority.' An *auctor* 'performed' the act of writing. He brought something into being and caused it to 'grow.' In the more specialised sense related to *auieo*, poets like Virgil and Lucan were *auctores* in that they had 'tied' together their verses with feet and metres. To the ideas of achievement and growth was easily assimilated the idea of authenticity or 'authoritativeness.'" A. J. Minnis, *Medieval Theory of Authorship* (London: Scholar Press, 1984), 10. We note the relation between authority and authenticity. Kierkegaard is authentic not through his own authority, but through the reinscription of the "authoritative text."

93. While speaking about authority, Kierkegaard uses two Danish words, *auctoritet* and *myndighed*; there does not seem, however, to be a semantic difference of any importance in the way these two expressions are used.

94. Kierkegaard extends his critique of authority also to Church (*Instance*). In this respect it is somewhat ironical when he says that upbuilding discourses are not sermons, because he speaks without authority. Even if he were a priest and if his religious discourses were, commonly speaking, legitimately called sermons, it would not mean they would be authoritative. In the strictest sense, perhaps only the Sermon on the Mount is for Kierkegaard a sermon.

95. This is probably related to the recurrent problem of language for him, namely whether the concept is rightly applicable only if the signified corresponds "perfectly" to the ideality of the concept. The best example is his unwillingness to say that he is a Christian, because he considers himself an imperfect Christian.

96. This would have a huge impact on the understanding of the aesthetic and the religious in Kierkegaard's authorship, since, by some strange twist of interpretation, quite often scholars present the argument that pseudonymous works are *just* aesthetic and nothing more, precisely because they employ indirect communication (as if that were some kind of defect or deficiency).

97. That one cannot make this rigid distinction between the pseudonymous/indirect communication/aesthetic and the veronymous/direct communication/religious we see also from what Kierkegaard (and this in spite of his own distinction drawn in *The Point of View*) says about the pseudonymous book *The Sickness unto Death:* "It was granted to me to illuminate Christianity on a scale greater than I had ever dreamt possible; crucial categories are directly disclosed here" (Pap. X 1 A 147; JP 6361).

98. George Pattison, *Kierkegaard: The Aesthetic and the Religious, from the Magic Theatre to the Crucifixion of the Image* (New York: St. Martin's Press, 1992), 92.

99. With regards to the essential communication and *Kunnen*, one can think of an interesting recent discussion in Kierkegaard scholarship concerning second ethics (most notably in the writings of Pia Søltoft).

100. Mark C. Taylor, preface to Patrick Bigelow, *Kierkegaard and the Problem of Writing* (Tallahassee: Florida University Press, 1987), xi. Doubting the directness of the *Point of View*, Mackey says, "But maybe the communication is not so direct after all. Craftiness remains" (Mackey [1986], 182). I suggest that it is not so much a craftiness as impossibility, since there is always a residue of the unexpressed, the gap between language and reality.

101. Bigelow (1987), 11.

102. In Chapter 6, we will attempt to clarify "appropriation" both by concrete analysis of the biblical quotations and by discussion of repetition and reduplication.

103. Adorno says that "Kierkegaard's existential doctrine can be called realism without reality. It proves the identity of thinking and being, but it does not seek reality outside the thinking." Theodor W. Adorno, *Kierkegaard's Construction of the Aesthetic*, trans. R. Hullot-Kentor (Minneapolis: University of Minnesota Press, 1989), 86. One can say that when Kierkegaard speaks of realism he speaks of a kind of spiritual realism, where the reality of idea, faith, and internal action (intention) has a priority over the reality of fact.

104. Among other reasons for the use of indirect communication in Kierkegaard's journals we curiously also find this one: "For me indirect communication has been as if instinctive within me, because being an author I no doubt have also developed myself, and consequently the whole movement is backwards" (Pap. X 3 A 413).

105. David F. Swenson, *Something about Kierkegaard*, ed. L. M. Swenson (Minneapolis: Augsburg Publishing House, 1956), 117–118.

106. Taylor (1975), 59.

107. An explicit example of dialogue can be found, for example, in *Philosophical Fragments* in the hypothetical dialogues after each chapter. For more on this, see Chapter 6.

108. Strictly speaking one cannot, of course, say that the Greeks had a notion of subjectivity.

Chapter 3

1. Prickett draws attention to the fact that reading of the Bible was affected not only by changes and development of biblical scholarship and theology, but also by the romantic hermeneutics: "[The Bible] had, in the process [of Romantic appropriation], been so irrevocably altered by the new hermeneutic assumptions it had engendered that it became for the nineteenth century virtually a different book from that of a century before" (Prickett 1996, xi).

2. Hal Koch and Bjørne Kornerup, *Den Danske Kirkes Historie*, vol. 6 (Copenhagen: Gyldendalske Boghandel, 1954), 25.

3. A couple of words need to be said about Kierkegaard's theological education in general. Kierkegaard was, of course, deeply schooled in Christian dogmatic theology. He was particularly interested in Patristic authors, especially ante-Nicene writers such as Tertulian. The Pietist tradition of the seventeenth and eighteenth centuries (Johann Arndt, Johann Gerhard, Philipp Spener, A. H. Francke, Gerhard Tersteegen) was also influential on Kierkegaard. Gouwens notes that their writings shaped his understanding of identification of the believer with Christ's sufferings in the imitation of Christ, but that he was critical of the tendency toward moralism and external strictures (Gouwens [1996], 49). The important references for him were works of Martin Luther and Blaise Pascal. Dupré locates Kierkegaard historically and systematically as an intermediary figure between Reformation Protestantism and Roman Catholic theology, because of his emphasis on subjectivity and individual conscience on the one hand, and freedom's role in faith and grace on the other. Louis Dupré, *Kierkegaard as Theologian: The Dialectic of Christian Existence* (New York: Sheed and Ward, 1963), x–xi.

4. Bruce H. Kirmmse, *Kierkegaard in Golden Age Denmark* (Bloomington: Indiana University Press, 1990), 102.

5. Ibid., 130. To be fair, one has to mention that at the same time Mynster outspokenly defended Jewish rights in relation to 1817 anti-Jewish riots in Denmark.

6. Kirmmse, 103.

7. Thulstrup (1985), 132.

8. For the discussion, see Chapter 5 of this book..

9. Kirmmse, 177.

10. J. Pedersen, "Kierkegaard's View of Scripture," in *Bibliotheca Kierkegaardiana*, ed. N. Thulstrup and M. Mikulova Thulstrup (Copenhagen: Reitzel, 1978), 33.

11. For example, "ikke jeg lever, men Christus lever i mig." Hans Larsen Martensen, *Den Christelige Dogmatik* (Copenhagen: Reitzel, 1883), 46; Gal 2:20) or "dersom I blive i mit Ord, da ere I mine Disciple" (Martensen, 417; Jn 8:31).

12. Kierkegaard plays with words: *old-nordisk* (old Norse) and *øl*, beer, ale). He has in mind Gruntvig's translation of Eph 5.15–21.

13. Kirmmse, 213

14. Thulstrup (1985), 250.

15. N. F. S. Gruntvig, *Udvalgte Skrifter*, vol. 3, *Bibelshe Proedikenes* (Copenhagen: Glydendalshe Boghandel, 1905, original 1816), 272–280.

16. Henrik Nikolai Clausen, *Det Nye Testaments Hermeneutik* (Copenhagen: Reitzel, 1840), 27.

17. Ibid., 399.

18. Ibid., 407.

19. J. Pedersen (1978), 32.

20. The Cambridge History of the Bible (1987), 275.

21. Hans W. Frei, *The Eclipse of Biblical Narrative: A Study in Eighteenth and Nineteenth Century Hermeneutics* (New Haven: Yale University Press, 1974), 224.

22. David F. Strauss, *The Life of Jesus Critically Examined*, trans. G. Eliot (London: SCM Press, 1973), 52.

23. Kierkegaard says that mythological interpretation is a form of indifference when one makes no difference between the mythological in non-Christian religions and the divine in Christianity (SKS K18, 338).

24. Strauss, 64.

25. Ibid., 88.

26. Ibid.

27. Ibid., 89.

28. Robert Morgan, *Biblical Interpretation* (New York: Oxford University Press, 1988), 50.

29. In some journal entries where he does speak about Strauss, Kierkegaard says that Strauss is incoherent when he claims that the whole human race is God-manly, but that at the same time no individual human being can be a God-man. Kierkegaard says that in this case it is not clear how an individual can participate in the God-manly. This leads to the problem of how the human race as the universal (*Almindelige*) relates to the individual (*den Enkelte*), and vice versa (SKS K18, 327).

30. For a study of Kierkegaard as interpreter of Scripture, see Timothy H. Polk, *The Biblical Kierkegaard: Reading by the Rule of Faith* (Macon, Ga.: Mercer University Press, 1997).

31. In the historical approach there are two main streams: philological scholarship and critical theological. Kierkegaard does not seem to mind the philological so much (indeed, it can even be admired), because "it has no bearing on faith" (CUP 28). Sometimes he mocks the pedantry with respect

to the Bible: "If the attackers, in order to deny the personality of the Holy Spirit, can try their hand at New Testament exegesis, they can just as well adhere to the distinction expounded by Lindberg—whether the Creed should read 'the holy spirit [*den hellige Aand*],' or 'the Holy-Spirit [*den Hellig-Aand*]'" (CUP 42).

32. It is interesting to note that the moment of decision is a sort of imitation of *the* moment in time, of the "fullness of time."

33. By "subjective" we mean not psychologically "subjective," but such that helps the individual to become a subject.

34. Even though he stresses subjective appropriation of the Bible, Kierkegaard does not mean just "any" interpretation. Sometimes he speaks about the wrong interpretation, thus presupposing that some distinction between a right and wrong reading is possible. An example of Kierkegaard speaking about the "true" or the "real" meaning is the following sentence: "So it is with the unconditional demand: if I must lift it, I am crushed. But *this is not the meaning* of the gospel; *its meaning is* that in humiliation I am to be lifted up by it in faith and adoration—and then I am as light as a bird" (SV XIII, 492, my emphasis).

35. We note that this is a transformed biblical quotation, Gal 3.24: "Wherefore the law was our schoolmaster to bring us unto Christ."

36. According to Kierkegaard, inspiration is not a guarantee; there is always uncertainty, and the dialectical can never be excluded (CUP 24). It is so because "inspiration is indeed an object of faith, is qualitatively dialectical, not attainable by means of quantification" (CUP 28).

37. This quotation entails a critique of the biblical plot. What it implies is that the biblical story could have been told in a different, even a better manner. This shatters the traditional view that plot is not an essential category in a sacred text, since what is narrated is ever more important than how it is done, at least from the point of view of a believer. The fact that Kierkegaard could speak of improvements to a biblical passage indicates that he subjected the Bible to the universal hermeneutical critical rules, that is, he advocated the collapse of the distinction between *hermeneutica sacra* and *hermeneutica profana*. On the other hand, it is clear that he upheld such a distinction on the level of personal engagement, since an individual can be infinitely and passionately interested only in texts pertaining to faith, and therefore reading a religious text always remains different from any other kind of reading.

38. However, in *Works of Love* Kierkegaard says: "Holy Scripture is very consistent in its use of language. It does not name as hope any and every expectancy, the expectancy of a multitude of things; it knows only one hope, the hope, the possibility of the good" (WL 262). This implies that Scripture gives us a very concrete content with a unified and simple meaning (which is not something we arrive at through the process of reading, but something already given, provided we read "correctly").

39. There is, of course, no strict mutual exclusivity between literal and nonliteral meanings (not to mention the basic sense in which all nonliteral interpretations are to some degree dependent on the literal). A fine example of the convertibility of literal and figurative values (how literal turns figurative to become literal again in a different context) is Hollander's analysis of Abraham's story: "But the Christian reading of this episode [Abraham] (not the akeda of the Hebrew Bible, but the first figurative sacrifice foreshadowing the trope of Christ as lamb), gives the literalness another dimension. What Abraham offers figuratively, the narrative literalizes when the ram is discovered entangled in the thicket. But the literalization is only a movement into the fullness of antitype: the foreshadowing will be literally fulfilled in the typological completion of the episode in the New Testament when the lamb of God is finally provided by, and of, him." John Hollander, *The Figure of Echo: A Mode of Allusion in Milton and After* (Berkeley and Los Angeles: University of California Press, 1981), 50.

40. Paul Ricoeur, *Essays on Biblical Interpretation*, ed. L. S. Mudge (London: SPCK, 1981), 55.

41. Frei, 268.

42. J. Pedersen (1978), 27–57 (30).

43. Kierkegaard says: "I do not begin by having the consolation of eternity and now only have to lose, to give up all earthly, no, I start by having to give up the earthly, and it is in this suffering that eternity appears to me. As soon as eternity consoles me, I have given up the earthly" (Pap. X 4 A 572).

44. An obvious proof of such a concern is Kierkegaard's preoccupation with translation issues; see the section "Translation" in Chapter 5.

45. As regards the problem between literal and nonliteral reading, Kierkegaard emphasizes that what matters is the idea, the spirit. But even when he stresses the spirit, he acknowledges the weight of the letter in the Bible and warns against slavery to it: "That the letter kills can be seen in the Sadducees, who adhered so strictly to the letter of the law that they denied the immortality of the soul" (Pap. II A 424; JP 1947). That is, Kierkegaard thinks that a too literal reading of the Bible can lead to destroying the essence of faith.

On the other hand, in his journals, speaking about language as a potentially dangerous enemy of every man, more dangerous perhaps than flesh and blood, Kierkegaard says: "This explains the entire nonsense of Christendom. If the New Testament had been taken literally, this confusion would not have been possible. For what is Christendom? It is this indulgence continued from generation to generation, whereby first of all a little bit is knocked off of what it means to call oneself a Christian, and then the next generation knocks off a little more of the already reduced price" (Pap. XI 2 A 128; JP 2334). According to this entry, a literal understanding is essential for Christianity and plays a particularly important role in its unfolding in time. One could say that an evolution of views over time—we note that the first entry is from 1839, while the second from 1854—could explain this seeming contradiction. But one could also say that the two above-quoted entries in Kierkegaard's journals do not form a real tension, because they speak about different types of literal understanding: the first deals with a literal reading of a text, the second with the need to take the spirit of Christianity literally.

46. Speaking about Kierkegaard's understanding of literal and metaphorical meaning, one could fruitfully exploit the literal meaning of the metaphor "to transfer." One could thus understand metaphor as transference of meaning to ourselves (and not far from ourselves), thus making it concrete. The believer could himself be called a metaphor of God's Word, the bearer of it.

47. For more about "violence" in the New Testament, see David McCracken, *The Scandal of the Gospels: Jesus, Story, and Offense* (New York: Oxford University Press, 1994).

48. Gouwens (1996), 129.

49. He further relates offense to the moment: "All offense is in its essence a misunderstanding of the *moment,* since it is indeed offense at the paradox and the paradox in turn is the moment" (PF 51).

50. In his journals Kierkegaard notes: "He who does not hate his father and mother for my sake, etc., is not worthy of me. How does this conflict appear in 'Christendom,' for surely it cannot mean that we should begin right off by hating them?" (Pap. X 5 A 33; JP 6831). He adds that it is so because Christianity is made into something other than it is according to the New Testament. Regarding the question of how to understand hatred, Kierkegaard says: "Think about a collision in passion. There is a person, whom I love with all my passion, but I know that if I presented him with what Christianity really is, he would turn bitter, would cease to be my friend. And yet Christianity makes it my duty to do this" (Pap. X 5 A 33). While it makes sense that hatred is judged to be necessary only in a situation where there is a choice between human love and divine love, this is not a satisfactory answer because, contrary to Lk 14.26, it is the others who hate. Thus while you provoke hatred, you do not hate yourself (or do you, if you provoke?), which seems to be a simpler task. In the New Testament two forms of hatred are present: being hated and hating.

51. Strauss, 43.

52. The term "ethical-literal" is used by J. Pedersen (1978), 42.

53. For a stimulating discussion of will in relation to faith, see Ferreira (1991), chapter 2, "Pathos-Filled Transitions: Will and Imagination."

54. For a commentary of this journal entry, see Polk, 54–60.

55. Ricoeur (1981), 5. In his journals Kierkegaard mocks this circle, remarking that the theologians of the Reformation kept on going around the circle, because faith is extracted from the Bible and the Bible should be interpreted according to the faith, which is gained from the Bible. Thus the door is open for any interpretation (Pap. II C 14, p. 326). For Kierkegaard, it is possible to break this circle through the moment of decision.

Chapter 4

1. "By repetition of a fundamental problem we understand the disclosure of the primordial possibilities concealed in it. The development of these possibilities has the effect of transforming a problem and thus preserving it in its import as a problem. To preserve a problem means to free and to safeguard its *intrinsic powers, which are the source of its essence and which make it possible as a problem.*" Martin Heidegger, *Kant and the Problem of Metaphysics*, trans. J. S. Churchill (Bloomington: Indiana University Press, 1962), 211–212.

2. Likewise, we are repeatedly told that the opening of the *Sickness unto Death* is an extremely dark passage or a parody on Hegel, and few have noted that its first lines are not those about the self relating itself, but rather a quotation from Jn 11.4: "This sickness is not unto death." It may be retorted that these lines are found in the introduction and therefore are not a proper opening of the book (but what is more of a beginning than an author's introduction?). Nevertheless, the fact that it has been almost universally overlooked is symptomatic of the tendency to exclude the religious in the philosophical and vice versa.

3. Christopher D. Stanley, *Paul and the Language of Scripture* (Cambridge: Cambridge University Press, 1992), 352. Also: "A similar approach can be seen in those Jewish materials that modern investigators call 'rewritten Bible.' Included here are such diverse works as the book of *Jubilees*, the *Temple Scroll* and *Genesis Apocryphon* from Qumran, Pseudo-Philo's *Biblical Antiquities*, and Josephus' *Jewish Antiquities*. Similar reworkings of the biblical text to serve a later interest can be seen in the testamentary literature of early Judaism (e.g., the *Testament of Abraham, Testaments of the Twelve Patriarchs*, etc.) and such documents as the *Life of Adam and Eve* and *Joseph and Aseneth*" (Stanley, 353).

4. It is true not only of fictitious stories, but also, for example, of splicing. See Chapter 5.

5. For the most striking examples see Chapter 5 of this book, on misquotations. Changes to the biblical material and the play with diverse variations on the biblical themes are not unique to *Fear and Trembling*. For example, in *For Self-Examination* (written under his own name) Kierkegaard writes: "Then one day a prophet came to King David. *Let us make the situation really contemporary and modernize a bit*" (FSE 37, my emphasis). This, among other things, enables us to question the line usually drawn between Kierkegaard's aesthetic and religious writings, as well as the role of pseudonyms in his works. The argument for *Fear and Trembling* being an aesthetical work is—crudely put—usually twofold: it is signed by a pseudonym and it plays with possibilities, thus communicating indirectly.

What would be a better example of the play with possibilities than four variations of the biblical story; what would better support the thesis that an aesthete, a pseudonym, does not take seriously the crucial issues, the religious? Yet when we discover that in *For Self-Examination* Kierkegaard allows himself to play with the Bible in fundamentally the same way, the whole argument collapses. It therefore needs to be rethought in other terms, or perhaps abandoned. It can be, however, acknowledged that there may be some differences between biblical variations in pseudonymous and in non-pseudonymous works. In the case of *For Self-Examination*, the story itself is not changed but is recontextualized or reenvisioned. In *Fear and Trembling* and *Stages on Life's Way*, the basic story itself is reinvented and even allows such radical departures from the "original" text as the break with the tradition of Abraham's silence, listed above. However, even if there were no comparable examples in the veronymous works, the fact is that the so-called "play" in *Fear and Trembling*—far from being irresponsibly indifferent—engages with the religious in a decisive way.

6. "Fictitious stories" are thus fictitious in the second degree insofar as they rediscover the authenticity of the "original" story and exploit the multiple levels of reading.

7. This suggestion sits awkwardly with Kierkegaard's repeated statements that age is indifferent in respect to the religious; on the other hand, it is quite typical of Kierkegaard to use a distinctively developmental psychology.

8. This is related to the discussion in *Remember Your Creator*, as well as to the difference between first and second immediacy.

9. Mulhall draws our attention to the fact that the man in "Exordium" focuses exclusively on his relation with Abraham rather than his own relation with God. Stephen Mulhall, *Inheritance and Originality: Wittgenstein, Heidegger, Kierkegaard* (Oxford: Clarendon Press, 2001), 373. Mulhall suggests that this is a fundamental error since, instead of wanting to be present in another person's relation with God, he should attempt to create his own relation. This criticism is not really valid given the subjunctive mode of the book, in which everything is presented as a possibility, and not as actuality (see the last sections of this chapter). The man therefore did not want to be a spectator, but to become present in the story and "go along," follow [*følge med*].

10. The best account of "contemporaneity" can be found in *Philosophical Fragments*.

11. Later in the text, doubt features prominently in the example of Faust (FT 107–110).

12. Let us, then, look at the 1740 Old Testament: "Og det skete derefter, at Gud fristede Abraham, og sagde til ham: Abraham, og han sagde: see, her er jeg. Og han sagde: tag nu din Søn din eneeste, som du haver kier, Isaak, og gak du til Moria Land; og ofre ham der til Braend-Offer paa eet af Biergene, som jeg vil sige dig." Kierkegaard: "Og Gud fristede Abraham og sagde til ham, tag Isaak, Din eneste Søn, som Du elsker, og gaae hen i det Land Morija og offer ham der til Braendoffer paa et bjerg, som jeg vil vise Dig" (SKS 4, 107).

The Hongs' translation can be misleading on this point. Thus Mulhall has based an important moment of his interpretation (Mulhall [2001], 362) on the supposed difference between "*as* a burnt offering" (Hongs) and "*for* a burnt offering" (English Authorized Version and King James Version). There is not such a difference in Danish: both the Old Testament 1740 and Kierkegaard say *til*. There are other differences between the Danish Bible and the way it is quoted by Kierkegaard, but not this one. Among these differences are: "and then it came to pass after these things" is omitted in Kierkegaard's text (but this is a very standard practice); the exchange between God and Abraham, as mentioned above; "one of the mountains" becomes "the mountain"; instead of "which I will *tell* thee of," Kierkegaard has "which I will *show* you."

13. There is another strange detail, this time in the text of Old Testament—the difference between the original command and then the second command. While in Gn 22.1 God "said unto him," in Gn 22.11 we read: "And the angel of the Lord called unto him out of heaven, and said, Abraham, Abraham: and he said, Here am I." A distance is implied first by mediation of God's voice through his angel, and then by adding "out of heaven" and the double address "Abraham, Abraham," which could indicate the effect of an echo. (We cannot be sure of this; it could as well be due only to the standard form of address in the original.)

14. For a detailed discussion of cases of compilation and splicing, see Chapter 5.

15. Jdt 10.10. *The Anchor Bible*, trans. C. A. Moore (New York: Doubleday, 1985).

16. Could this be connected to a hidden feminine point of view in this episode?

17. We should also observe that Kierkegaard quotes Jdt 10.10 in *Concluding Unscientific Postscript* in relation to decision, anxiety, and transition. "One almost forgets the decisiveness of the transition because it lasts so long. In narrative and description, in the rhetorical address, the abstract 'so long until' evokes a very illusory effect, whether as an optical illusion (for example, the book of Judith, chapter 10, verse 10: 'And Judith went out, she and her maid with her, but the men of the city watched her *until* she had gone down the mountain and *until* she passed through the valley and they could no longer see her')" (CUP 336).

18. Another case of interaction between a Greek reference and a biblical one can be found, for example, in *Stages on Life's Way:* "Whether the gods took a part of him while he was sleeping out of fear of waking him by taking too much, or whether the gods divided him in half and the woman was the other half, it was the man, after all, who was divided" (SLW 76; Gn 2. 21–24). We can see that even while dealing with one of the most important anthropological questions—that of creation—no preference is given to the biblical account on this issue over the second reference: Plato's *Symposium* 189d-193b.

19. The word "idolator" may be very important, since that is how Abraham evaluates the act of human sacrifice, speaking as it were from a post–Old Testament perspective. And because, according to the logic of the story, calling himself an idolator Abraham obviously is telling an untruth, this may be an interpretative clue—namely that human sacrifice is not how Abraham understands God's command.

20. Ambiguously, *Lyst* in Danish means both "desire" and "pleasure." The Hongs translate it as "desire."

21. For the discussion of the suspension of truth in indirect communication, see Chapter 2.

22. There is another version (five) of Abraham's sacrifice in the subsequent text, which we shall discuss later.

23. De silentio says about Abraham that "his response to Isaac is in the form of irony, for it is always irony when I say something and still do not say anything" (FT 118). We note that according to this definition, irony is not "saying the opposite" but "saying nothing."

24. As Louis Jacobs observes, it is improbable that Kierkegaard knew it, but in fact there is a Midrashic exposition of the Akedah, which says that Satan threw a challenge to God that Abraham had not sacrificed anything in relation to the feast. L. Jacobs, "The Akedah in Jewish Thought," in *Kierkegaard's "Fear and Trembling": Critical Appraisals*, ed. Robert L. Perkins (Tuscaloosa: University of Alabama Press, 1981), 1–10 (5).

25. Hope is usually attributed to Abraham, since Isaac is his "haab i alle Slaegter." It also reminds us to what degree Abraham's decision affects Sara's fate.

26. E. F. Mooney, "Understanding Abraham: Care, Faith, and the Absurd," in Perkins, 100–114 (108).

27. It can be noted that in the Qu'ran it is Ishmael, not Isaac, who is subject to Akedah.

28. I take this to mean also that Kierkegaard was familiar with the "precedent" of child sacrifice in Jewish religious writings, but thought that it by no means exhausted the meaning of Abraham's story.

29. It is interesting to note that Kierkegaard elaborates on Abraham's intercession on behalf of Sodom and Gomorrah in an upbuilding discourse, "Love Hides the Multitude of Sins," published on the same day as *Fear and Trembling*.

30. Interestingly it has the same structure as a promise: when we promise, we take upon ourselves the future. To God's promise Abraham responds with the corresponding structure, namely with the responsibility not only afterward but also before.

31. The paradigm of "echo" rather than of voice is also helpful in understanding the moment of "obedience" in Abraham's relation to God's Word. "Hearing" and "obedience" are indistinguishable; they blend together in the effort of listening, in "active listening." There is a lot of textual evidence that even though Abraham did what he was told, it was not a "simple" blind obe-

dience. For example, as we have seen (FT 18), even though Abraham would have done what he was asked to do, he would not thereby have proved his faith. Obedience without acceptance and law without love cannot bring about the double movement of faith.

32. "Self-sacrifice" would, however, not be a correct term because it is done "for his own sake."

33. Garrett Green, *Imagining God: Theology and the Religious Imagination* (San Francisco: Harper and Row, 1989), 149.

34. "Quidam's Diary" ends with an observation presumably made by Frater Taciturnus, which very adequately sums up what is going on in the text: "Here the diary ends for the time being. It deals with nothing, yet not in the sense of Louis XVI's diary, the alternating contents of which are supposed to have been: on one day, went hunting; the second day, *rien* [nothing]; the third day, went hunting. It contains nothing, but, as Cicero says, the easiest letters deal with nothing, then sometimes it is the hardest life that deals with nothing" (SLW 397).

35. In his journals Kierkegaard gives a curious explanation of the origins of this piece: "I am going to try to get rid of the gloomy thoughts and black moods that still live in me by writing something which will be called: A leper's self-contemplation" (Pap. IV A 110; JP 5666).

Thus, already in May 1843 Kierkegaard planned a dialogue between two lepers. One of them is sympathetic—he hides himself and does not want to cause anxiety for others—the other wants to take revenge by making people afraid. The fact that this was meant to provide some sort of personal relief does not, however, tell us why it takes the form that it does, nor how it relates to its immediate context amid the surrounding entries of Quidam's diary. It is interesting nevertheless, since it seems that storytelling can perform a kind of therapeutical function for Kierkegaard, even when mediated by the pseudonym. Therefore this explanation is relevant from the point of view of a "pseudonym problem."

36. For examples and details, see Chapter 5.

37. Gn 2.18.

38. A similar case of "forgetting forward" can be found in the *Philosophical Fragments:* "What else is repentance [*Anger*], which does indeed look back, but nevertheless in such a way that precisely thereby it quickens its pace toward what lies ahead!" (PF 19). For analysis see Chapter 5.

39. In some cases it is difficult to understand whether it is a reference at all. For example, "So Solomon lived happily with the prophet Nathan" (SLW 251), in the commentaries, is usually marked as a reference to 1 Kgs 1.8–46. But in 1 Kgs it is only said that Nathan interfered and reminded King David of his promise to make Solomon the king after him. In no other way did Nathan and Solomon live happily together.

40. For an interpretation focused on the father-son relationship (which also transfers it to Kierkegaard's biography), see Poole (1993), 115–125. It

gives the whole story a sexual overtone and concludes that Solomon-Quidam-Kierkegaard has become impotent.

41. Kierkegaard explains that what he had in mind was the question of guilt: "I must get at my Antigone again. The task will be a psychological development and motivation of the presentiment of guilt. With that in mind I have been thinking of Solomon and David, of the relation of Solomon's youth to David, for no doubt both Solomon's intellect (dominant in the relationship) and his sensuousness are the results of David's greatness" (Pap. IV A 114; JP 5669). Is it the question of guilt or rather that of a debt (of course, in Danish *skyld* and *skylder*, the concepts of guilt and debt, are united)? And is the guilt not the dream itself?

42. We remember that in *Fear and Trembling*, being old is equivalent to not having or having lost faith, and that Abraham is young despite his age.

43. This recalls Solomon's dream, when he is terrified by the thought of God and the man in the "Exordium" in *Fear and Trembling*, who shuddered at the horror of thought about Abraham.

44. See, for example, how Kierkegaard uses the New Testament to describe Abraham: "And yet he was God's chosen one in whom the Lord was well pleased!" (FT 17). This refers to Mt 12, 18: "Behold my servant, whom I have chosen; my beloved, in whom my soul is well pleased," and to Lk 23, 35: "Let him save himself, if he be Christ, the chosen of God" See also "So maybe it is not your will that this should be" (FT 18), which is likely to be an allusion to Christ's words in Mt 26, 39: "Not as I will, but as though wilt."

45. It is interesting to observe a parallel between *Nebuchadnezzar* and "A Leper's Self-Contemplation" with respect to the conflict between the internal and the external and the motif of transformation. In both a reconciliation with God is achieved, but whereas in "A Leper's Self-Contemplation" it is provoked by a secret action (which turns into inwardness), namely the concoction of the salve that makes leprosy invisible, in *Nebuchadnezzar* it is an outward action — God turns a human being into a beast of the field — that brings about the change in consciousness. It is also remarkable that all three fictitious stories in Quidam's diary are related to dreaming, or sleep.

46. Another reason for which essential communication should take the form of possibility is grounded in Kierkegaard's understanding of language and its relation to reality and truth. Kierkegaard says, for example: "Immediacy is reality; language is ideality; consciousness is contradiction [*Modsigelse*]. The moment I make a statement about reality, contradiction is present, for what I say is ideality. . . . In ideality by itself there is no possibility of doubt; when I express it in language, contradiction is present, since I do not express it but produce something else" (*Johannes Climacus or De Omnibus Dubitandum Est*, PF 168). Thus, in order to avoid contradiction and "opposite sense," it is necessary to present "truth" in a subjunctive mood as a possibility.

47. In a slightly different sense, Kierkegaard speaks about the possibility of reality. In his letter to the reader, Frater Taciturnus explains the structure of the experiment in "Quidam's Diary." The dialectical religious subjectivity finds expression in ideality (possibility) after reality (precisely not before, as a kind of illusionary anticipation, but after), which is an act of freedom, and then again in terms of communication, Quidam can only express his own innermost subjectivity (*Indeslutethed*) indirectly, that is to say, as a possibility. Frater Taciturnus also says that "faith is the ideality that resolves an *esse* into its *posse* and then conversely draws the conclusion in passion. If the object of faith is the absurd, it is ideality that resolves an *esse* in a *non posse* and now wills to believe it" (SLW 440).

48. Instead of a literal interpretation, some have, of course, proposed an allegorical one. For example: "If we accept de Silentio's suggestion that the task of reading the New Testament is exemplary for reading the Old, this would mean looking beyond the literal significance of the tale of Abraham's ordeal in search of its symbolic or allegorical meaning" (Mulhall 1999, 379). This is how Abraham's story has been always read in the Christian tradition, that is, as a prefiguration of the sacrifice of Jesus.

But after all, the typological or allegorical interpretation only postpones a hermeneutical task (for how are we to understand an allegory?), but does not turn it into an existential task. Kierkegaard's version of Abraham, though not necessarily excluding this New-Testamental dimension, is somewhat more radical. It is true that we need to go beyond the literal meaning, but we can do so also by redefining the literal as a possibility and not as a factual actuality, thus making it relevant for us.

49. See Polk on substitutionary logic, 193–196.

50. We note, however, that working on the Letter to the Romans, Kierkegaard argues, "As it is written, Jacob have I loved, but Esau have I hated" (Rom 9.13). Here *misein*, "to hate," should be understood not in its principal sense (*positivus*), but in its partial, weakened (*privativus*) sense, because in Hebrew "to hate" is often used merely to say "love less." Kierkegaard here is probably following Tholuck, who suggested that it could mean *ein Minderlieben* (SKS 18, 362).

51. This should not, however, be confused with the only "true" and "real" objective story.

52. David Law observes that "there is a strong affinity between Kierkegaard and the negative theologians in their conception of God, treatment of the knowledge of God, Christology, and employment of indirect communication. On this basis, it would seem that, despite differing ontological presuppositions, it is possible to regard Kierkegaard as a negative theologian." David R. Law, *Kierkegaard as Negative Theologian* (Oxford: Clarendon Press, 1993), 210.

The problem is that Kierkegaard has a very different concept of language and communication from the medieval theologians. The other difference is

Kierkegaard's emphasis on ethical/active and subjective *versus* contemplative and metaphysical in negative theology. This is not the place to discuss how radical is the moment of negative theology in Kierkegaard, whether it does not fall back into "metaphysics of presence," although my guess is there is a truly negative element. This would be a direct consequence of Jn 1.18 or Ex 33.23, as well as a consequence of Kierkegaard's view that God cannot be known conceptually.

53. Nicolas of Cusa, *Of Learned Ignorance*, trans. G. Heron (London: Routledge, 1954), vol. 1, 8.

54. David J. Gouwens, *Kierkegaard's Dialectic of Imagination* (New York: Peter Lang, 1989), 233.

55. The role of the negative in Kierkegaard's indirect communication can be hardly overestimated also because "negative" is related to his understanding of human beings as beings-in-becoming. How indirect communication is built upon the negative (elimination) is discussed in Chapter 2.

56. Frei drew the distinction between literal meaning and historical reference, thus encouraging discussion about the importance of imagination for reading the Bible. Imagination is now often held to be one of the key modes of religiousness. There is a general confusion between imagination as a cognitive capacity for making the absent present to mind (in a Kantian sense) and romantic imagination. Sometimes imagination is also seen as a kind of Kierkegaardian second immediacy, as, for example, when Green says, "The imaginative world of the Bible can be theologically appropriated in such a way as to enable a second naiveté" (126).

57. Ferreira (1991), 57.

58. Ibid., 4.

59. Gouwens (1989), 246–247. Kierkegaard makes a distinction between religiousness A, pagan relation to God; and religiousness B, based on paradox when the believer believes in the incarnated God.

60. In terms of reader-orientated strategy, this construction allows the reader to come to the "true" stories for himself, because there is no such story in the text, but only a diffusion and a suggestion of the story.

61. He related this kind of imagination to allegorical interpretation (Pap. X 2 A 548).

Chapter 5

1. Francis Woodbury Fulford, *Søren Aabye Kierkegaard: A Study* (Cambridge: Wallis, 1911), 63.

2. One should note that Kierkegaard makes mistakes not only when he quotes or alludes to the Bible, but also, for example, when he quotes Shakespeare in German. Nevertheless, we need to take into account the special status of the Bible as the sacred book of the religion of the Word, and as an authoritative text that is meant to make the reader act.

3. Rosas, 61.

4. Hartshorne, 11.

5. "Disanalogous" use is a part of Kierkegaard's use of exception as paradigm, as discussed in *Fictitious Stories*. It occurs when he uses the Bible either in a directly inverse sense or as a negative parallel: "It is not like . . ." Some references have undergone such transformations that one wonders whether they really are references or perhaps a completely independent segment of text that just happens to resemble a biblical passage. For example, in the *Postscript* in the discussion about the confusion of knowledge and faith, probably criticizing Hegelianizing theology, Kierkegaard says, "Therefore it is also taught that faith is abolished in eternity" (CUP 30; 1 Cor 13.8–13).

The argument can be reconstructed as follows: since it has been assumed that uncertainty and passion feed faith, in an absolutely perfect world passion would be excessive (because passion is understood as a striving for the infinite), and thus faith would also be impossible or redundant. The commentators refer us to 1 Cor 13.8–13, but in this chapter of the Bible we find the contrary sense in 8, "Whether there be knowledge, it shall vanish away," and in 13, "And now abideth faith, hope, charity, these three; but the greatest of these is charity." That is, it is knowledge and not faith that is abolished. The word "taught," however, clearly suggests that it is a reference to the Bible. But does the complete reversal of the sense still allow us to recognize it as such? On the other hand, the very presence of an inverted quotation is interesting because it means that in the course of a philosophical-theological discussion, Kierkegaard sometimes attributes the opposite sense to the Bible. In turn, this indicates that Kierkegaard's attitude to the Bible is very complex and far from either straightforward devotion or disrespect.

6. A good example of how even insignificant mistakes can inform us of certain aspects of Kierkegaard's authorship relates to the notorious question of pseudonyms. In *Stages on Life's Way*, Kierkegaard says, "Or did not the wise virgins stay awake longer than the foolish ones?" (SLW 140; Mt 25.1–13). Actually they did not: in the biblical story, all the virgins "slumbered and slept" and then awoke together, but the foolish ones did not have oil for their lamps. This mistake is repeated later in the text: "If I only had to stay awake like one of the bridesmaids, only keep my lamp lit" (SLW 254; Mt 25.1). This is, as noted, wrong—all the virgins slept, and then arose.

This mistake is not significant in the sense that it changes or distorts the meaning, indeed one could say that the "mistake" is simply due to a kind of metaphorical extension. What makes it significant is the fact that in the first case, the mistake is made by the Married Man; in the second instance by Quidam. Does this not suggest that the mistake is made by the author of both, particularly because it is made even by Kierkegaard in one of his upbuilding discourses?

We should note, however, that this particular mistake about virgins seems to be a popular mistake made by many people, so in this case one can probably speak about a "secondary" mistake brought about by reliance on the tradition (though this is curious in its turn, given that Kierkegaard usually emphasizes the need to read the primary sources). There are several places where Kierkegaard does get the same quotation right. However, even if we assume that it is a secondary mistake, it is nevertheless interesting from a hermeneutical perspective. It illuminates the author's relation to the source text and its reception, and also relates several of Kierkegaard's "sub-authors" to one another. The most remarkable thing about it is that it betrays a certain identity of "the" author through the continuity of the "mistake" across pseudonymous and signed works.

7. For an analysis, see, for example, George W. Savran, *Telling and Retelling: Quotation in Biblical Narrative* (Bloomington: Indiana University Press, 1988).

8. J. Carpzov, *A Defense of the Hebrew Bible*, trans. M. Marcus (London: Bernarg Lintot, 1729), 112.

9. For an overview see Stanley, 18–20.

10. K. Stedahl, *The School of St. Matthew*, ASNU 20 (Copenhagen: Munksgaard, 1954), 194–201.

11. Blaise Pascal, *The Provincial Letters*, trans. A. J. Krailsheimer (London: Penguin Books 1967), 22.

12. The best example of such an approach in nineteenth century Denmark is Gruntvig (see Chapter 3). It seems that there was no specific policy in the Danish Church with respect to biblical quotations.

13. There are many more examples to illustrate each of the "types" of use. Unfortunately it was not possible to include them due to the restrictions on this volume. Of course, "types" are relative; many of the examples could be analyzed from several different perspectives. Because of the rather technical nature of this chapter I will use Danish more extensively than elsewhere.

14. In an unpublished article, H. Politis has discussed the interesting fact that sometimes one finds exact quotations (biblical or other) in the journals, while the same quotation is not exact in the published books.

15. B. R. Dewey, "Kierkegaard and the Blue Testament," *Harvard Theological Review* 60 (1967): 391–409 (391). There is a dispute about the dating of the markings: P. A. Heiberg and V. Kuhr assert that they date from the period 1847–1848; Dewey argues that they are likely to have been made earlier.

16. Dewey, 394.

17. Among the courses he attended at the University of Copenhagen were Professor H. N. Clausen's lectures on the synoptic gospels (1832–1833), Clausen's 1833–1834 winter term lectures on dogmatics (Kierkegaard took many notes on these, see Pap. I C 19), and, in summer

1834, E. C. Scharling's lectures on the two Epistles to the Corinthians. For a detailed description of the many courses Kierkegaard attended, see W. von Kloeden, "Biblestudy," *Kierkegaardiana* 1 (1978): 16–39.

18. Dewey, 395.

19. Kierkegaard casts some doubt on the number of days (forty) traditionally assigned to Jesus' temptation in the wilderness in Lk 4. He reconstructs the Lukan account (Lk 4.1–3) as follows. First, Jesus was led by the Spirit for forty days in the wilderness without food; no temptations occurred during this period. When the forty days of fasting were *completed*, Jesus was hungry, and at this point the devil began to tempt him ("If you are the Son of God, command this stone to become bread," etc.). In the margin near Lk 4.2, Kierkegaard comments, "Thus the temptation did not last forty days at all; for 'he was hungry' only when the forty were over" (Pap. VIII 2 C 3, 27).

20. Another good example from the same discourse is: "When love lives in the heart, the eye is shut and does not discover the open act of sin, to say nothing of the concealed act, 'for the one who winks his eye has evil in mind' (Proverbs), but the one who understands the wink of eye is not pure" (EUD 60) ("den, der vinker med øiet, har Ondt i Sinde," Ordsprog (SKS 5, 70). Kierkegaard here refers his reader to *Proverbs* but does not give an exact reference. According to commentators, this can refer to two possible places, Prv 10.10, "He that winketh with the eye causeth sorrow: but a prating fool shall fall"; or Prv 6.14, where it is said of the one who blinks his eye, "Forwardness is in his heart, he devises mischief continually; he soweth discord." Kierkegaard makes an insignificant substitution, using *vinker* instead of the original *blinker*, probably because later he uses *vink* as a noun.

21. "Om Du nogensinde bliver Menneske mere, istand til at frigjøre Dig i Isolationens Enkelthed, eller Du beholder et Minde om, at Du er et Lem paa et større Legeme" (SKS 4, 27).

22. At the same time we note: "Humor is always a revocation (of existence into the eternal by recollection backward, of adulthood to childhood, etc., see above), it is the backward perspective; Christianity is the direction forward, to becoming a Christian and becoming that by continuing to be that" (CUP 602).

23. We have already touched upon the semantics of listening/hearing in relation to Abraham. Later we will also draw attention to reading aloud as appropriation and the relation between hearing and obedience; see Chapter 6.

24. Polk (150) suggests that such harmonization can only be done by either a "precritical" or "postcritical" exegete:

> For if Kierkegaard's harmonization of traditions seems naive, how much more his citation of "the apostle Paul" in the first place: "All of God's creation is good if it is received with thankfulness" (1 Tm 4.4). What makes the move so dubious to critical eyes is that the passage is not "authentic" Paul by historical reckoning, but *deutero*-Pauline.

Kierkegaard not only blurs the sharp lines separating Pauline Christianity from the Jewish Christianity of "James" (not to mention the sectarian-inclined Johanine Christianity); he even mixes the former with its hierarchically stratified offshoot of more than a half-century later.

We need to be clear about this: Kierkegaard's move is not one any form-, tradition-, or redaction-critic could make *per se*. It is a move only a "precritical" or "postcritical" exegete would make, or a historical critic who forgets the rules of his game.

25. Such as in the elaborate constructions of Rom 3.10–18 and 2 Cor 6.16–18.

26. Stanley, 256.

27. There are, of course, numerous examples of simpler splicing. In *Philosophical Fragments* we read: "For it is indeed less terrifying to fall upon one's face while the mountains tremble at the god's voice than to sit with him as his equal, and yet the god's concern is precisely to sit this way"(PF 35): "thi det er mindre forfaerdeligt, at falde paa sit Ansigt, medens Bjerge skjaelve for Gudens stemme, end at sidde hos ham som hos sin Lige, og dog er dette jo Gudens Bekymring netop at sidde saaledes" (SKS 4, 240).

In fact, the mount quaked not because of the voice of God, but because the Lord descended upon it in fire (Ex 19.18). The voice comes in the next line, first the loud trumpet, then Moses, and finally God's voice. This kind of splicing is not, however, as radical as the incorporation of one book of the Bible into another, and it could be a natural outcome of quoting by heart.

28. One could wonder whether this is not an allusion to the title *Philosophical Fragments/Filosofiske Smuler.*

29. One could also note that many of the alterations in the biblical quotations are grammatical adaptations (alterations in person, number, tense, mood, preposition, etc.). Their function is merely to create a smoother transition from the host text to the quote. However, Danish is an analytical language, and even such small parts of speech as prepositions play a very important structural role and may involve significant points of meaning. Kierkegaard often plays with the tiny details of language. For example in *The Moment,* he plays with prepositions and makes an important difference between *et billede paa livet* and *et billede af livet*.

30. There are many cases of resonance and very close interactions, which create fine metaphorical laceworks. A good example is found in *Either/Or* I, pages 28 and 41. The connection between the two passages becomes apparent only in relation to Ex 12 and 14. "My life achievement amounts to nothing at all, a mood, a single color. My achievement resembles the painting by that artist who was supposed to paint the Israelites' crossing of the Red Sea, and to that end painted the entire wall red and explained that the Israelites walked across and that the Egyptians were drowned" (E/O I 28; Ex 14.21–31).

The author speaks about color and immediately connects it to the Red Sea, and then it is further connected to blood on page 41: "My misfortune is this: an angel of death always walks at my side, and it is not the doors of the chosen ones that I sprinkle with blood as a sign that he is to pass by—no, it is precisely their doors that he enters—for only recollection's love is happy" (E/O I 41, Ex 12. 23). See further in Ex 12.23: "For the Lord will pass through to smite the Egyptians; and when he seeth the blood upon the lintel, and on the two side posts, the Lord will pass over the door, and will not suffer the destroyer to come in unto your houses to smite you."

31. For example, one of the features of the use of biblical quotations in *Philosophical Fragments* is what we could call a cluster of quotations. There are three clusters with ten or more quotations on the same page: see PF 32–33/SKS 4, 239 (as many as sixteen references), and PF 56–57/SKS 4, 259. Of course, a page is an accidental unit, but it does help to imagine how concentrated the use is in some parts of the text. In general there is a tendency to have several quotations in one place (for example, there are five on PF 32/SKS 4, 238; seven on PF 58/SKS 4, 260; and so on; otherwise on pages immediately before and after). The quotations seem to invoke or provoke each other. In some cases one can speak of a certain synonymity.

We note a similarity to a rhetorical figure in the rabbinical tradition known as *charaz*, which means to string pearls in order to make a necklace. The practice was taken up by St. Paul, for example in Rom 10.19–21; see also "concatenation," unknown to the Jewish sources but introduced by Philon of Alexandria, as used by St. Paul in Rom 3.10–18.

32. See for example "Psalms 10.14. The Vulgate translated this: *tibi* (namely *Deo*) *derelictus pauper*. Scriver (pt. 1, p. 35) explains this as follows: that the world chose all the distinguished, powerful, etc.—thus there was nobody left for God but the poor and the forsaken. Our translation translates it differently: the poor entrusts himself to You" (in the English translation: "The poor committeth himself unto thee") (Pap. X 4 A 197; JP 2325).

33. The English Jb 13.15 is: "Though he slay me, yet will I trust in him," but the Danish Old Testament 1740 did have "hope": "See, vil han slaae mig ihiel, skulde jeg [dog] ikke haabe?"

34. Another example of attention to such subtle differences is the following entry in his journals: "Thomas a Kempis (bk. IV, ch 6) quotes Ezekiel 33.16 this way: None of his sins shall remember him [*skal komme ham ihu*]. Usually it reads differently: None of his sins shall be remembered against him [*skal huskes ham*]. It would be remarkable if the first translation is correct, for it is a far stronger expression of the forgiveness of sins" (Pap. A 282, p. 207; JP 4787).

35. Kloeden, 16–39.

36. An example of a serious concern with text criticism and the possibilities of manipulation is the following remark in *Stages on Life's Way:* "This in

turn is like a well-known passage in the book of Genesis, *where it says that Esau kissed Jacob,* and the learned Jews who did not credit Esau with this mentality but did not dare to change the consonants, either, merely inserted other dots, *so that it read: he bit him*" (SLW 97; Gn 33.4, my emphasis).

37. SKS K 17, 284–285.

38. Of course Kierkegaard was not only influenced by Luther, but also criticized him on more than one occasion. For example, in Pap. X 1 A 419; JP 2495, he criticized Luther's translation of 2 Thes 3. 2: "Faith is not everyone's business" (in standard English, "For all men have not faith"), saying that Luther's translation made faith into some sort geniality. "Faith is thereby superficially defined as a kind of genius, a disposition, a talent." This point was important for Kierkegaard, for whom everybody was equally capable of having a passionate and personal relationship with God.

39. Another case can be found in SKS 5, 63. The commentary tells us that it is probably Kierkegaard's own translation. The 1740 Old Testament says: "Ligesom en Sneebolt paa Hostens Dag, er et trofast Bud for dem, som sendte ham; thi han vederqvaeker sine Herrers Siel" (Prv 25.13).

40. "Han [den skalkagtige] nedslaaer sit Ansigt, og lader som han var doed, og hvor han ikke kiendes, skal han forraske dig." Or, in the same discourse: "When stinginess lives in the heart, when one gives one eye and looks with seven to see what one obtains in return, one readily discovers the multiplicity of sin" (EUD 61), "naar man giver med eet øie og med syv øine seer efter, hvad man har faaet igjen" (SKS 5, 70; Sir 20.14). Here the author again relies on Luther's translation of Sir 20.14.

41. It needs to be remarked that I have not performed a thorough comparison of the use of biblical quotations in the pseudonymous and signed works, so the evidence should be treated as suggestive, not conclusive.

42. Heb 4.15: "For we have not a high priest which cannot be touched with the feeling of our infirmities; but was in all points tempted like as we are, yet without sin."

43. For example, Kierkegaard quotes "those who are past feeling" (CA 94; Eph 4.19) in Greek, changing the sentence slightly. In a very interesting footnote Kierkegaard says: "By this I by no means say that evil is merely negative, *das Aufzuhebende* [that which is to be annulled]; on the contrary, that God knows nothing of evil, that he neither can nor will know of it, is the absolute punishment of evil. In this sense the preposition *apo* [away from] is used in the New Testament to signify removal from God or, if I dare put it in this way, God's ignoring of evil . . . Here I shall quote a passage from Scripture, II Thessalonians 1.9, where it is said of those who do not know God and do not obey the gospel [here Kierkegaard quotes in Greek: 'They shall suffer the punishment of eternal destruction and exclusion from the presence of the Lord and from the glory of his might']" (CA 112). It is worthy of note that in the center of this particular reading is a preposition.

44. Remarkably, in *Concluding Unscientific Postscript* Johannes Climacus quotes Vigilius Haufniensis. The biblical quotation remains embedded in the quotation from the *Concept of Anxiety*. "When a person has prostituted himself by speaking in this way about enthusiasm and love, has betrayed his obtuseness, which is not, however, a matter of understanding, since the cause of it is just that the understanding has become too large, in the same sense as the cause of liver disease is that the liver has become too large, and therefore, as another author has remarked, 'It is the dumbness that salt takes on when it loses its strength'—then one phenomenon still remains, and that is Christianity" (CUP 229). In Kierkegaard's works there are several instances of such double quoting or second-hand quoting, when the quotation is attributed to the author who himself has quoted and not to the original source. We note also that Vigilius Haufniensis is quoted freely.

45. Jurgis Baltrusaitis, *Anamorphic Art*, trans. W. J. Strachan (New York: Abrams, 1977), 1.

Chapter 6

1. Cf. PV, his journals, etc.

2. Cf. Longinus, whose *Essay on the Sublime* "is not only a text making abundant use of quotation but also a metadiscourse on quotation. As such, it questions the subsidiary status of quotation and the relationship between the quoted text and the text quoting in order to address the notion of authority." Claudette Sartiliot, *Citation and Modernity* (Norman: University of Oklahoma Press, 1993), 6.

3. On the other hand, one can note that the claim that *Philosophical Fragments* is a hypothetical project fits in the discussion about the importance of subjunctive mode and representation in the form of possibility; see Chapter 4.

4. At the same time the dialogues provide us with a superb example of a technique that, in my opinion, occupies a central place in Kierkegaard's mode of writing. This rhetorical strategy can be called a kind of self-mortification that aims at self-protection. To put it very briefly, Kierkegaard's strategy comes down to this: whatever criticism may be made, it has been already preempted by the author himself. The most obvious means of achieving this is precisely the creation of imagined enemies or accusers (such as the Probable Accuser in the dialogues in *Philosophical Fragments*). Kierkegaard creates a whole army of marionette enemies with their marionette weapons, that is to say, arguments against him, and then shoots them down one by one.

In his response to these imagined critiques, he attempts to invalidate the contra-arguments, sometimes simply by ridiculing them, other times by exposing them to a typical Socratic interrogation or overruling the arguments (cf. Bakhtin, double-voiced discourse). This creates an illusion of thorough control and mastery over all his text, and of complete transparency: nothing has been left out, everything has been thought about. Thus an omnipresence of the absent Author is created.

5. Minnis, 10. We will see later that in this light, Kierkegaard's famous claim that he is an author without authority could also be understood to mean that he is without authority in the sense that he is deprived of "authenticity" (note—not originality) of creation, since he is "copying" the Bible.

6. Some of these worries may, of course, be interpreted as irony with respect to the rationalistic inquiry.

7. This refers not only to the presence of the many references, but also to the way in which they are employed. For example, when Climacus says: "If I pleaded with him to change his resolution, to manifest himself in some other way, to spare himself, then he would look at me and say: Man, what have you to do with me; go away, for you are of Satan, even if you yourself do not understand it!" (PF 33).

It is interesting to note that Climacus presents this situation played by "I" hypothetically, although it actually happened in very much the same terms to Peter (even if in *Philosophical Fragments* there is, as it were, more emphasis on appearance, on the form of revelation, rather than on the fate of the incarnated God). See Mt 16.23: "But he turned and said unto Peter, Get thee behind me, Satan: thou art an offense unto me: for thou savorest not the things that be of God, but those that be of men." The first half of Climacus's imagined response is also a real reference: "Jesus said unto her, Woman, what have I to do with thee?" (Jn 2.4).

8. We have discussed Kierkegaard's understanding of authority of the author in Chapter 2.

9. We note, of course, that Climacus chooses to ignore the solution presented by his age, namely, that it was a human creation, a creation of the whole human race, as suggested by the mythological school.

10. Notice a smooth transition from hermeneutical issues to ontological ones, a typical Kierkegaardian feature and one of the aspects that makes Kierkegaard so contemporary.

11. It is, of course, very appropriate of him to hold this view when he himself is a pseudonym.

12. What he means by "poem" here is the biblical element in *Philosophical Fragments*, that is, *Philosophical Fragments* inasmuch as the book echoes and repeats the Bible.

13. S. Mulhall, "God's Plagiarist: 'The Philosophical Fragments' of Johannes Climacus," *Philosophical Investigations* 22, no. 1 (1999): 1–34 (7).

14. Analogously, the only thing we have but do not own is God's Word, as a gift of love.

15. Mulhall (1999), 27.

16. In Chapter 5 we have already mentioned that sometimes Kierkegaard puts biblical sayings in a chain as well, by a kind of third-hand attribution.

For example, in *Stages on Life's Way:* "Hamlet says he has conceived his grandiose plan of being the avenger to whom vengeance belongs" (SLW 453). Even though it is true that Shakespeare puts these words in the mouth of Hamlet, their origin nevertheless is in the Bible, Dt 32.35, Rom 12.19, Heb 10.30. This could hardly have escaped Kierkegaard's attentive reading of the Bible, so it is likely to be a conscious choice.

17. Mulhall (1999), 31.

18. This remark can be useful for the question of pseudonyms.

19. See, for example, Mulhall (1999) and Poole.

20. He continues: "And you have not put [the words] in the mouth of the one speaking, and not even put [them] into the speaker's mouth" (it is worth noticing the distinction between the words of an author and the words an author puts in the speaker's mouth).

21. I will concentrate mainly on reduplication (*Reduplikation*), but some points apply to redoubling (*Fordoblelse*) as well. Reduplication is a part of redoubling: "While *redoubling* is a perfection for ever achieved in the Divine, which thus for ever is itself 'infinitely' by denying itself 'finitely,' *reduplication* seems to be a task that we perform in time: for it is becoming what we know or truly say, to the best of our ability, as we strive to accomplish or approximate it." Martin Andic, "Love's Redoubling and the Eternal Like for Like," in *International Kierkegaard Commentary*, vol. 16, *Works of Love*, ed. Robert L. Perkins (Macon, Ga.: Mercer University Press, 1999), 9–37 (37).

22. We have already drawn attention to this feature in relation to fictitious stories and some of the deviations.

23. For example, Kierkegaard has often suggested that if one is willing to understand the Bible, the meaning is "obvious," it somehow presents itself. We should recall, however, that the will in question is not a volition, but a broadened concept of will that includes imagination and "coming forth."

24. In this respect one could perhaps read differently Wittgenstein's claim in the penultimate section of the *Tractatus:* "My prepositions are elucidatory in the following way: anyone who understands me eventually recognizes them as nonsensical, when he has used them—as steps—to climb up beyond them. (He must, so to speak, throw away the ladder after he has climbed up it)" (6.45). One could understand non-sense as an expression of a negativity of production that does not produce any sense, but reproduces something already familiar to the reader, thus Wittgenstein's project is also a tautological project.

25. Stanley Cavell, *Themes out of School* (San Francisco: North Point Press, 1984), 225.

26. It is important to remember that, as has been shown, Kierkegaard inscribes the Bible not through transcription, that is to say, direct, unreflected transmission, but by subjunctive diffusion and deviations.

27. For example, St. Thomas, answering question I 13, article 11 "Whether this name, HE WHO IS, is the most proper name of God?"—says that since

the existence of God is his essence itself, it is also his name. He quotes Damascene: "He who is, is the principal of all names applied to God; for comprehending all in itself, it contains existence itself as an infinite and indeterminate sea of substance" (St. Thomas Aquinas, *The "Summa Theologica,"* trans. Fathers of the English Dominican province [London: Washbourne, 1911]).

28. "Predicate-less Being. Jehova says: I am who *I* am; I am. This is the supreme being. But *to be* in this way is too exalted for us human beings, much too earnest [*alvorligt*]. Therefore we must try to become something; to be *something* is easier. . . . Most men, or at least almost everyone, would die of anxiety about himself [*for sig selv*] if his being should be—a tautology; they are more anxious about this kind of being and about themselves than about seeing themselves. So their situation is mitigated. The alleviation might be, for example, I am Chancellor, Knight of Denmark, member of the Cavalry Purchasing Commission, Alderman, Director of the Club. In a deeper sense all this is—diversion. But to repeat, man is probably not able to bear true earnestness . . . But no doubt all these numerous predicates are actually diversions, distractions, which prevent a man from the deepest impression of this *to be*" (Pap. XI 1 A 284; JP 200).

29. See Pap. III B 177; Pap. III B 179.

30. Pap. IV C 62.

31. Pap. X 4 A480.

32. See, for example, what Kierkegaard says about love in *Works of Love:* "What love does, that it is; what it is, that it does" (WL 280).

33. Gadamer (1999), 114.

34. Clement of Alexandria, "Stromates" V, 12, 78, 3, in *Ante-Nicene Fathers,* vol. 2 (Grand Rapids: Eerdmans Publishing Co., 1983), 463.

35. Deleuze, 271.

36. Deleuze has suggested that "Difference itself is therefore between two repetitions: between the superficial repetition of the identical and instantaneous external elements that it contracts, and the profound repetition of the internal totalities of an always variable past, of which it is the most contracted level" (Deleuze, 287).

37. As we will see later, this possibility created through the impossible relates repetition to gift. Derrida says that gift can "be" through the impossible.

38. Frye comments on this forward-orientated remembering: "Kierkegaard's very brief but extraordinarily suggestive book *Repetition* is the only study I know of the psychological contrast between a past-directed causality and a future-directed typology. The mere attempt to repeat a past experience will lead only to disillusionment, but there is another kind of repetition which is the Christian antithesis (or complement) of Platonic recollection, and which finds its focus in the Biblical promise: 'Behold, I make all things new' (Rv 21.5). Kierkegaard's 'repetition' is certainly derived from, and to my mind identifiable with, the forward-moving typological

thinking of the Bible." Northrop Frye, *The Great Code: The Bible in Literature* (London: Routledge and Kegan Paul, 1982), 82.

39. Speaking about "concrete," we should bear in mind its etymological sense: *con-cresco*, "to grow together (with oneself)." We notice how tautology meets repetition here. While "I AM WHO I AM" applies to God, the perfection of our being consists in becoming who we are. Interestingly "recollection," although it seems to be opposed to Kierkegaard's understanding of "repetition," also could mean gathering oneself together.

40. "Er der da ikke en Gjentagelse? Fik jeg ikke Alt dobbelt? Fik jeg ikke mig selv igjen, netop saaledes, at jeg dobbelt maatte fole Betydningen deraf" (SKS 4, 87).

41. We emphasize "internal," private quoting, not a public manifestation, which would moreover have the pretence of authority. This is one of the features that set quoting the Bible apart from other quoting. On the other hand, speaking about repetition of inwardness, Kierkegaard says: "There is inwardness when what is said belongs to the recipient as if it were his own" (CUP 260).

42. Tautology is, of course, a natural element of quotation, because one of its functions is to make an affirmation by means of reduplication, that is to say, to affirm that which has already found a "perfect" expression (when there is nothing to add and nothing to subtract). Speaking about quoting Job's words for himself and as his own, the young man exclaims in *Repetition*: "I cannot do more, for who has such eloquence as Job, who is able to improve upon anything he said" (R 205).

43. Deleuze, 291.

44. Tautology is a perfect expression of reduplication; in fact, in the philosophical vocabulary it is often used synonymously.

45. For the "fat of rams" reference, see 1 Sm 15.22.

46. See also reading as writing in *Repetition*: "Have you really read Job? Read him, read him again and again. I do not even have the heart to write one single outcry from him in a letter to you, even though I find my joy in transcribing over and over everything he has said, sometimes in Danish script and sometimes in Latin script, sometimes in one format and sometimes in another. Every transcription of this kind is laid upon my sick heart as a God's hand-plaster" (R 204).

47. Especially important is, of course, reading the Bible aloud. For example, in *Repetition* the young man stands upright and reads in a loud voice so that Job's words will become his (R 205).

48. In Danish: *at lyde*, "to sound" or "to listen," or, in an archaic use, "to strain one's mind in order to understand something"; and *ad-lyde*, "to obey." Interestingly, the word for belonging also enters into the paradigm of hearing, *at tilhøre* (Kierkegaard often addresses his reader as *tilhører*, listener or perhaps follower).

The proximity exists also in German: *horchen*, "to listen"; *gehorchen*, "to obey." And in Lithuanian: *klausyti*, "to listen"; and *paklusti*, "to obey." And in Latin: *ob-oedio*, "to hearken/listen," "to be obedient."

49. Although at the same time he is fully conscious of the next step: "But be ye doers of the word, and not hearers only, deceiving your own selves." At the same time, as we have already said, for Kierkegaard it is not really a next step, because any "hearing" that is not reduplicated as action is not even a hearing (Jas 1.22).

50. Mulhall (1999), 7. 51. It is what we already have, not what we have taken, which would be theft. However, the play between "gift" and "theft" can be retained: by not taking God's Word as a gift, we steal from ourselves.

51. What we already "have," not what we have taken, which would be a theft. However, the play between gift and theft can be retained: by not taking God's Word as a gift, we steal from ourselves.

52. For example, see a recent publication of the collection of the articles *The Logic of the Gift: Toward an Ethic of Generosity*, ed. Alan D. Schrift (London: Routledge, 1997). The current discussion rediscovers the ancient theological thought of gift and grace, like Augustine's "Deus est qui Deum dat" (God is He Who gives God) in the modern context.

53. Marcel Mauss, *The Gift: The Form and Reason for Exchange in Archaic Society*, trans. W. D. Halls (London: Routledge, 1990), 13.

54. Ibid., 17.

55. Yet another likely source is Husserl, with his concept of *Gegebenheit* in *Logical Investigations*. However, there is a heated discussion between Marion, Ricoeur, and Derrida as to whether its relation to gift is merely an equivocal one.

56. Derrida's critique of Heidegger is that this is a Greek gift and that there is no "dissemination without return."

57. "Non pas impossible mais l'impossible," Jacques Derrida, *Given Time, I: Counterfeit Money*, trans. P. Kamuf (Chicago: University of Chicago Press, 1991), 19. We should note, however, that this does not mean that there is no gift. As Derrida says himself: "So the gift does not exist and appear as such; it is impossible for the gift to exist and appear as such. But I never concluded that there is no gift. I went on to say that if there is a gift, through this impossibility, it must be the experience of this impossibility, and it should appear as impossible" (in J. D. Caputo and M. J. Scanlon, eds., *God, the Gift, and Postmodernism* [Bloomington: Indiana University Press, 1999], 59).

58. Caputo (1997), 163.

59. Ibid.

60. Jacques Derrida, *Given Time* (1991), 21.

61. In *Philosophical Fragments*, Kierkegaard speaks about a moment that has the peculiar nature that it is both quintessentially temporal as a moment

is, but at the same time full of the eternal (see, for example: "The moment is not properly an atom of time but an atom of eternity," CA 88). The author proceeds by saying that this moment requires a special name, and suggests "let us name it": "Et saadant ïeblik maa dog have et saerligt Navn, lade os kalde det: *Tidens Fylde*" (SKS 4, 226), "Let us call it: the *fullness of time*" (PF 18).

This corresponds to Gal 4.4: "But when the fullness of time was come, God sent forth his son, made of a woman, made under the law," where it is not a metaphor to express a significant moment, but a reference to a very particular event. This connects also to what we have said about the collapse of the hypothetical nature of *Philosophical Fragments*.

62. Deleuze, 1. We have already drawn attention to the connection between repetition and gift through "impossibility," which is the condition of their "being there for us."

63. This does not mean that Kierkegaard did not think about "impossible" in this context; on the contrary, as his discussion of forgiveness (which I think is in many ways parallel to gift) shows, he was very close to Derrida in stressing gift or forgiveness as impossible. But then he made a second movement—transformation in faith and by faith, which makes the impossible possible: "It is proclaimed that there is forgiveness of sins, but one says, 'It is impossible' . . . Oh, blessed refreshment, that the one who was brought close to despair because it was impossible now believes it, blessedly believes it, but in his soul's wonder continues to say, 'It is impossible!'" (CA 107).

64. Jb 1.21: "And said, Naked came I out of my mother's womb, and naked shall I return thither: the Lord gave, and the Lord hath taken away; blessed be the name of the Lord."

65. Caputo (1997), 160.

66. Analogously: "Repetition is never so perfect in time as in eternity, which is the true repetition" (R 221).

67. Except one debt—the debt of loving another: "The equality in love, which lasts and is the only thing that lasts, the equality that does not allow any human being to be another's debtor, except, as Paul says, in the one debt, the debt of loving one another" (EUD 158; Rom 13.8). But this debt is so peculiar that it could be itself called a gift.

68. Ferreira points to the mistake of assuming (1) that because faith is not the result of unconditioned human activity it cannot require human activity; (2) that its character as "gift" is exclusive of its involving any describable human activity (Ferreira, 53).

69. We note the stress on the ethical action: Kierkegaard emphasizes that if a person is not able to thank the one he sees, how can he be able truly to thank God, whom he does not see.

70. Interestingly, Prickett relates the ambiguity of appropriation to the Bible: "Indeed it will be our argument that the primeval tension between theft and creative acquisition is not an accident of the written word, but in

some way endemic to it. Genesis begins with the Fall and ends with the story of Jacob. At some very deep level that tension may actually be essential to our idea of what constitutes a book, as if the original sin of Eden were not merely part of the foundation myth of Western civilisation, but was also somehow encapsulated, even mirrored, within the form by which that myth has been transmitted" (Prickett, 34).

71. This is explicitly expressed through deviations.

72. In *The Concept of Irony,* Kierkegaard suggests that echo is crucial for indirect communication: "With Socrates, rejoinder was not an immediate unity with what had been said, was not a flowing out but a continual flowing back, and what one misses in Xenophon is an ear for the infinitely resonating reverse echoing of the rejoinder in the personality (for, as a rule, the rejoinder is straightforward transmission of thought by way of sound) (CI 18).

73. Which was, of course, partly initiated by the division from the time of Reformation between a traditional account of divine agency and the affirmation of free, active creatures.

74. Jerome B. Schneewind, *The Invention of Autonomy: A History of Modern Moral Philosophy* (Cambridge: Cambridge University Press, 1998), 486.

75. For the "as Scripture speaks" reference, see Rom 7.3; Rom 6.20; 1 Cor 9.21.

76. This contains the reference to 1 Cor 3.1-2: "And I, brethren, could not speak unto you as unto spiritual, but as to carnal, even as unto babes of Christ. I have fed you with milk, and not with meat: for hitherto ye were not able to bear it, neither yet now are ye able."

77. "The inwardness and the unutterable sighs of prayer (Romans 8.26) are incommensurable with the muscular" (CUP 91).

Bibliography

Works by Kierkegaard

Journals and Papers, ed. and trans. Howard V. Hong and Edna H. Hong, assisted by Gregor Malantschuk, 7 vols. Bloomington: Indiana University Press, 1967–1978.

Kierkegaard's Writings, ed. and trans. Howard V. Hong and Edna H. Hong (except vol. 1, ed. and trans. Julia Watkins; vol. 8, ed. and trans. Reidar Thomte in collaboration with Albert B. Anderson; vol. 9, ed. and trans. Todd W. Nichol; vol. 26, prepared by Nathaniel J. Hong, Kathryn Hong, and Regine Prenzel-Guthrie), 26 vols. Princeton: Princeton University Press, 1978–2000.

Vol. 1, *Early Polemical Writings: From the Papers of One Still Living; Articles from Student Days; The Battle between the Old and the New Cellars* (1990).

Vol. 2, *The Concept of Irony; Shelling Lecture Notes* (1989).

Vol. 3, *Either/Or I* (1987).

Vol. 4, *Either/Or II* (1987).

Vol. 5, *Eighteen Upbuilding Discourses* (1990).

Vol. 6, *Fear and Trembling; Repetition* (1983).

Vol. 7, *Philosophical Fragments; Johannes Climacus* (1985).

Vol. 8, *The Concept of Anxiety* (1980).

Vol. 9, *Prefaces* (1997).

Vol. 10, *Three Discourses on Imagined Occasions* (1993).

Vol. 11, *Stages on Life's Way* (1988).

Vol. 12, *Concluding Unscientific Postscript* (2 vols., 1992).

Vol. 13, *The Corsair Affair* (1982).

Vol. 14, *Two Ages* (1978).
Vol. 15, *Upbuilding Discourse in Various Spirits* (1993).
Vol. 16, *Works of Love* (1995).
Vol. 17, *Christian Discourses; Crisis (and a Crisis) in the Life of an Actress* (1997).
Vol. 18, *Without Authority; The Lily in the Field and the Bird of the Air; Two Ethical-Religious Essays; Three Discourses at the Communion on Fridays; An Upbuilding Discourse; Two Discourses at the Communion on Fridays* (1997).
Vol. 19, *The Sickness unto Death* (1980).
Vol. 20, *Practice in Christianity* (1991).
Vol. 21, *For Self-Examination; Judge for Yourself* (1990).
Vol. 22, *The Point of View: The Point of View for My Work as an Author; Armed Neutrality; On My Work as an Author* (1998).
Vol. 23, *The Moment and Late Writings; Articles from Faedrelandet; The Moment; This Must Be Said, So Let It Be Said; Christ's Judgment on Official Christianity; The Changelessness of God* (1998).
Vol. 24, *The Book on Adler* (1998).
Vol. 25, *Kierkegaard: Letters and Documents* (1978).
Vol. 26, *Cumulative Index* (2000).

Samlede Vaerker, ed. A. B. Drachmann, J. L. Heiberg, and H. O. Lange, 20 vols., 3d ed. Copenhagen: Gyldendalske Boghandel, 1962.

Søren Kierkegaards Papirer, ed. P. A. Heiberg, V. Kuhr, and E. Torsting, 16 vols. in 25 tomes; 2d ed., ed. N. Thulstrup, with an index by N. J. Cappelørn. Copenhagen: Gyldendal, 1967–1978.

Søren Kierkegaards Skrifter, ed. N. J. Cappelørn, J. Garff, J. Kondrup, A. McKinnon, F. H. Mortensen. Copenhagen: Gad, 1997–2001. SKS1-SKS6, SKS 17-18, K1-K6, K17-K18.

Works on Kierkegaard

Adorno, Theodor W. *Kierkegaard's Construction of the Aesthetic,* trans. R. Hullot-Kentor. Minneapolis: University of Minnesota Press, 1989.

Agacinski, Sylviane. *Aparté: Conceptions and Death of Søren Kierkegaard,* trans. K. Newmark. Tallahassee: Florida State University Press, 1988.

Anderson, B. "Kierkegaard's Despair as a Religious Author," *International Journal for Philosophy of Religion* 4 (1973): 241–254.

Andic, M. "Love's Redoubling and the Eternal Like for Like," in *International Kierkegaard Commentary,* vol. 16, *Works of Love,* ed. Robert L. Perkins. Macon, Ga.: Mercer University Press, 1999.

Bigelow, Patrick. *Kierkegaard and the Problem of Writing.* Tallahassee: Florida State University Press, 1987.

———. *The Conning, the Cunning of Being: Being a Kierkegaardian Demonstration of the Postmodern Implosion of Metaphysical Sense in Aristotle and the Early Heidegger.* Tallahassee: Florida State University Press, 1990.

Bloom, Harold, ed. *Søren Kierkegaard*. New York: Chelsea House Publications, 1989.

Cappelørn, N. J. "Kierkegaards eget 'synspunkt": "At leve forlaens men forstå baglaens," *Studier Teologi* 31 (1973): 45–53.

Come, Arnold B. *Kierkegaard as Theologian: Recovering Myself*. Montreal: McGill-Queen's University Press, 1997.

Conant, J. "The Anxieties of Reason: Kierkegaard, Wittgenstein, and Nonsense," in *Pursuits of Reason: Essays in Honor of Stanley Cavell*, ed. T. Cohen, P. Guyer, and H. Putnam. Lubbock: Texas University Press, 1993.

Deuser, H., and N. J. Cappelørn. "Perspectives in Kierkegaard Research," in *Kierkegaard Studies, Yearbook 1996*, ed. N. J. Cappelørn and H. Deuser. Berlin: Walter de Gruyter, 1996.

Dewey, B. R. "Kierkegaard and the Blue Testament,"*Harvard Theological Review* 60 (1967): 391–409.

Diem, Hermann. *Kierkegaard's Dialectic of Existence*, trans. H. Knight. Edinburgh: Oliver and Boyd, 1959.

Dunning, Stephen N. *Kierkegaard's Dialectic of Inwardness: A Structural Analysis of the Theory of Stages*. Princeton: Princeton University Press, 1985.

Dupré, Louis. *Kierkegaard as Theologian: The Dialectic of Christian Existence*. New York: Sheed and Ward, 1963.

Emmanuel, Steven M. *Kierkegaard and the Concept of Revelation*. Albany: State University of New York Press, 1996.

Evans, C. Stephen. *Passionate Reason: Making Sense of Kierkegaard's Philosophical Fragments*. Bloomington: Indiana University Press, 1992.

Fenger, Henning. *Kierkegaard: The Myths and their Origins*, trans. G. C. Schoolfield. New Haven: Yale University Press, 1980.

Ferreira, M. Jamie. *Transforming Vision: Imagination and Will in Kierkegaardian Faith*. Oxford: Clarendon Press, 1991.

———. *Love's Grateful Striving*. New York: Oxford University Press, 2001.

Fulford, Francis Woodbury. *Søren Aabye Kierkegaard: A Study*. Cambridge: Wallis, 1911.

Garff, Joakim. "Min Kære Læser!" Kierkegaard læst med afmålt hengivelse," *Fønix* 14 (1990): 2–20.

———. *Den Sovnløse: Kierkegaard læst aestetisk/biografisk*. Copenhagen: Reitzel, 1995.

Gouwens, David J. *Kierkegaard's Dialectic of Imagination*. New York: Peter Lang, 1989.

———. *Kierkegaard as Religious Thinker*. Cambridge: Cambridge University Press, 1996.

Hannay, Alastair. *Kierkegaard: The Arguments of the Philosophers*. London: Routledge and Kegan Paul, 1982.

Hartshorne, M. Holmes. *Kierkegaard, Godly Deceiver: The Nature and Meaning of His Pseudonymous Writings*. New York: Columbia University Press, 1990.

Holm, Isak Winkel. *Tanken i Billedet: Søren Kierkegaard's Poetik*. Copenhagen: Gyldendal, 1998.

Jacobs, L. "The Akedah in Jewish Thought," in *Kierkegaard's "Fear and Trembling": Critical Appraisals*, ed. Robert L. Perkins. Tuscaloosa: University of Alabama Press, 1981.

Kallas, E. "Kierkegaard's Understanding of the Bible with Respect to his 'Age,'" *Dialog* 26 (winter 1987): 30–34.

Kellenberger, James. *Kierkegaard and Nietzsche*. New York: St. Martin's Press, 1997.

Kirmmse, Bruce H. *Kierkegaard in Golden Age Denmark*. Bloomington: Indiana University Press, 1990.

Kloeden, W. von. "Biblestudy," *Kierkegaardiana* 1 (1978): 16–39.

Law, David R. *Kierkegaard as Negative Theologian*. Oxford: Clarendon Press, 1993.

Lowrie, Walter. *Kierkegaard*. New York: Oxford University Press, 1938.

Mackey, Louis. *Kierkegaard: A Kind of Poet*. Philadelphia: University of Pennsylvania Press, 1971.

———. *Points of View: Readings of Kierkegaard*. Tallahassee: Florida State University Press, 1986.

Malantschuk, Gregor. *Kierkegaard's Way to the Truth*, trans. M. Michelsen. Minneapolis: Augsburg, 1963.

———. *Kierkegaard's Thought*, trans. H. V. and E. H. Hong. Princeton: Princeton University Press, 1971.

McKinnon, A. "Kierkegaard's Interpretation of His 'Authorship': Some Statistical Evidence," *Inquiry* 27 (1984): 225–233.

McKinnon, A., and R. Webster. "A Method of 'Author' Identification," *Computer Studies in Humanities and Verbal Behavior* 2 (1969): 19–23.

Minear, Paul S., and Paul S. Morimoto. *Kierkegaard and the Bible*. Princeton: Princeton Theological Seminary, 1953.

Mooney, Edward F. "Understanding Abraham: Care, Faith, and the Absurd," in *Kierkegaard's "Fear and Trembling": Critical Appraisals*, ed. Robert L. Perkins. Tuscaloosa: University of Alabama Press, 1981.

———. *Selves in Discord and Resolve*. London: Routledge, 1996.

Mulhall, Stephen. *"God's Plagiarist: 'The Philosophical Fragments' of Johannes Climacus," Philosophical Investigations* 22, no. 1 (1999): 1–34.

———. *Inheritance and Originality: Wittgenstein, Heidegger, Kierkegaard*. Oxford: Clarendon Press, 2001.

Müller, Paul. *Søren Kierkegaards Kommunikationsteori*. Copenhagen: Reitzel, 1984.

Nordentoft, Kresten. *Kierkegaards Psykologi*. Copenhagen: GAD, 1972.

Norris, Christopher. "Fictions of Authority: Narrative and Viewpoint in Kierkegaard's Writing," in *The Deconstructive Turn:Essays in the Rhetoric of Philosophy*. London: Methuen 1983.

———. "De Man Unfair to Kierkegaard? An Allegory of Non-Reading," in *Kierkegaard: Poet of Existence*, ed. B. Bertung. Copenhagen: Reitzel, 1989.

Parkov, Peter. *Bibelen i Søren Kierkegaards Samlede Vaerker.* Copenhagen: Reitzel, 1983.

Pattison, George L. *Kierkegaard: The Aesthetic and the Religious, from the Magic Theatre to the Crucifixion of the Image.* New York: St. Martin's Press, 1992.

———. "If Kierkegaard Is Right about Reading, Why Read Kierkegaard," in *Kierkegaard Revisited*, ed. N. J. Cappelørn and J. Stewart. Berlin: Walter de Gruyter, 1997.

Pedersen, B. "Fictionality and Authority: A Point of View for Kierkegaard's Work as an Author," *Modern Language Notes* 89 (1974): 938–956.

Pedersen, J. "Kierkegaard's View of Scripture," in *Bibliotheca Kierkegaardiana*, ed. N. Thulstrup and M. Mikulova Thulstrup. Copenhagen: Reitzel, 1978.

Perkins, Robert L., ed. *Kierkegaard's "Fear and Trembling": Critical Appraisals.* Tuscaloosa: University of Alabama Press, 1981.

Plekon, M. "Kierkegaard as Theologian: The Roots of His Theology in *Works of Love*," in *Foundations of Kierkegaard's Vision of Community: Religion, Ethics, and Politics in Kierkegaard*, ed. G. B. Connell and C. S. Evans. New Jersey and London: Humanities Press, 1992.

Pletsch, C. "The Self-Sufficient Text in Nietzsche and Kierkegaard," *Yale French Studies* 66 (1984): 160–188.

Pojman, Louis P. *The Logic of Subjectivity: Kierkegaard's Philosophy of Religion.* Tuscaloosa: University of Alabama Press, 1984.

Polk, Timothy H. *The Biblical Kierkegaard: Reading by the Rule of Faith.* Macon, Ga.: Mercer University Press, 1997.

Poole, Roger. *Kierkegaard: The Indirect Communication.* Charlottesville: University Press of Virginia, 1993.

———. "'My Wish, My Prayer': Keeping the Pseudonyms Apart, Preliminary Considerations," in *Kierkegaard Revisited*, ed. Cappelørn and Stewart.

Ree, Jonathan, and Jane Chamberlain, eds. *Kierkegaard: A Critical Reader.* Oxford: Basil Blackwell, 1998.

Rosas, Joseph L. III. *Scripture in the Thought of Søren Kierkegaard.* Nashville: Broadman and Holman, 1994.

Schleifer, Ronald, and Robert Markley, eds. *Kierkegaard and Literature*: Irony, Repetition, and Criticism. Norman: University of Oklahoma Press, 1984.

Swenson, David F. *Something about Kierkegaard*, ed. L. M. Swenson. Minneapolis: Augsburg, 1956.

Taylor, Mark C. *Kierkegaard's Pseudonymous Authorship*: A Study of Time and the Self. Princeton: Princeton University Press, 1975.

———. *Journeys to Selfhood: Hegel and Kierkegaard.* Berkeley and Los Angeles: University of California Press, 1980.

Thompson, Josiah. *The Lonely Labyrinth: Kierkegaard's Pseudonymous Works.* Carbondale: Southern Illinois University Press, 1967.

Thulstrup, Niels. *Kierkegaard's Relation to Hegel*, trans. G. L. Stengren. Princeton: Princeton University Press, 1980.

_____. *Kierkegaard og Kirken i Danmark.* Copenhagen: Reitzel, 1985.

Thulstrup, Niels, and M. Mikulova Thulstrup, eds. *Bibliotheca Kierkegaardiana.* Copenhagen: Reitzel, 1978–1988.

Walsh, Sylvia. *Living Poetically: Kierkegaard's Existential Aesthetics.* University Park: Pennsylvania State University Press, 1994.

Westphal, Merold. "Kierkegaard and the Anxiety of Authorship," *International Philosophical Quarterly* 34 (1994): 5–22.

Other Works

Adorno, Theodor W. *Noten zur Literatur II.* Berlin: Suhrkamp, 1961.

Altieri, Charles. "Toward a Hermeneutics Responsive to Rhetorical Theory," in *Rhetoric and Hermeneutics in Our Time: A Reader*, ed. W. Jost and M. J. Hyde. New Haven: Yale University Press, 1997.

Altman, C. F. "Intertextual Rewriting: Textuality as Language Formation," in *The Sign in Music and Literature*, ed. W. Steiner. Austin: University of Texas Press, 1981.

Aquinas, St. Thomas. *The "Summa Theologica,"* trans. Fathers of the English Dominican province. London: Washbourne, 1911.

Austin, John Langshaw. *Philosophical Papers.* Oxford: Clarendon Press, 1970.

Authier-Revuz, Jacqueline. *Ces Mots qui ne vont pas de soi: Boucles réflexives et non-coincidences du dire.* Paris: Larousse, 1995.

Baltrusaitis, Jurgis. *Anamorphic Art*, trans. W. J. Strachan. New York: Abrams, 1977.

Barthes, Roland. *The Pleasure of the Text*, trans. R. Miller. New York: Noonday Press, 1975.

_____. *Image Music Text*, ed. S. Heath. London: Fontana, 1977.

_____. "From Work to Text," in *Textual Strategies: Perspectives in Post-Structuralist Criticism*, ed. J. V. Harari. Ithaca: Cornell University Press, 1979.

_____. *Le Bruissement de la langue.* Paris: Seuil, 1984.

Bataille, Georges L. *Expérience intérieure.* Paris: Gallimard, 1953.

Beaumont, C. A. *Swift's Use of the Bible: A Documentation and a Study in Allusion.* Athens: University of Georgia Monographs 14, 1965.

Ben-Porat, Z. "The Poetics of Literary Allusion," *A Journal for Descriptive Poetics and Theory of Literature* 1 (1976): 105–128.

Beugnot, B. "Contexts and Quotation," *Linguistische Berichte* 39 (1975): 1–21.

Bloom, Harold. *A Map of Misreading.* New York: Oxford University Press, 1975.

_____. *Anxiety of Influence.* New York: Oxford University Press, 1997.

Boller, P. F. *Quotemanship: The Use and Abuse of Quotations for Polemical and Other Purposes.* Dallas: Southern Methodist University Press, 1967.

Borges, Jorge Luis. *Fictions.* London: John Calder, 1985.

Bruns, Gerald. *Hermeneutics Ancient and Modern.* New Haven: Yale University Press, 1992.

Bultmann, Rudolf. *Jesus Christ and Mythology.* New York: Charles Scribner's Sons, 1958.

_____. *Kerygma and Myth: A Theological Debate*, rev. trans. R. H. Fuller. New York: Harper and Row, 1961.

_____. "Das Problem der Hermeneutik,"*Glauben und Verstehen*, vol. 2. Tubingen: Mohr, 1961.

Cambridge History of the Bible, vol. 3. Cambridge: Cambridge University Press, 1996.

Caputo, John D. *Radical Hermeneutics: Repetition, Deconstruction, and the Hermeneutical Project.* Bloomington: Indiana University Press, 1987.

_____. *The Prayers and Tears of Jacques Derrida: Religion without Religion.* Bloomington: Indiana University Press, 1997.

_____ and M. J. Scanlon, eds. *God, the Gift, and Postmodernism.* Bloomington: Indiana University Press, 1999.

Carpzov, J. *A Defense of the Hebrew Bible*, trans. M. Marcus. London: Bernarg Lintot, 1729.

Cavell, Stanley. *Themes out of School.* San Francisco: North Point Press, 1984.

Church, Alphonso. *Introduction to Mathematical Logic.* Princeton: Princeton University Press, 1964.

Clark, H. H., and R. J. Gerrig. "Quotation as Demonstration," *Language* 66, no. 4 (1990): 764–802.

Clausen, Henrik Nikolai. *Det Nye Testaments Hermeneutik.* Copenhagen: Reitzel, 1840.

Clement of Alexandria. "Stromates" V, 12, 78, 3, in *Ante-Nicene Fathers*, vol. 2. Grand Rapids: Eerdmans Publishing Co., 1983.

Compagnon, Antoine. *La Seconde Main, ou le travail de la citation.* Paris: Seuil, 1979.

Coombs, J. H. "Allusion Defined and Explained," *Poetics* 13 (1984): 475–488.

Crenshaw, James L. *Ecclesiastes.* London: SCM Press, 1988.

Cresswell, M. J. "Quotational Theories of Propositional Attitudes," *Journal of Philosophical Logic* 9 (1980): 17–40.

Cusanus, Nicolas. *Of Learned Ignorance*, trans. G. Heron. London: Routledge, 1954.

Davidson, Donald. "Quotation," in *Inquiries into Truth and Interpretation*, ed. D. Davidson. Oxford: Clarendon Press, 1984.

Deleuze, Gilles. *Difference and Repetition*, trans. P. Patton. London: Athlone Press, 1994.

De Man, P. "Hypogram and Inscription: Michael Riffaterre's Poetics of Reading," *Diacritics* 11 (winter 1981): 17–35.

Derrida, Jacques. "Living On/Border Lines," in *Deconstruction and Criticism*, ed. H. Bloom, P. de Man, J. Derrida, et al. London: Routledge and Kegan Paul, 1979.

———. *Limited Inc.* Evanston, Ill.: Northwestern University Press, 1988.

———. *Donner le Temps.* Paris: Galilée, 1991.

———. *Given Time, I: Counterfeit Money*, trans. P. Kamuf. Chicago: University of Chicago Press, 1991.

Dilthey, Wilhelm. "The Rise of Hermeneutics," trans. Frederic Jameson, in *The Hermeneutic Tradition: From Ast to Ricoeur*, ed. Gayle L. Ormiston and Alan B. Shrift. Albany: State University of New York Press, 1990.

Drahos, Peter. *A Philosophy of Intellectual Property.* Aldershot: Darthmouth, 1996.

Eliot, Thomas Searns. "Tradition and the Individual Talent," in *Selected Essays.* London: Faber, 1932.

———. "Ulysses, Order, and Myth," *Dial* 75 (1923): 480–483.

Emerson, Ralph Waldo. "Quotation and Originality," in *The Works of Ralph Waldo Emerson*, vol. 8. Boston: Jefferson Press, 1911.

Fish, Stanley. *Is There a Text in This Class? The Authority of Interpretative Communities.* Cambridge: Harvard University Press, 1980.

Fletcher, H. "Milton's Use of Biblical Quotations," *Journal of English and Germanic Philology* 26 (1927): 145–165.

Foucault, Michel. *Language, Counter-Memory, Practice: Selected Essays and Interviews*, ed. D. F. Bouchard. Ithaca: Cornell University Press, 1977.

Fowler, R. "Who Is 'the Reader' in the Text?" *Semeia* 31 (1985): 5–23.

Frei, Hans W. *The Eclipse of Biblical Narrative: A Study in Eighteenth and Nineteenth Century Hermeneutics.* New Haven: Yale Univeristy Press, 1974.

Frye, Northrop. *The Great Code: The Bible in Literature.* London: Routledge and Kegan Paul, 1982.

Gadamer, Hans-Georg. "Rhetoric, Hermeneutics, and the Critique of Ideology: Metacritical Comments on 'Truth and Method,'" in *The Hermeneutics Reader*, ed. K. Mueller-Vollmer. New York: Continuum, 1994.

———. *Truth and Method*, trans. J. Weinsheimer and D. G. Marshall. London: Sheed and Ward, 1999.

Genette, Gerard. *Palimpsestes: La Littérature au second degree.* Paris: Seuil, 1982.

———. *Paratexts: Thresholds of Interpretation*, trans. J. E. Lewin. Cambridge: Cambridge University Press, 1997.

Goodman, N. "On Some Questions Concerning Quotation," *The Monist: An International Quarterly Journal of General Philosophical Inquiry* 58 (1974): 294–306.

Green, Garrett. *Imagining God: Theology and the Religious Imagination.* San Francisco: Harper and Row, 1989.

Greisch, Jean.*Herméneutique et grammatologie*. Paris: Editions du CNRS, 1977.

Gruntvig, N. F. S. *Udvalgte Skrifter,* vol. 3, *Bibelske Praedikener.* Copenhagen: Gyldendalshe Boghande, 1905, original 1816.

Harari, Josue V., ed. *Textual Strategies: Perspectives in Post-Structuralist Criticism*. Ithaca: Cornell University Press, 1979.

Harweg, R. "Einige Besonderheiten von Zitaten in linguistischer Rede," *Zeitschrift fur vergleichende Sprachforschung* 84 (1970): 288–298.

Hawkins, P. S. "Resurrecting the Word: Dante and the Bible," *Religion and Literature* 16, no. 3 (1984): 59–71.

Hebel, U. J. *Intertextuality, Allusion, and Quotation: An International Bibliography of Critical Studies*. New York: Greenwood Press, 1989.

Hegel, Georg Wilhelm Friedrich. *Phenomenologie des Geistes*, ed. J. Hoffmeister. Hamburg: Felix Meiner, 1952.

_____. *Lectures on the Philosophy of Religion*, ed. P. C. Hodgson, 3 vols. Berkeley and Los Angeles: University of California Press, 1985.

_____. *Elements of the Philosophy of Right*, trans. H. B. Nisbet. Cambridge: Cambridge University Press, 1991.

Heidegger, Martin. *Being and Time,* trans. John Macquarrie and Edward Robinson. New York, Harper and Row, 1962.

_____. *Kant and the Problem of Metaphysics,* trans. J. S. Churchill. Bloomington: Indiana University Press, 1962.

Hernadi, G. "More Questions Concerning Quotations," *Journal of Aesthetics and Art Criticism* 39 (1981): 271–273.

Hirsch, E. D., Jr. *Validity in Interpretation*. New Haven: Yale University Press, 1967.

Hollander, John. *The Figure of Echo: A Mode of Allusion in Milton and After.* Berkeley and Los Angeles: University of California Press, 1981.

The Holy Bible. Cambridge: Cambridge University Press, 1997.

Hurry, D. "Style, Allusion and the Manipulation of Viewpoint," *Critical Quarterly* 23 (1981): 61–71.

Iser, Wolfgang. *The Implied Reader: Patterns of Communication in Prose Fiction, from Bunyan to Beckett*. Baltimore: John Hopkins Universtiy Press, 1974.

Jauss, Hans Robert.*Pour une Herméneutique littéraire,* trans. Maurice Jacob. Paris: Gallimard, 1982.

Jenny, L. "The Strategy of Form," in *French Literary Theory Today: A Reader*, ed. T. Todorov. Cambridge: Cambridge University Press, 1982.

Jost W., and M. J. Hyde, eds. *Rhetoric and Hermeneutics in Our Time: A Reader.* New Haven: Yale University Press, 1997.

Judith. The Anchor Bible, trans. C. A. Moore. New York: Doubleday, 1985.

Kant, Immanuel. *The Metaphysics of Morals,* trans. M. Gregor. Cambridge: Cambridge University Press, 1996.

Koch, Hal, and Bjørne Kornerup. *Den Danske Kirkes Historie,* vol. 6. Copenhagen: Gyldendalske Boghandel, 1954.

Krause, W. "Versuch einer allgemeinen Theorie des Zitats," in *Die Stellung der Fruehmittelalterlichen Autoren zur Heinischen Literatur.* Vienna, 1958.

Kurihaha, T. "The Syntax and Semantics of Quotation Reconsidered," *Language and Culture 7* (1985): 67–89.

Laugaa, Maurice. *La Pensée du pseudonyme.* Paris: PUF, 1986.

Levenson, Jon Douglas. *The Death and Resurrection of the Beloved Son.* New Haven: Yale University Press, 1993.

Longinus. *On the Sublime,* trans. J. A. Arieti and J. M. Crossett. New York and Toronto: Edwin Mellen Press, 1985.

Martensen, H. *Den Christelige Dogmatik.* Copenhagen: Reitzel, 1883.

Mauss, Marcel. *The Gift: The Form and Reason for Exchange in Archaic Society,* trans. W. D. Halls. London: Routledge, 1990.

McCracken, David. *The Scandal of the Gospels: Jesus, Story, and Offense.* New York: Oxford University Press, 1994.

Meijer, J. M. "A Case of Quoting," *Slavia* 45 (1976): 187–191.

Meyer, Herman. *The Poetics of Quotation in the European Novel,* trans. T. and Y. Ziolkowski. Princeton: Princeton University Press, 1968.

Meyer, K. A. "Zitate und Plagiate," *International Journal of Professional Ethics* 1 (1955): 54–58.

Mieder, W. *Sprichwort, Redensart, Zitat: Tradierte Formelssprache in der Moderne.* Bern: Lang, 1985.

Miller, Jacqueline T. *Poetic License: Authority and Authorship in Medieval and Renaissance Context.* New York: Oxford University Press, 1986.

Minnis, A. J. *Medieval Theory of Authorship.* London: Scholar Press, 1984.

Montaigne, Michel de. *Essais.* Paris: Garnier-Flammarion, 1969.

Morawski, S. "The Basic Functions of Quotation," in *Sign, Language, Culture,* ed. A. J. Greimas and R. Jakobson. The Hague: Mouton, 1970.

Morgan, Robert. *Biblical Interpretation.* New York: Oxford University Press, 1988.

Morgan, T. E. "Is There an Intertext in This Text? Literary and Interdisciplinary Approaches to Intertextuality," *American Journal of Semiotics* 3, no. 4 (1985): 1–40.

Mueller-Vollmer, Kurt. *The Hermeneutics Reader: Texts of the German Tradition, from Enlightenment to the Present.* Oxford: Basil Blackwell, 1986.

Nadel, A. M. "Translating the Past: Literary Allusions as Covert Criticism," *Georgia Review* 36 (1982): 639–651.

Nehamas, Alexander. *Nietzsche: Life as Literature.* Cambridge: Harvard University Press, 1985.

The New Jerome Biblical Commentary, trans. and ed. R. E. Brown. London: Geofry Chapman, 1990.

Norton, David. *History of Bible as Literature*. Cambridge: Cambridge University Press, 1993.

Oxford Latin Dictionary. Oxford: Clarendon Press, 1968.

Parsons, T. "What Do Quotation Marks Name? Frege's Theories of Quotations and That-Clauses," *Philosophical Studies* 42 (1982): 315–328.

Pascal, Blaise. *The Provincial Letters*, trans. A. J. Krailsheimer. London: Penguin Books, 1967.

Perlina, Nina. "The Role and Function of Quotation in F. M. Dostoevsky's Works," *Forum* 3 (1980): 33–47.

———. "Varieties of Poetic Utterances: Quotation in the Brothers Karamasov." Lanham, Md.: University Press of America, 1985.

Plett, H. F. "The Poetics of Quotation," in *From Verbal Constitution to Symbolic Meaning*, ed. J. S. Petoefi and T. Olivi. Hamburg: Buske, 1988.

Prickett, Stephen. *Words and the Word: Language, Poetics, and Biblical Interpretation*. Cambridge: Cambridge University Press, 1986.

———. *Origins of Narrative: The Romantic Appropriation of the Bible*. Cambridge: Cambridge University Press, 1996.

Quine, W. V. *Mathematical Logic*. Cambridge: Harvard Univeristy Press, 1951.

Quintilian. *Institutio Oratoria*, trans. Harold Edgeworth Butler. London: William Heinemann, 1958.

Ricoeur, Paul. *The Conflict of Interpretations: Essays in Hermeneutics*, ed. D. Ihde. Evanston, Ill.: Northwestern University Press, 1974.

———. *Interpretation Theory: Discourse and the Surplus of Meaning*. Fort Worth: Texas Christian University Press, 1976.

———. *The Rule of Metaphor*. Toronto: University of Toronto Press, 1977.

———. *Essays on Biblical Interpretation*, ed. L. S. Mudge. London: SPCK, 1981.

———. *Hermeneutics and the Human Sciences*, trans. J. B. Thompson. Cambridge: Cambridge University Press, 1981.

Rorty, Richard. *Philosophy and the Mirror of Nature*. Princeton: Princeton University Press, 1979.

Ryan, Alan. *Property and Political Theory*. Oxford: Basil Blackwell, 1984.

Said, Edward W. "Molestation and Authority in Narrative Fiction," in *Aspects of Narrative*, ed. H. J. Miller. New York: Columbia University Press, 1971.

———. *Beginnings: Intention and Method*. New York: Basics, 1975.

Sartiliot, Claudette. *Citation and Modernity*. Norman: University of Oklahoma Press, 1993.

Savran, George W. *Telling and Retelling: Quotation in Biblical Narrative*. Bloomington: Indiana University Press, 1988.

Schleiermacher, Friedrich D. E. *Hermeneutics: The Handwritten Manuscripts*, ed. H. Kimmerle. Missoula, Mont.: Scholars Press, 1977.

———. *Hermeneutics and Criticism*, ed. A. Bowie. Cambridge: Cambridge University Press, 1998.

———. *The Christian Faith*, ed. H. R. Mackintosh and J. S. Stewart. Edinburgh: T. and T. Clark, 1999.

Schneewind, Jerome B. *The Invention of Autonomy: A History of Modern Moral Philosophy.* Cambridge: Cambridge University Press, 1998.

Schrift, Alan D., ed. *The Logic of the Gift: Toward an Ethic of Generosity.* London: Routledge, 1997.

Soskice, Janet Martin. *Metaphor and Religious Language.* Oxford: Clarendon Press, 1985.

Stanley, Christopher D. *Paul and the Language of Scripture.* Cambridge: Cambridge University Press, 1992.

Starobinski, J. *L'œil vivant.* Paris: Gallimard, 1961.

Stedahl, K. *The School of St. Matthew*, ASNU 20. Copenhagen: Munksgaard, 1954.

Sternberg, Meir. *The Poetics of Biblical Narrative: Ideological Literature and the Drama of Reading.* Bloomington: Indiana University Press, 1985.

Stillinger, Jack. *Multiple Authorship and the Myth of Solitary Genius.* New York: Oxford University Press, 1991.

Strauss, David F. *The Life of Jesus Critically Examined*, trans. G. Eliot. London: SCM Press, 1973.

Suleiman, Susan Ruban, and Inge Crosman Wimmers, eds. *The Reader in the Text: Essays on Audience and Interpretation.* Princeton: Princeton University Press, 1980.

Tanner, Katherine. *God and Creation in Christian Theology: Tyranny or Empowerment?* Oxford: Basil Blackwell, 1988.

Tarski, Alfred. *Logic, Semantics, Mathematics.* Oxford: Clarendon Press, 1956.

Taylor, Charles. *Philosophy and the Human Sciences: Philosophical Papers.* Cambridge: Cambridge University Press, 1985.

Thiselton, Anthony C. *New Horizons in Hermeneutics.* London: HarperCollins, 1992.

Tillich, Paul. *A History of Christian Thought.* London: SCM Press, 1986.

Tuomarla, Ulla. *La Citation mode d'emploi: Sur le fonctionnement discursif du discours rapporté direct.* Annales Academiae Scientiarum Fennicae, 2000.

Vanhoozer, Kevin J. *Biblical Narrative in the Philosophy of Paul Ricoeur: A Study in Hermeneutics and Theology.* Cambridge: Cambridge University Press, 1990.

Vattimo, Gianni. *Ethique de l'interpretation*, trans. Jacques Rolland. Paris: Editions la découvertes, 1991.

———. *Beyond Interpretation: The Meaning of Hermeneutics for Philosophy*, trans. D. Webb. Stanford: Stanford University Press, 1997.

Whittaker, J. "The Value of Indirect Tradition in the Establishment of Greek Philosophical Texts or the Art of Misquotation," in *Editing Greek and Latin Texts*, ed. J. N. Grant. New York: AMS Press, 1989.

Wierzbicka, A. "The Semantics of Direct and Indirect Discourse," *Papers in Linguistics*, no. 7 (1974): 267–307.

Wilss, W. "Beobacttunger zur Anspielungstechnik in der deutschen Gegenswartssprache," *Grazer linguistische Studien* 11–12 (1980): 368–390.

Wimsatt, William K., and Monroe C. Beardsley. "The Intentional Fallacy," in *The Verbal Icon: Studies in the Meaning of Poetry*, ed. W. K. Wimsatt. New York: Noonday, 1966.

Wittgenstein, Ludwig. *Culture and Value*, trans. P. Winsh. Oxford: Basil Blackwell, 1977.

―――. *Tractatus Logico-Philosophicus*. Frankfurt am Main: Suhrkamp, 1989.

Index

Perspectives in Continental Philosophy Series
John D. Caputo, series editor